SECOND LIFE

SECOND LIFE

Having a Child
in the
Digital Age

AMANDA HESS

Doubleday | New York

Published in the United States by Doubleday, a division of Penguin Random House LLC, 1745 Broadway, New York, NY 10019.

DOUBLEDAY and the portrayal of an anchor with a dolphin are registered trademarks of Penguin Random House LLC.

Library of Congress Cataloging-in-Publication Data
Names: Hess, Amanda (Journalist), author.
Title: Second life: having a child in the digital age / Amanda Hess.
Description: First edition. | New York: Doubleday, [2025] | Includes bibliographical references.
Identifiers: LCCN 2024036416 (print) | LCCN 2024036417 (ebook) | ISBN 9780385549738 (hardcover) | ISBN 9780385549745 (ebook)
Subjects: LCSH: Hess, Amanda (Journalist) | Motherhood. | Internet—Social aspects. | Information society.
Classification: LCC HQ759 .H6447 2025 (print) | LCC HQ759 (ebook) | DDC 306.874/3092 [B]—dc23/eng/20250120
LC record available at https://lccn.loc.gov/2024036416
LC ebook record available at https://lccn.loc.gov/2024036417

penguinrandomhouse.com | doubleday.com

Printed in the United States of America
1st Printing

The authorized representative in the EU for product safety and compliance is Penguin Random House Ireland, Morrison Chambers, 32 Nassau Street, Dublin D02 YH68, Ireland, https://eu-contact.penguin.ie.

For my guys

If the tongue of the reject is wide on its throat and hangs down from its mouth, an enemy will seize my border city through revolt.

——ANCIENT MESOPOTAMIAN OMEN

I feel as if I've been looking for you for a very long time.

——REYNOLDS WOODCOCK, *PHANTOM THREAD* (WRITTEN BY PAUL THOMAS ANDERSON)

Contents

Note

This book is an account of a relationship with technology. My personal experiences have been reconstructed based on thousands of contemporaneous screenshots, text messages, and recordings, and my personal data archives, medical records, and notes. Other details are based on my own recollections. The internet moves quickly, and some of the apps, websites, and products discussed in these pages have undergone changes since I first used them.

SECOND LIFE

Alma

On the website FactsBuddy.com, you can find a short biography of me, the American journalist Amanda Hess. Facts Buddy describes itself as an *optimistic website that targets to build a large audience for information,* which means that it scans the internet for personal data and drops it into the template of a life.

According to the internet, Amanda Hess is *a woman of average stature.* She was *born to her caring and supportive parents in the United States of America.* She writes about the internet, for which she *receives satisfying pay.* She is *happily married to her handsome husband Marc,* and *the duo resides in Brooklyn along with their son Alma born in October 2020.* It's all true—my height, my job, my spouse. Except for the bit about my son.

In fact, I have two sons. The first was born in 2020, but not in the month of October. And his name is not Alma. When I first found my biography on Facts Buddy, it felt like I had accessed an alternate universe. Early in that pregnancy, I walked with Marc along the edge of a pond, our secret news crackling between us, and I told him that if the baby was a girl, I might want to name her Alma. Then a prenatal test found a Y-chromosome in fetal cells circulating in my blood, and my imagination scampered to another list of names. I mentioned Alma to no one else.

I have tried to figure out why Facts Buddy would think that I called my son that, and this is my best guess. In October of 2020, I posted his baby picture to Instagram. He is pink and small, and rests easily between the crook of Marc's elbow and the palm of his hand. He wears a sky-blue bib that Marc commissioned from Etsy as an inside joke. Across the chest it says: *For the hungry boy.*

That's a quote from *Phantom Thread*, Paul Thomas Anderson's 2017 film, for which I harbor a near-deranged affection. *Phantom Thread* is about a meticulous and obsessive dressmaker named Reynolds Woodcock, and upon its release, it quickly became one of our relationship source texts. Marc and I each often mimicked Reynolds's bleating voice—*I cannot begin my day with a confrontation, please*—to slyly ask the other to leave them alone. In the movie, Reynolds is charmed by a waitress named Alma when she serves him an obscenely large breakfast, along with a note that says: *For the hungry boy. My name is Alma.* I posted a screenshot of Alma's note alongside the picture of the bib. Facts Buddy likely skimmed the data from those twin images and conflated them.

For all that the internet thinks it knows about me—and I have volunteered a great deal—there are certain things that it can never know. It thinks, for example, that a meme is my son. When Facts Buddy calls him Alma, it makes me feel like I have, in some small way, evaded the internet's unblinking eye. And that is how my son makes me feel all the time. Like I've gotten away with something.

Confrontation

I did not know that anything was unusual until I was seven months pregnant. *This week your baby can cry,* my pregnancy app said. *Yes, in the uterus!* I waited in the lobby of the prenatal imaging center, stroking my phone until I depleted its stock of inane facts. My baby cried inside my body for the same reasons that it would cry outside of my body, *like if they hear a loud noise or are bothered by something,* the app said. *Just as you might be starting to prepare for their arrival, they're constantly preparing for life in the outside world.* The app handed me a drawing of a frowning baby, a teardrop slipping down its cheek.

Inside the exam room the technician wore a stumpy ponytail and an annoyed expression. I wore a sheet of paper with armholes. She dimmed the lights and stood astride her mysterious station. I could see plastic scepters and orbs, a basket of serums, a keyboard with hieroglyphic markings. The technician unsheathed her wand. She slathered cold gel on my skin and worked her probe into the hard rind of my stomach. I assumed various poses at her command, bobbing and craning my neck to keep one eye focused on my young. On the screen, static rained on little ribs and fists. As the technician worked, she offered selections from her trove of professional small talk: do you know the sex, have you picked a name.

I wanted to slice her out of the scene, to watch my baby with silent focus, but I also wanted to seem normal and good. I told her the baby was a boy without a name. Then she said, "He's sticking his tongue out," so I said, "Awwww."

The technician fussed with the machine. She twisted its dials and clacked at its keys and then left the room. The gel grew thick on my skin. I missed my phone. I wondered if there were any new work emails in there. When the technician returned, she ordered more poses, captured more shots. I had reported to the doctor's office for a routine scan, but as in a dream, the routine kept repeating. We passed the plausible length of a standard procedure, then lapped it. Again, the technician left the room and returned. "The doctor is busy with another patient," she said. "That's why it's taking so long. I might as well get more photos while we wait."

On her livestream of my body, she conjured a craggy amber landscape, a cave of mineral spires. I asked her what it was.

"An ear," she said.

"Weird!" I said.

My bright tone hung awkwardly in the darkened air. The technician's store of conversation was picked clean. She now communicated in the perfunctory style of a deposition, answering only when strictly necessary. I searched her glassy eyes for clues. Were they always fixed so intensely on the screen? Dread pooled in my brain and danced in liquid shapes. Stupid, stupid. The doctor was not with another patient and the technician was not taking more pictures for fun. I watched her map my baby's ear for secret reasons. When she directed me to lie on my side, I gratefully accepted. I turned my back to her and the monitor. I turned my back on my baby.

Later I would read a report of the ultrasound and learn that this phase of the examination had lasted for one hour. For an hour I lay on the table, playing dead. I imagined that if I could stay completely still, the skeletal hand of complication might pass me by. It would crack the door to the next ultrasound room and tap on some other pregnant body. The moment would slink away like so many of the anxious thoughts that had visited me during my pregnancy. I was always anticipating the worst, imagining the plane dropping from the sky, the shooter breaching the office door. Soon the doctor would arrive smiling, apologizing for the delay. The technician would hand me a roll of keepsake photos. I would escape past the reception desk and rise through the elevator into the sun.

Why did I say that: WEIRD! I said it out loud and welcomed the complication into the room. I upset the tacit rules of the procedure—the technician takes the photographs, the doctor interprets them, I smile through my mask. Alone with the technician, I could imagine my baby as a nymph exploring the womb. Only when the doctor arrived did he become a specimen pinned behind the window of my skin. If I had said nothing, I still would have known that my pregnancy had been recategorized as a special medical case. But I could have pretended for a few more minutes that it had not.

The errors I made during my pregnancy knocked at the door of my mind. I drank a glass and a half of wine on Marc's birthday, before I knew I was pregnant. I swallowed a tablet of Ativan, for acute anxiety, after I knew. I took a long hot bath that crinkled my fingertips. I got sick with a fever and fell asleep without thinking about it. I waited until I was almost thirty-five years old to get pregnant. I wanted to solve the question of myself before bringing another person into the world, but the answer had not come. Now my pregnancy was, in the language of obstetrics, geriatric.

For seven months we'd all acted like a baby was going to come out of my body like a rabbit yanked from a hat. The same body that ordered mozzarella sticks from the late-night menu and stared into a computer like it had a soul. The body that had, just a few years prior, snorted a key of cocaine supplied by the party-bus driver hired to transport it to Medieval Times. This body was now working very seriously to generate a new human. I had posed the body for Instagram, clutching my bump with two hands as if it might bounce away. I had bought a noise machine with a womb setting and thrown away the box. Now I lay on the table as the doctor stood in his chamber, rewinding the tape of my life.

My phone sat on an empty chair, six feet away. Smothered beneath my smug maternity dress, it blinked silently with text messages from Marc. If I had the phone, I could hold it close to the exam table and google my way out. I could pour my fears into its portal and process them into answers. I could consult the pregnant women who came before me, dust off their old message board posts and read of long-ago ultrasounds that found weird ears and stuck-out tongues. They had dropped their babies' fates into the internet like coins into a fountain and I would scrounge through them all, looking for the lucky penny. For the woman who returned to say, *It turned out to be nothing. Trick of light.*

It was ludicrous, but in my panic, it felt incontrovertible: if I searched it smart and fast enough, the internet would save us. I had constructed my life through its screens, mapped the world along its circuits. Now I would make a second life there, too. As I write this, four years later, I see my hour on the table as the moment that my relationship with technology turned, its shadows shifting around me. I reached for a sense of control and gripped tightly to my phone. It would not give me the answers I was looking for, but it would feed me wrong answers from its endless supply. It would serve me facts and conspiracies, gadgets and idols, judgments and tips.

The baby tapped at my stomach. I rubbed my hand against it, returning the signal. The technician handed me a spray of paper towels and left me alone in the room. I heaved myself up and faced the exit. My stomach hung over the table's edge, waiting for the door to open.

Chapter 1

Cycle

Every month it came as a surprise. A fine morning lurched into a shaky afternoon. My boyfriend would irritate me in a way I could not articulate, and in response, I would reach back in my memory for some previous incident to twist into a complaint. In the evening, I might cry inexplicably while watching a British murder show, get a stomachache, and flop unhappily in bed until a sticky feeling bubbled between my legs. Still, the reality of the situation would not become clear to me until I saw the blood spattered in the toilet.

Right: my period. I could never keep track of when it had left and when it was due to return. Most of the time I tried not to think about having a body at all. It was too easy to remember that my insides were made of creepy interlocking ligaments and bones, like a skinned cadaver from *Bodies: The Exhibition*. Sometimes I would scroll past an inspirational quote on Instagram, like *The body expresses what the mind suppresses,* posted by a user calling herself @medicine_mami, and I would think, *Shit. Should I do something about that?* No! The suppression was working fine. I lay in bed at night, my rigid arms suspending the screen inches from my face, and disassociated into my phone. I reread the Wikipedia page for the missing Malaysian airplane. I watched a pore strip pull the blackheads from a Reddit user's nose. Finally, I retreated to a meditation app, where a woman's voice hissed commands at my muscles until I forgot that I existed.

And yet my period kept arriving unannounced, whining for my attention. Then one day I heard about an app that would track my cycle for me. Maybe I wouldn't have to cultivate bodily awareness after all: I could just outsource it to my phone. The app was called Flo. She beckoned me from the App Store to download her and—as she put it—*become an expert on you.*

Flo was named after an old euphemism for menstruation and styled like my childhood diary. She was medicine-pink and stocked with digital stickers for illustrating the symptoms of my reproductive life. I could conjure a frowning rain cloud when I was angry and make tiny squiggles radiate from tiny underpants when my stomach hurt. She asked me to report my vaginal discharge and its consistency; she wanted to know when I had sex and how. I logged my cramps and feelings in her as if she could convert my PMS into a cool stream of data.

As Flo learned more about me, she began to not only predict my period dates but foretell the emotional contours of my days based on my expected hormone mix. *Increased understanding of negative emotions is linked to the luteal phase,* she told me on day twenty-one of my cycle, *so this could be a good day to tackle thorny conversations with colleagues or managers.*

I did not believe in Flo's woo-woo prognostications, at least not enough to factor my luteal phase into my relationship with my boss. But I scanned her dispatches occasionally, whenever I felt like pulling the handle on her animatronic fortune-teller machine and receiving a weird menstruation-themed prophecy. When I read an article in *The Wall Street Journal* accusing Flo of sharing sensitive user data with Facebook (a claim Flo denied), I didn't delete the app. Online advertisers already profited off the assumption that I hated myself, I reasoned. Would it really make a difference if they found out exactly when I hated myself the most? I kept Flo in my pocket, checking in with her every couple of weeks. I even consulted her as I selected the date that I would marry my boyfriend Marc, making sure it fell during a week of emotional stability and minimal bloating.

As Flo shepherded me through my cycles, I became, almost against my will, highly aware of my capacity to become pregnant. When I had downloaded Flo to predict my periods, I hadn't been thinking of the app's other, obvious use case: it is a fertility-tracking assistant. Deep in its App Store sales pitch, Flo's language of data-driven self-discovery flowered into a homily on childbearing. *Discover a personal journey to motherhood with Flo*, it said. *Get pregnant as soon as naturally possible for you*. Flo made conception feel like an appealingly dull video game. Each month, she circled a date on the calendar in dots of robin's-egg blue: my predicted *day of ovulation*. In the days leading up to the egg's purported release, Flo advised me of my *high chance to get pregnant*. Then a desperate alert burst onto the screen: *Your body is at its most fertile today*.

I had spent most of my adulthood trying to avoid pregnancy, and for years I wore a breezy ambivalence about the possibility of ever having kids. My use of Flo coincided with the year in my life when that cover story was blown, revealing a sudden urge to get pregnant—*as soon as naturally possible for you*. When Marc and I first met, in our late twenties, he knew that he wanted children, and I was less sure. But by the time we got engaged, our positions had shifted. I was finally ready and now he wanted us to take our time. At dinner, I counted out the years under the table on my fingers, projecting how old I might be by the time we got around to the baby's conception, its birth, its high school graduation.

It's not that Flo made me want to have kids, or to do it right away. But she sharpened my imagination around how it could go down. Pregnancy had once been an idea drifting in a hazy future. Now it was a plot that could be executed by following a few simple commands. Each month, Flo laid out the plans for me and slipped them into my pocket. Each month, I ignored them. When my period came, I imagined Flo's digital egg flushing down the drain.

I resented the cliché that, as I neared thirty-five, I was driven mad by the sound of my biological clock. Now the app itself seemed to be ticking in the background everywhere I went. I could sense my body syncing to its calendar, my brain bending to its logic. Soon Marc had folded, too. In November of 2019—seven months before I turned thirty-five, two weeks after we married, and thirteen days since my last period began—we had sex on a date that Flo circled for us. Afterward, I scrolled through Flo's menu of reproductive activities and pressed on a glyph of an open padlock representing unprotected sex. My phone screen was seized by a preset animation, as if to suggest that Flo was a participant in the act. A trio of ovular forms danced around, and then a tiny pink heart materialized, stamped on the calendar. A sex heart from Flo.

I was at work one day when my phone startled awake with a message from Flo. *Hi there!*, she said. *Based on my predictions, your period may be late. Do you have 5 minutes for a quick Q&A to look at potential causes?* I had tried only once. I knew that it would be absurd to expect instant results. I would never say it out loud, to another person, even to myself, and yet here was Flo, screaming it in my face: *ARE YOU PREGNANT?* I tapped through her quiz, reporting on my weight, my medications, my stress. The next day, when my period gushed into the toilet, I was surprised by how hard I cried.

Flo had carved out a digital space where I could envision a conception, like some kind of online hysterical pregnancy. She had told me that I was at my *most fertile*. Already I felt that I had failed. I'd downloaded the app to help me to relieve the burden of my reproductive cycle, to think even less about its events. But every time I opened her, she pulled me again into her reproductive psychodrama.

My phone started working like a dream. All my sublimated thoughts surfaced there. Desperation over my age, my fertility—that was a costume of womanhood that I would never wear in public. But there in the dark closet of my phone, I slipped it on.

The next month brought another fertility window, another attempt, another sex heart stamped on Flo's sex calendar. A few days later, on the last day of 2019, Marc and I dumped out all the credit card points in our virtual wallets and flew to Paris on a last-minute honeymoon, as if we knew that our days of spontaneous movement would soon be numbered. We were out at breakfast one morning when my stool screeched urgently away from the table. A passing waitress recoiled into a stunned exclamation point. I told Marc to meet me back at the hotel, threw open the café door, and puked a geyser of juice onto the sidewalk. I sensed a crowd of cool French people parting around me. I looked into the orange puddle at my feet, wondering why it had come out of me.

I wove back to our sardine-can room at the Moxy, a Marriott brand targeted at millennials. Its rooms were set *at an affordable price point*, the ad copy said, so that we could *save on space and splurge on experiences*. I lay on the bed, experiencing something. Then I pulled out Flo and counted back on the calendar to its last sex heart. I couldn't be experiencing morning sickness yet, and it was too soon for a test to detect a pregnancy, but if a fertilized egg was going to lodge itself in my uterine lining, now would be the time. Google explained, *Some women do notice signs and symptoms that implantation has occurred. But,* it warned, *many of these signs are very similar to PMS.* I was pregnant in Paris, or I was going to get my period in Paris, and that was romantic or vaguely annoying.

One week later, back in our apartment, I crouched over the toilet, lowered the tip of a pregnancy test into the bowl, and peed on my hand. I was trying to get pregnant, to finally seize command of my body, but I was not quite sure where the pee came out—not a good sign. I wagged the test wand beneath the stream until I achieved contact. Then I set it on the lip of the sink and watched the liquid crawl across the test window. A vivid pink line appeared, and then a dim one, like waves drifting from a skipped stone. I peed on another test, and when I could pee again, I peed on one more. Marc was out of town for work, and I wanted to tell him in person, to watch the information hit his face. I wrapped the tests together in a square of paper and vibrated across our apartment.

For a moment, I was the only person in the world who knew that it existed.

Then I grabbed my phone, logged a positive pregnancy test in Flo, and pressed a button to unlock a new level of the app: *Pregnancy mode.*

If you activate the pregnancy mode, a countdown to the birth of your baby will be shown instead of cycle predictions, Flo warned me. I agreed to her terms. The screen mutated into a mineral orange color, like the sky at the lip of a storm. A cluster of cells burst to life and drifted lazily around a veiny orb.

Back in period mode, I hadn't even known that Pregnancy mode existed. Now it felt like I had slipped into my phone's astral plane. I thumbed across the new interface, mesmerized by Flo's pocket reconstruction of my womb. She was busy generating primers and tasks and stacking them in little notecards that refreshed each day. *Know your do's and don'ts,* she advised me. *Get healthy nutrition tips. Learn how to stay active.*

Later, I asked Marc how he felt about us using Flo to get pregnant. "I didn't use the app," he reminded me. "You used the app." I was the one who was always gazing at the screen as if it were a scrying mirror. But when I got so sad after our first try, Marc was startled, and he paid attention. He made sure he knew when my fertility window opened and when it slammed shut. He knew which dates on the sex calendar were for messing around and which ones required that we be, as he joked, "good at sex." I had embedded Flo in my flesh, traded my self-knowledge for her computer vision. Now I passed her projections on to him.

As he made his way home, I later learned, Marc charted my ovulation calendar in his mind. He knew that my period was almost due, knew that I might have already taken a test, and, when he walked in the door and I presented him with the wrapped package, knew what was inside. In bed that night, I opened Flo to show him our little cartoon blastocyst, then swatted it away. We talked with our faces close together. There was something inside me that we had made. The reality of the situation coalesced between us, flowed through the apartment, flooded everything. My period app suddenly seemed mawkish and insane. Its artificial interface had given way to real cells dividing in my actual body. But when I turned over to go to sleep, I opened Flo again and swiped intently through her offerings. Marc and I had been navigating each other for so long, waiting for our intentions to align. But now it felt like my body, or my phone, was leading me to a place that I alone could go.

· · ·

In the beginning, you're not supposed to tell anyone you're pregnant, so I spoke about it only with Flo. I lied to my friends about why I couldn't go out, to my bosses about why I couldn't think. Doctors did not want to see me until I was more pregnant. I didn't know anything about pregnancy, except that I was supposed to urgently reform all my personal habits—I should be eating differently, moving intentionally, suppressing nothing. Already I had fallen behind. I imagined tiny bones fusing and brain matter multiplying carelessly under my ignorant stewardship.

Immediately, Flo offered herself up as my virtual pregnancy helpmeet. She served me meal recommendations and prompted me to absorb facts about human development. *When does a fetus develop a brain?* Flo asked. Around week seven, *the brain will grow at a rate of 250,000 neurons per minute,* Flo answered. A few weeks earlier I had viewed Flo's recommendations as ingratiating nonsense. Now I was shaking her by the shoulders, demanding that she tell me everything she knew.

Flo's voice had a stiff, alien pitch. *Labor is a very important process that marks the end of pregnancy,* she told me. And, *Newborn babies are not like adults at all.* Her articles were illustrated with photographs of household objects arranged to suggest various sexual scenarios: a split-open grapefruit, a flower drooling purple nectar, a spurt of cottage cheese. Sometimes the articles were marked as "reviewed" by a doctor, often a woman pictured in a white lab coat. But they felt like they had come from nowhere, like they had been automatically generated in the hull of the app.

Flo spoke like an astrologer of the body, and her pronouncements were sometimes grammatically unwell. But this only deepened her lobotomizing effect. She didn't sound like a person. She sounded like a machine trying to sound like a person, and that made her seem, in a roundabout way, like an authority—an omniscient being that floated somewhere outside the realm of human expertise. I was lucky to have gotten pregnant easily; Marc and I knew so many people who had tried for years, lost pregnancies, cycled through fertility treatments, given up. But my easy luck also conferred a power to Flo. She had told me just what to do, and it had worked, had it not? She had waved her magic wand and made it so.

Now she was making the whole course of my pregnancy feel preordained. She chopped it into events, shaped it into episodes, dropped them over the course of a season that built toward my September due date. Every Sunday morning, I eagerly opened the app to "see" the thing she called *your baby*, to watch its animated cells morph into a new configuration. Soon it was a veiny muscle with a pale twisted cord. A balloonlike appendage unfurled from its rump and then dissolved. It sprouted flippers and pebbly eyes. Its smoothed CGI features reminded me of the molded fetus trinket that a mournful antiabortion protester once pressed into my palm outside of a Manhattan Planned Parenthood. I knew the app was engineered to offer only a slightly differentiated experience to each of the hundreds of millions of people who downloaded it, but in my mind, it took on the medical force of a sonogram. I watched it like it was a porthole to my womb.

That's it for today!, Flo told me when I depleted her offerings. *But*, she added, *we have a secret space for anonymous discussions with other users.* When I was done staring at my imaginary baby, I thumbed one tab over to Flo's "Secret Chats," where the app's users converged into a thrumming pregnant unconscious. Inside Flo, we did not have online handles or photo avatars. Instead, we were randomly assigned tiny cartoon animal heads, like a bespectacled sheep or a satisfied bear. I appeared as a sad white dog. Only when I studied a comment thread closely, inching my eye to the screen, could

I differentiate one user's contributions from another. It made it feel like we were speaking in one singular voice.

A typical Secret Chats user seemed to be young, sincere, devoutly religious, and very horny. No matter where she was from—Lithuania, Pakistan, New Zealand, New Jersey—she spoke in a hasty English warped by autocorrect. *Baby dust to all,* she offered to those still hoping to conceive. *Let's wait for God's time,* she counseled those awaiting genetic testing results. She called everyone *dear,* as in: *Let's update each other daily on what is happening to us dear* and *The God that answer me will answer u dear.* I felt like I had found the one online community untouched by the sorting mechanisms that usually guided me toward people who were just like me: thirtysomething, white American women who wore clogs and didn't believe in God. On Flo, I was urgently elbowed into a new demographic—anybody pregnant—and now it was like we shared a bloodstream. I weaved in and out of conversation with a pregnant auto body attendant, a pregnant cop, a pregnant farmer's wife.

The chatter on Flo was destabilizing and asynchronous. Even as she served me content pegged to my pregnancy stage, she kept pulling me back to confront the past again and again. She would lead me to a thread about being nine weeks pregnant and then, months later, ping me with a new comment from a woman who was now in *her* ninth week. On Flo, dire practical concerns—*I live in Pakistan and I think I'm pregnant and there's no safe way of getting abortion here and I cant keep the baby because im only 19*—drifted by, unanswered. The Secret Chats were for thoughts that stretched beyond science and law. Like: *Have you ever sensed implantation?* And: *Is there anything you'd never discuss with anyone else no matter what?* The forum had the old-internet thrill of a nameless message board, and the posts could be intimate and startling. It felt illicit, like 4chan for people who were growing other people. I came across the account of a woman who had a miraculous pain-free hospital birth and one whose birth became an emergency brain surgery and one whose baby's arm snapped during delivery and one who went into labor while she was harvesting beans. *I felt like my anus will crack and I was very angry,* she said.

The space thrummed with wild power. But Flo made sure our energies never escaped the walls of the app. To *avoid unwanted anxiety and maintain a safe space for everyone,* the rules of Secret Chats prohibited *politics, preaching, hate,* and *private information.* Flo set the topics herself and made all wayward chats disappear. She asked: *What's your love language?* But not: *Have you experienced medical trauma?* If a user searched the Secret Chats for "Black," she would find an article on banishing blackheads. If she searched "abortion pill" she would find one about pregnancy pillows. She could not send a direct message or share her phone number with another user. She could not even post an image of a birthmark or a tattoo, lest it lead to her real-life identification.

It was impossible, given these conditions, to compare notes on an abortion provider or drop by one afternoon with a frozen dish. All we could do was *share our stories.* Inside Flo, every identity marker could be scrubbed, every difference leveled, every advantage obscured in the pursuit of evergreen content. We flowed into a stream of experience and sensation. We dissolved into baby dust.

One day, long after my pregnancy was over, I got curious about Flo. I wanted to know who had made her. I pulled up her website and navigated to the "About Us" page, where I found a baffling mission statement: *Flo exists to empower women by giving them a space they can access the knowledge and support they need to prioriti͡e their health and wellbeing.* An illustration showed a multicultural group of angular women, sketched in a style that had become ubiquitous among brands targeting feminine millennial audiences: bodies built from geometric shapes, drawn in thick lines, tinted shades of earthenware. The Flo girls wore minimalist separates and crossed their arms proudly over their half-moon breasts. A few masculine figures lurked among them, assuming deferential postures.

Google revealed who was really behind Flo: men. Specifically, Yuri and Dmitry Gurski, twin brothers from Belarus. Previously, Yuri had helped launch apps with names like All-In Pedometer and FoodMeter: Good Food or Bad Food? Now he was the cofounder and CEO of Palta, a wellness technology company that developed Flo, a fasting app called Simple, an AI fitness app called Zing, and a *digital skincare product* called Lovi. I navigated to Yuri's LinkedIn page, where he boasted of his *extraordinary number of business exits*, selling off apps to Google, Facebook, and a Russian platform called Mail.Ru. I clicked to enlarge his headshot. He wore a smartwatch around one wrist and a beaded bracelet around the other.

Flo's origin story had long been scrubbed from the site, but I found it using the Internet Archive Wayback Machine, a service that preserves images of old websites. I paged back through its scans as if rubbing a pencil on a notepad to reveal a secret message etched into the paper. In the post, Max Scrobov, the company's chief product officer, described Flo's inception this way: It began with *a bunch of geeks who wanted to better understand our beloved ones—our wives and girlfriends,* he wrote. *At some point, we realized the app not only helped us feel more confident about our relationships, but also helped women feel happier, be in charge of their own body, and plan ahead.*

I scrolled back through Flo's girlish diary. Its prompts—asking if I was *frisky,* if I felt guilty, if I had practiced my yoga, taken my pills, logged my weight—had been born from a desire to make men feel confident. As an unexpected side effect, women were thrilled.

The story sounded creepy but also a little contrived. *Flo exists to empower women*, the company motto assured me. But Flo was a business, so it also existed to make money. Backed by venture capitalists, it was meant to grow aggressively to assure its investors handsome returns. By 2024, the company had raised over $290 million and reached a valuation of $1 billion. It had tracked 2.2 billion menstrual cycles, and facilitated more than 35 million pregnancies, including my own. According to financial disclosure forms, Flo brought in $111 million in revenue in 2023.

"Our vision is for every girl, woman and person who menstruates to use Flo on a daily basis, learning more about their health and feeling more empowered as a result," Dmitry Gurski said in a 2021 interview. They would not rest until they had tracked every day of every menstrual cycle on Earth. When I asked to interview Flo's founders, I was instead directed to speak to some of their female employees. They materialized on a Zoom call from the company's far-flung offices, and I asked them what it was like to work for a menstruation tracker run by cisgender men. "It's potentially one of the reasons why Flo became a success," Cath Everett, Flo's VP of product, replied. She explained that as they built the app, the founders interviewed gynecologists to answer basic questions about the menstrual cycle. The app's "beauty," its "simplicity and ease," may have sprung from "their own lack of knowledge," Everett said. "Perhaps that means they made fewer presumptions, as well."

Flo had not invented the period-tracking app, though you would not know that by reading its website. Clue, developed by the Danish internet entrepreneur Ida Tin, launched in 2013, two years before Flo. Its logo was not pink but red, like blood. Tin ushered in a new category of women's health technology and coined the term "femtech" to describe it. In doing so, she built on a long tradition of women marshaling data about menstruation for political ends. In

1876, the English-American doctor Mary Putnam Jacobi published the pamphlet "The Question of Rest for Women During Menstruation." Jacobi interviewed hundreds of women about their periods and produced a statistical analysis that disproved the then-ascendant idea that mental or physical exertion during menstruation was dangerous and must be suppressed. In 1913, the British botanist Marie Stopes started producing what she called "rhythm charts," graphing her waning and waxing libido over the course of her monthly cycle and recruiting other women to join her. She published the results in a 1918 advice book, *Married Love*, invoking the language and iconography of data science to legitimize women's sexual desires.

Data presents itself as neutral, but these projects were not. Jacobi was a socialist who wanted to pry open educational opportunities for women and girls. Stopes was a eugenicist who wanted to improve the stock of human babies. She created her rhythm charts to support her first-wave feminist politics, but even as she asserted the normalcy of women desiring sex, she drew the boundaries of what constituted a "normal" woman. In an early draft of *Married Love*, Stopes specified that her calculations of the "normal sex-sequence" applied to any "healthy, well-fed, middle-class woman of northern European nationality." She wanted such women to have more children, as soon as naturally possible for them. In her next book, *Radiant Motherhood*, Stopes complained that "the diseased, the racially negligent, the thriftless, the careless, the feeble-minded, the very lowest and worst members of the community" were free to "produce innumerable tens of thousands of stunted, warped, and inferior infants," while the "superior artisan classes" paid taxes to support them.

Once I learned that Stopes was a eugenicist, I tunneled through the historical record until I found her most disgusting parts. Off the success of her advice books, Stopes created a network of women's clinics, called the Society for Constructive Birth Control and Racial Progress, to discourage births from "the worst end of our community" and encourage births from "the better end." For the "hopelessly rotten," she favored sterilization. To Stopes, a great many people were hopeless. When her son Harry got engaged to a nearsighted woman named Mary, Stopes complained in a letter that their union would make a mockery of their "lives' work for Eugenic breeding and the Race." He married her anyway. Later Mary had this to say about her mother-in-law: "I honestly thought she might poison us both."

Finally, I reached the rock bottom of Stopes's biography: On August 12, 1939, she mailed a book of her romantic poems to a man she admired. "Dear Herr Hitler," she wrote, "Love is the greatest thing in the world."

I was, in the words of Marie Stopes, a healthy, well-fed, middle-class woman of northern European heritage. But I was also, in her view, racially negligent for procreating with a Jew. "Empowering women" was an easy gloss, but the work of turning bodies into information was not as straightforwardly liberating as Flo made it seem. The synthesis of the app's various origin stories—a "bunch of geeks" created a global menstrual surveillance tool that they claimed would inspire a mass empowerment event—recalled the naïve promise of the "Quantified Self movement," which took the tech press and the TED conference stage by storm in the early 2000s. The *Wired* editors Kevin Kelly and Gary Wolf laid the movement's groundwork in a 2007 blog post in which they argued that tools like *psychological self-assessments* and *non-invasive probes* would produce data that could unlock the meaning of life. *Unless something can be measured,* they wrote, *it cannot be improved.*

The Quantified Self movement was criticized, early on, for its alpha-nerd masculinity. When Apple released an expansive self-monitoring app called Health in 2014, it allowed users to track their blood alcohol content and their body temperature but not their periods. The publicity around the oversight was an embarrassment, but it also signaled a market opportunity. Women's bodies were available to be measured, calibrated, and sold back to them, too. Even fetuses could be optimized before birth.

When Flo debuted the next year, it brought the biohacking tech-bro ethos to menstruation data. Now Flo was the handmaiden inducting me into her ideology of pregnancy. She numbed me to the idea that my pregnancy was a public event. She got me used to the feeling of an external authority charting my progress and correcting my behavior. She suggested that I conduct my pregnancy with exacting self-control, and then she pointed to her fetus cam, reminding me of the stakes of my choices. I wondered what Flo was really hoping to improve with her measurements. Did she want to make me into a good mommy? Did she want me to gestate a better baby? Or did she just want me to open the app again and again? Flo made it seem like I was making the empowered choice by surveilling myself. But it was a choice that ultimately enriched Flo.

If Flo was a video game, Pregnancy mode was one zillion times harder than Period mode. It felt like booting up an old Nintendo and finding that its laser blaster had transformed into a loaded gun. Flo stopped directing me toward threads like *How loud are you during sex?* and into ones like *What do you use on your pregnancy stretch marks? Share some tips* and *Managing weight during pregnancy for health reasons: Share your experience.* She became an accountant of the flesh, pushing statistical averages at every stage of pregnancy. She told me when to expect swollen gums, frequent urination, a dip in my sex drive, a visible bump. She instructed me to eat dried fruits one week, then fortified cereals, then sweet potatoes, lentils, sunflower seeds, calcium, seaweed. Always floating in the background was her photorealistic fetus. Flo informed me when it was beginning to develop a voice box, eyelashes, facial expressions. It smiled at me from inside the app.

Flo covered many of the same beats as a book like *What to Expect When You're Expecting* did, but she did not function like a book. A book didn't jump in front of a pregnant woman while she was checking her work email and say: *Your baby can hear your heartbeat.* I could pick up a book and put it down. I could leave it at home and walk out the door. Flo was always with me, navigating my pregnancy from my pocket. Even when I switched off her notifications, she kept drawing me back in. In the early weeks of my pregnancy, I found myself pressing her pink feather icon as many as ten times a day. My neck was always bent cranelike over my phone, peering into my womb console.

I sensed that for some women who were facing substandard medical care, Flo was the artificial nurse who could fill in some of the gaps. Occasionally Flo users would take to the Secret Chats and plead for help. *I have symptoms of depression according to the health assistant but IT WONT LET ME KNOW WHAT IS GOING ON WITH ME AND MY BODY BECAUSE I HAVE TO BUY THE PREMIUM!!*, one of them wrote. A fissure emerged around how helpful Flo really was. *I know we're all from different parts of the world and different cultures have different sex education but please remember, WE ARE NOT DOCTORS HERE!!! None of us can do bloodwork to check your hormone levels or give you a sonogram to check your organs through this app!!* one user said. To which another replied, *Believe it or not, not everyone has the resources to go running to a doctor.*

Flo was for women who could not run to a doctor, and it was also for women who raced between their doctors and their phones, pounding on an accelerating treadmill of information. The sickest thing about my relationship with Flo was that I ignored all her advice. I did not modify my diet based on the gestational week. I did not track my symptoms against her calendar. Still my fingers led me back to the app, where I thumbed through her updates without even reading them. Her offerings scratched at a deeper itch. The drumbeat of recommendations tapped out an unconscious message: pregnant women ought to think about being pregnant all the time. I checked Flo out of anxiety, or maybe just boredom. I could no longer tell the difference.

When I was just a few weeks pregnant, I considered deleting Flo altogether, but the idea made me weirdly superstitious. Should I really just . . . delete my baby? I tried out a different pregnancy app, one that did not feature a creepily realistic CGI fetus. Instead, it translated my fetus's size into a parade of Parisian bakery items. *You're beautiful!* it said when I opened it in bed. But the app could not see me, did not know me, and did not know my baby. It had just swallowed my expected due date and crapped out a drawing of a macaron. Obviously, Flo didn't know me, either. (Obviously, obviously.) But she had been there. Marking her calendar, making her predictions, wielding her fantasy endoscope. From the very beginning.

Chapter 2

Bump

It took forty-eight hours for the brands to find me. Two days after I got my positive pregnancy test, Instagram served me an ad for a mobile game called Lily's Garden. In the game, a down-on-her-luck city girl inherits her great-aunt's ramshackle country home, and now you, the Lily's Garden player, must perform wearisome tile-matching exercises to help Lily buy a new birdbath or whatever. The gameplay required Lily to have zero interiority, but in this ad, she was inexplicably holding a pregnancy test—one that looked identical to the one I had just peed on.

I lowered my phone very slowly. Did it know? It couldn't have known. Or else . . . Lily's Garden had instantly processed my pregnancy into marketing data and responded in a deranged manner. Could it be so desperate for me to download a game about landscaping, it impregnated a cartoon? I watched Lily make goo-goo eyes at the test and hug it proudly to her breast. I felt, I guess, happy for her. Our synchronized moment played out over the course of a sponsored Instagram story, and then it was gone.

More ads followed. A manicured hand squeezed a pair of golden capsules between two fingertips: a *reimagined* prenatal vitamin. A model wore a frilly smocked dress in an all-white kitchen, pressing an infant to her chest. I'm guessing that digital ad networks found out about my pregnancy through my highly unsubtle online activities. As soon as I got pregnant, I typed *What to do when you get pregnant* into my phone, and now advertisers were supplying their own answers.

I imagined my test's pink dye spreading across Instagram, Facebook, Amazon. All around me, a techno-corporate infrastructure was locking into place. I could sense the advertising algorithms recalibrating and the branded newsletters assembling in their queues. Pregnant exercise instructors beckoned to me from YouTube thumbnails. Digital clothing companies offered confusing bras. More brands knew about my pregnancy than people did. They all called me *mama*.

I knew that I was supposed to think of targeted advertising as evil, but I had never experienced it that way. The personalization felt hapless and lazy. Brands hand-delivered me the same millennial slop they plastered all over the New York City subways—boxed mattresses and rebranded SSRIs. Now when I opened Instagram, I was confronted by a slender white lady dressed as a pregnant milkmaid and sipping a Topo Chico from a straw. The model reached through the phone and bonked me on the forehead. I hated the ad and I wanted the dress.

It had felt like Flo was coaxing me into a costume of womanhood, and now the costume was literal. My feed cleared into a runway of bump-friendly styles. Fleets of pregnant models appeared in lush microclimates. They executed stretches and danced like inflatable tube people with their arms flouncing above their smiling heads. They seemed dazed by the beauty of their own clothing, as if it had been crafted by helpful birds. If they encountered one another, they bumped their bumps together. Often the models' heads were cut off at the necks, like porn actors', so that I could imagine more easily that I was them.

Maternity lines once had cutesy puns for names, like A Pea in the Pod and Take Nine, but now my cursor pointed me toward companies branded with severe abstractions, like Ripe and Storq. The company that engaged me the most tirelessly throughout my pregnancy was called Hatch. In addition to selling maternity clothes and a *bump care* regimen of belly oils, belly sheet masks, and temporary belly tattoos, Hatch published a digital magazine on pregnancy and motherhood called *Babe by Hatch*. I subscribed to its newsletter in exchange for a 10 percent discount code. *We got you, mama*, Hatch assured me as my email address slipped from my fingers.

Each week, the newsletter addressed me in smarmy baby talk, the native dialect of millennial digital brands. Hatch opened by comparing my baby to a consumer item—like, *Week 8: your baby is the size of a CBD gummy*—then served me some *real talk*. She wanted to know if I had picked out the baby's name yet or if I was waiting to *assess their vibe*. She assured me that my moods were fluctuating while *preggo* because *HCG*—a hormone produced by the placenta—was *en fuego*. Circumcision was *totally your call mama*, she said, while genetic testing was *a loaded convo*. Either way, I was *large and in charge* and ready to *crush the whole "mom" thing* and I should probably buy a flask of belly oil for $64.

For six days out of the week, I forgot that Hatch existed. On Thursday, the email arrived. I would start hate-reading it only to realize several minutes later that I had absorbed a primer on lymphatic drainage and was now wandering vacantly through the jumpsuit section. Over the next few years, the newsletter would prove so successful that it would become the model for how maternity clothes were sold. "It really does take a community to do this, but many of us live far from our own parents and families," Hatch's founder, Ariane Goldman, said in a 2021 interview. Hatch styled itself as the pregnant community's virtual village, and in 2019, its emails generated about 35 percent of the brand's sales. "Our customers need it; women around the world need it," Goldman said. In 2023, she was named CEO of a new megamaternity brand called the Hatch Collective, which absorbed the legacy maternity brands A Pea in the Pod, Motherhood Maternity, and Destination Maternity (a line sold at Walmart) in order to, as its website put it, *unite all women under a common thread of motherhood.* Pregnancy had a new voice, and it sounded like *Babe by Hatch.*

I did not need new clothes, not yet. I reported to my office every morning, pretending as if I were unchanged. As if the phone in my back pocket were not slick with images of lubricated stomachs. As if my mind were laser-focused on, uhhh, work. My baby was the size of *a mood ring.* My baby was the size of a *pasty.* Every night I came home and lifted my shirt for the mirror, waiting for my new body to arrive.

When I was fourteen weeks pregnant *(your baby is the size of a tube of Glossier Boy Brow),* I came home from the office and did not return for two years. Covid sealed Marc and me into our one-bedroom apartment. We didn't know what it was or how you got it, if it could sneak in through a vent or stick to the bottom of a cereal box. We didn't know if it could cross the placental barrier and harm a fetus. On my phone, I watched a shaky video filmed outside the hospital down the street. A forklift heaved bagged corpses into the bed of a semitruck. I watched another video of another forklift filling another corpse truck across town, this one filmed by a medical worker sealed into baby-blue protective equipment. "Bodies, bodies, bodies," he said.

A few weeks later *(your baby is the size of a Cronut)*, Uber aired a commercial thanking its customers for not using its services. A piano plinked over a montage of images signifying the indomitability of the human spirit: girls roller-skating through a kitchen; a dad doing push-ups with a baby; friends clinking glasses on a video call. Then a pregnant woman appeared, doing nothing. She just stood at a window, touching her belly with her hand.

Getting pregnant felt like stepping into a metaphor. The metaphor of all metaphors. People were always talking about conceiving ideas, gestating books, incubating startups. My body became the source of inspiration and genius. Art came from me. Now the corporate Covid ads stamped another new meaning onto my body: I was a symbol of hope and resilience in a time of mass death.

But I was not pregnant with meaning, I was pregnant with pregnancy, and I did not feel generative and alive, I felt itchy and full. Nausea snuggled into my chest. My scalp felt weirdly loose, like it was levitating just above my skull. At night I fell into dead sleep and awoke with numb legs. I gagged up vitamins and water. My eyeballs felt gritty and exposed. I went for such a long time without pooping that I was forced to develop advanced techniques for extracting the backlog of hardened shit from my ass. My shit required accessories: latex gloves, craft scissors, a stepstool, a little spoon filched from the honey jar. I swallowed stool softeners, probed and chipped at the blockage, cramped and strained on the toilet. I felt desperate and crazy, like it was never going to come out, like I would die of shit up my ass. Finally, it tore out of me in a slide of rock and sediment. I wondered whether delivering the shit was good practice for birthing a human being. Then I grabbed the scissors. After several rounds, I learned that I needed to cut up the biggest pieces of shit in the toilet bowl before I flushed to stop it from clogging my pipes. This happened once a week. It was the most creative thing I did during pregnancy, and all it produced was shit.

Locked away in my apartment, my body transformed. My stomach pushed past my hips and peeked from the bottoms of my shirts. It wasn't cute and round but boxy and thick, like a brutalist concrete slab. Soon it was making me bump into walls and squeeze around the living room couch. I opened my closet and surprised myself with the body that spilled from the mirror's frame. "I wonder if I've been changed in the night?" Lewis Carroll's Alice says after she drops down the rabbit hole and grows very large. I had a new body now, one known only to me and Marc. My laptop camera sliced me off at the neck and hid my pregnancy on virtual work calls and union meetings. When I left the house, I had to remind myself that people looked at me and saw a pregnant woman. I felt like a background actor in their movie montage, my growing bump marking the passage of time. Neighbors sat on the lips of their stoops or passed me on muddy paths and said, *Hey, mama!—Congratulations!—Good for you!—Sexy!—Thank you for creating life!*

It was actually really nice. My body pulled me into an intimacy with strangers at a time when nobody was supposed to get close. My good fortune was broadcast to the whole neighborhood. It could be spotted yards and yards away. Before I was pregnant, I heard the comedy duo Garfunkel and Oates's song "Pregnant Women Are Smug" and thought, *I'm not sure that's fair.* But now I was pregnant and very smug. I basked in the sense that my community was eager to welcome the future neighbor growing inside me. And yet the strength of the attention directed toward my body was, I had to admit, suspicious. I felt like a slug, but the commentary assured me that I was approaching my peak feminine state. The catcalling that had quieted as I entered my thirties roared back. "A woman is likely to glow and look more beautiful during this period while her body is fulfilling its ultimate physical function," read a Boston physician's pregnancy pamphlet, published around 1970. *Ultimate* meant "extreme" but also "final." It signaled an ending. It felt like everyone was humoring me, like they were all in on a plot to give my youthful sexuality one last charity spin before it expired.

One day I streamed *Seahorse*, a documentary about a British trans man, Freddy McConnell, who documented his experience conceiving and birthing a baby amid the highly feminine culture of pregnancy. (In seahorses, the female produces and lays her eggs in the male's "brood pouch," where he incubates them before rhythmically spraying them into the sea through an opening in the pouch. I watched a video on YouTube.) McConnell wanted to be a father, so he did what was necessary. "I'm going to have my own baby because it's the simplest thing to do. It's the most pragmatic option," McConnell said. But nothing about his experience was simple. He had to wean off testosterone, inject a new hormone into his abdomen, select and purchase a vial of donor sperm. Then he had to be pregnant.

I watched McConnell persevere through the months as medical personnel and acquaintances looked through him, unwilling to make sense of a pregnancy unraveled from the myths of femininity. "I thought it would feel like more of a natural thing, because it's my body," he said. Instead, "I feel like a man who is doing something really odd." Our experiences were not the same, but he unlocked exactly how I was feeling. Not a woman doing something natural or inevitable. A woman doing something odd.

Lockdown extended the illusion of my stable self a little longer. It delayed the looming confrontation between motherhood and me. I had willed this to happen; I had orchestrated it all on an app. But now the person who had made those plans had vanished and I was not sure when she would return. My smugness dissipated when I returned to the apartment and logged back in to my real life. One afternoon I returned from a walk, pulled the covers over my head, and visualized all the life choices that I had just strangled off. I brought them into bed with me: all the trucks I would never drive to all the cabins I would never enter on all the lakes I would never swim in with all the men I would never meet. Covid stuck me in a looping preview of parenthood: trapped in my apartment, cleaning things with a moist wipe. It was like my pregnancy had tripped a psychic wire. The whole world remapped to my anxious and isolated state. I cried a lot and then I asked my phone what happened to a fetus when you cried all the time.

"I feel like I'm dying," I told Marc. "I feel like my life is ending." He touched my hand and told me that made sense. My pregnancy was carrying me toward one of those hospitals overflowing with corpses. But when I opened Instagram, I found the pregnant mamas unchanged. They lounged restfully, their spindly fingers fondling their stomachs on an endless loop. Maternity clothing seemed to be the only advertising category that had not spontaneously converted into a corporate meditation on the triumphs of video chatting. The internet just kept winding up its mommy music box and making skirts twirl.

How could a pandemic disrupt their message? The ads were already built on a steely denial of death and decay. One of Hatch's recurring features was called "Mom Crush," in which a stylish and accomplished woman provided an account of her pregnancy and posed for a photo series wearing outfits by Hatch. The mom crushes had hypermodern jobs, like thought leader or plant-based meal-delivery service cofounder, and they described rigid regimes that seemed designed to preserve their forms as they passed through the veil of motherhood. One described her second-trimester diet as *mainly fresh fruits, veggies, avocados, and lean proteins*. Another said that she allowed herself *two cheat days a week*. When Hatch asked its mom crushes about their plans for taking maternity leave, many of them replied that it would not be necessary. One said that she had *never been so productive*. One was *texting a client between contractions!* One was looking forward to the *incoming opportunities* around *storytelling this particular time*. One of them said, *My business is also my baby*.

I had once imagined that maternity clothing brands sold super-stretchy pants and weirdly long shirts, but now I understood that they sold a resolution to the identity crisis of motherhood. One of Hatch's taglines was *Still you, just pregnant*. Storq put it this way: *Feel like yourself again, only more comfortable*. Never before had aspirational fashion brands tried to sell me such a meager vision for my future self. *Buy this dress and nothing will change for you*, they seemed to say. *Buy this dress and you will not disappear into motherhood, never to be heard from again!* Which is how I knew that the old me was really, truly gone.

When Instagram served me that Lily's Garden ad, it unlocked a memory of a 2012 *New York Times Magazine* story about how corporations were using predictive analysis to influence shoppers before they even knew what they were looking for. The story, by Charles Duhigg, centered on a Target statistician named Andrew Pole who created an algorithm for predicting which customers had entered a life stage that could prove extremely lucrative to Target: pregnancy. New parents were "a retailer's holy grail," Duhigg wrote. They were "exhausted and overwhelmed and their shopping patterns and brand loyalties are up for grabs." Companies like Target were now racing to interpret shifts in the purchasing habits of women of childbearing age, trying to identify the pregnant ones before their competitors did.

The story produced an infamous anecdote that became a part of internet lore, a cautionary tale for the age of digital ad tracking that was just coming into view. A concerned father purportedly stormed into a Target location, angry that the store sent his teenage daughter coupons for baby stuff. When a manager called him to apologize, the father was chastened. "It turns out there's been some activities in my house I haven't been completely aware of. She's due in August," Duhigg reported him as saying. The story taught Target's marketing team that it needed to be sneakier about how it served its predictive ads, seeding diaper and crib content with unrelated products, like lawn mowers. In a blog post, *Forbes* summarized the story this way: "How Target Figured Out a Teen Girl Was Pregnant Before Her Father Did."

Rereading the story, I was struck by the framing of the offense. The focus was not on the teenager's privacy; it was on her father's honor. Who should know about a pregnancy first: surveillance capitalism or your dad? I got pregnant just eight years after the story's publication, and by then, it seemed that the question had been answered definitively. A corporation did not need cutting-edge behavioral science to guess that I was pregnant. I plugged the information directly into my phone. Obviously, I told the internet before I told my parents.

And the internet was not shy about what it served back. Retailers were no longer worried about freaking me out with their knowledge of the blastocyst inside me. I had learned to regard what we now called *the algorithm* with a bemused familiarity, as if it were a personal shopping assistant who mildly sucked at her job, like I sometimes did. When the algorithm misjudged me, I was fake-offended. When she got me exactly right, hey, good for her. But now that

I was pregnant, advertising on Instagram became so personalized that it started to feel intimate, even though it was the opposite of that—it represented the corporate obliteration of my privacy. The pregnancy ads reached me before I had a doctor. Before I had a clue.

When I searched *What to do when you get pregnant* on a Chrome browser, I ended up on a WebMD article called "How Often Do I Need Prenatal Visits?" WebMD informed me that in the first trimester, my doctor would probably like to see me once a month. In return, WebMD invited ad trackers to follow me around. As I researched this book, I retraced my steps, using a tool that reveals tracking technology embedded in websites, and I found that WebMD had allowed 74 companies to track me, stored 153 cookies in my browser, and told Facebook where I had been. One of the companies with a tracker on WebMD was called 33Across, which described itself as *an addressable infrastructure designed for the open web* that built *identity resolution technology* and *programmatic monetization*, which meant that it compiled my personal data from a bunch of other ad-tech companies in order to profile me more thoroughly. When I requested my data from 33Across, I found that it had used my advertising profile with 29 brokers to add me to dozens of audience segments, including "Newlyweds," "Expecting Parents," and "Pregnancy and Birth."

WebMD alone directed dozens of ad companies toward my pregnancy, but the full scope of the ad-tech surveillance system was unquantifiable. When I asked Jen Golbeck, a professor of computer science at the University of Maryland, how many advertising profiles on me were floating around the ad-tech ecosystem, she replied, "So many that I don't know that it's possible to estimate." And when I asked Christo Wilson, a computer science professor at Northeastern University, how many advertising data points I had generated in my life, he said, "Billions and billions."

The ad-tech industry was like that Hieronymus Bosch painting, with shifting privacy laws continually casting its gluttonous players into regulatory hellscapes. But this only expanded the range of personal data that they sought to mine and exploit. The industry was capable of gleaning when I watched my British murder show on Roku, when I bought my pregnancy tests with a credit card at my local pharmacy, when I watched a bump progression video on TikTok, when I liked an Instagram influencer's pregnancy reveal, and when I walked, phone in my pocket, to the threshold of a baby-gear store. Immediately, it could know when I marked myself as pregnant in an app. NextMark, a digital marketing company, offers a list of pregnant women scraped from *pregnancy planning tools* and *app interactions that indicate stages of a pregnancy,* a list it said was *updated in real time.* Of course, it knew when I plugged my due date into a fancy maternity-brand website. *If you opt into our loyalty program, we also share your contact information, due dates, and other pregnancy related information (trimester and number of children) to partners who can provide you and your growing family with additional offers and services,* the Hatch privacy policy said.

When a data broker added me to an audience segment, it bundled thousands of pregnant people's data up with mine and shopped them to advertisers who wanted to sell us tent dresses and adult onesies, and a little later on, postpartum genital sprays and belly bands. These advertisers could target an existing audience segment, or they could command a platform to shop their wares to a "look-alike audience," so that even if I did not end up in one of these databases, I could be roped in by behaving similarly to someone who did. And an ad platform like Meta was so vast, its data stores so deep, its machine-learning processes so deft, it did not need to "know" explicitly about a pregnancy in order for its algorithms to send relevant ads my way.

As I scrolled through a website or swiped through Instagram, advertising networks ran continuous automated auctions in the background, each advertiser bidding for the chance to capture my attention in that moment. I visited WebMD again recently, this time with a plug-in installed to track bids, and found that Amazon had won an auction to populate the page with ads in 610 milliseconds. Pregnancy had turned me into a coveted consumer, and for a moment this felt like power. Brands wanted me to model their clothes! Stores wanted to swaddle my young in their diapers! But my pregnancy was only valuable in that it made these companies think that they could take my money. My data was not that plum of a prize after all. NextMark maintains a database of mailing lists separated by audience segment, and as I paged through its offerings, I discovered that one prenatal mailing list, called "Momsense! Moms to Be," charges $85 to reach one thousand pregnant consumers. Another list, "She's Having a Baby," costs $95. For another $8, an advertiser could filter the list by ethnicity, income, or age. And for an extra $10, it could buy one thousand due dates for one thousand babies.

By NextMark's metrics, my pregnancy was about as valuable as a list of CBD buyers suffering from obsessive-compulsive disorder ($95 per thousand). It was about as valuable as a list of "booming boomers" with erectile dysfunction ($85 per thousand). It was less valuable than a list of people who had purchased a Donald Trump–themed chess set ($120 per thousand) and a list of medical geneticists ($500 per thousand). My baby's due date—the one that I had calculated in Flo and surrendered to Hatch—represented one of the most tantalizing pieces of personal data that I had ever produced. It was the date that my life was expected to change forever, and the date that a new life was expected to begin. Through NextMark, it could be purchased for $10 along with the due dates of 999 other babies. I imagined the date tossed onto a squirming pile of baby data. Its value was one-tenth of one cent. Almost worthless.

The value of a pregnancy, in the online economy, was a topsy-turvy idea. News of my pregnancy might have been worth a fraction of a cent, but an influencer's pregnancy could compel brands to shell out tens of thousands of dollars. In February of 2024, I walked into Ghiaia Cashmere, a luxury menswear shop tucked into a Mission-style strip mall in Pasadena, California, to meet the fashion entrepreneur and digital creator Pia Baroncini, whose second pregnancy was currently being sponsored by various wellness and luxury brands. Ghiaia was founded by Baroncini's husband, Davide, and in addition to serving as the brand's chief marketing officer, she was the creative director of the womenswear brand LPA, the cofounder of the Italian goods company Baroncini Import & Co., the host of the podcast *Everything Is the Best,* and the star of her own Instagram account, where she broadcast her life with Davide to her more than two hundred thousand followers.

On the internet, Baroncini presented like a New York cool girl who had been improbably pulled into the cover shoot for an Italian romance novel. Her constellation of business ventures gravitated around her own body, and she let her followers in on the supplements she took, the pastas she cooked, and the romantic nightgowns she wore to bed. As she entered her thirties, she filled them in on new physical challenges—weight gains and losses, a diagnosis of polycystic ovary syndrome (PCOS), holistic fertility treatments, and eventually, a pregnancy. Her growing body, her expanding family, seemed only to lengthen her reach in the lifestyle space. In 2021, when she was pregnant with her first child, Hatch named Baroncini a mom crush, and she told the brand how she had *cycle synced* her diet and workouts to boost her fertility and ate yogurt to optimize her prenatal microbiome.

I thumbed to Baroncini's Instagram page while I waited for her to arrive. A photo stack of a recent Ojai staycation sponsored by Samsonite luggage sat atop her grid. In the main image, her toddler ate from a plate of tortilla chips as Baroncini lounged near a pool, hand on bump. As I looked at my phone, I ran my free hand over the sleeve of a cashmere coat, turned over its tag, saw a number exceeding $5,000, and backed away from the mannequin as if I might be detained for initiating physical contact. Baroncini appeared a few minutes later, willowy and relaxed in a crisp striped shirt and gauzy pants. She threw an arm around my shoulder and joined me on a stool in front of the shop's reclaimed tiki bar, where a young man who looked like he could play a vampire in a teen movie poured espressos from a machine. She was three months pregnant.

I wanted to know what it felt like to experience pregnancy in a body inscribed with so much value—to live in a body that stood to generate money through pregnancy, not lose it. Immediately after receiving her positive test, Baroncini told me, she alerted her representatives at the influencer management company DBA, who started pitching the event to their networks. That same day, Baroncini contacted one of her brand partners, the supplement startup Perelel Health, personally over text message. During my pregnancy, I had bought a generic prenatal gummy off a drugstore shelf, but Perelel believed that *women deserve better*. It offered a range of supplement packs that it claimed were tailored to various reproductive events, including a Cycle Support Pack for menstruation; an Egg Freeze Support Pack; a Conception Support Pack for those *thinking or trying;* a Recovery Support Pack for pregnancy loss; distinct packs for the first, second, and third trimesters of pregnancy; and a Mom

Multi Support Pack for the postpartum period. *The conception pack and PCOS formula gave me a child,* Baroncini texted that day. *It was absolutely the supplements.* A few months later, Perelel celebrated Baroncini's pregnancy announcement by posting a screenshot of the exchange to Instagram.

"I love being pregnant," Baroncini told me. "I love when people touch." Attention to her pregnant body represented "a warmth and a connection to humans," she said. "So it is extra hurtful when it has been turned into something extremely negative." She told me about a Reddit group where over a thousand members assembled to post screenshots of her Instagram feed with comments like *How have we normalized this level of narcissism?* and *She's a monster.* They speculated about the source of her weight loss and the age-appropriateness of her toddler's development. (Of the Perelel post, one said: *Sick sick sick.*) As Baroncini spoke of these people, a flash of annoyance pierced her open gaze. "I always say, if it weren't on the internet, it would be amongst the moms in a mom group. It's just on a larger scale," she said. She told me about a woman in her social circle who had recently speculated that Baroncini had fat pads surgically removed from her lower cheeks. "Because I'm a business, I view it as a business expense," she said of the commentary. "This is just the price of doing business. The world is disgusting."

I asked if the Pia Baroncini business offered any maternity leave, and she laughed. "Hell no," she said. "This is my big time. This is what people want to see." She jocularly handled her stomach. "This is baby Super Bowl."

A few weeks after my trip to Pasadena, I called Catie Li, a Chinese American model and fashion influencer with more than 370,000 followers on Instagram and more than 300,000 on TikTok. Li started her career doing publicity work for the Shade Room and BET before striking out on her own, styling and posing herself in plus-size outfits while pursuing brand partnerships and taking a cut of affiliate marketing sales. When we spoke, Li was newly postpartum with her first child. "I just hit the four-month sleep regression," she said. "So that's great." But on the internet, she still looked as dewy as a Disney character, like bells chimed when she blinked.

Before Li got pregnant, she and her husband thought deeply about whether it would be financially feasible for them to have a child. Li is also represented by DBA, and when she asked her management team how pregnancy and motherhood might impact her business, they assured her that it could be a profitable transition. She wasn't prepared for what happened next. When she informed some clients about her pregnancy, they responded, essentially: "Congratulations, but we're probably not going to continue this conversation." She said, "And now that I've had the baby, there's crickets on their end."

Li had been in the fashion business for a long time. It was rare for her to see plus-sized models who were pregnant, and rare to see pregnant models who were not white. "I'm in a niche already, being a plus-size woman and a woman of color," she said. Still, she says she "was a little naïve about it." There was no natural limit to Li's audience: plus-sized women get pregnant, they wear clothes when they are pregnant, and fashion icons like Rihanna had proven that a pregnant body need not be shoved into the maternity section, never to be seen again. But Li could not find any maternity brands that carried clothes in her size—"literally nothing," she said—and brands in the plus-sized space weren't interested in featuring a pregnant model. Li's look radiated "a young, refreshing vibe," she said, and she began to suspect that brands believed her pregnancy confused that message. "They were just shelving me for later," she realized.

"It's insane to say that we're inclusive," Li said of the fashion and beauty industries. She had staked her career on challenging their strict categories, but in motherhood she was thwarted. Four months postpartum, she wondered how long her influencer purgatory would last. She had been asking her manager, "How are we gonna bring it back? Because I don't think they know what to do either," she said. It seemed like the fashion world could stomach only one deviation from its ideal at a time. Which meant that if a brand was going to feature a pregnant model, she was probably going to be skinny and white.

During my pregnancy, I ravenously consumed images of other people's pregnancies. Even as the U.S. Covid response compelled "essential workers" to labor under dangerous conditions, it assured homebound "nonessential workers" like me that various antisocial behaviors, such as binge drinking and compulsive online shopping, were newly acceptable, even brave. Working from home severely reduced my need for maternity clothes—I never had to trudge into an office, dressed like a business-casual tent—but it gave me more time to sit around, shaking the internet's snow globe of maternal femininity. Every time I opened Flo, she showed me her stock image of a pregnant body: a thin, computer-generated white woman that looked like a Barbie doll with its head popped off. She was the avatar of the contemporary maternal ideal—the woman whose bump was grown under such exacting conditions that the rest of her body remained unchanged.

Once I had thought of pregnancy as a time when you were allowed to eat whatever you wanted, but now I could see that it was the Tour de France of restrictive eating. Strict diet and exercise during pregnancy were cast not just as aesthetic practices but moral achievements, conflated with the health of the pregnancy and the expression of superior mothering. Hatch asked its mom crushes about their *relationship with movement,* their *vision of wellness,* and their *self-care rituals*—gentle rebrands of the punishing diets once advised by the maternity industry.

A 1952 catalog for the high-end brand Page Boy Maternity, which advertised empire-waist suits "to help you build your little empire" and stoles to "camouflage your precious bulge," also solicited questions from subscribers and supplied answers from its "Page Boy Maternity consultant"—a kind of proto–mom board conducted through the mail. One client asked the consultant how much weight she could gain during pregnancy, and the consultant said that it should not exceed twenty pounds. "Many women nibble all day during pregnancy. This is not caused by the pregnancy but is the result of emotional problems," the consultant said. After all, "you do wish to gain back your before-baby-came figure rapidly, don't you? So watch your weight!" Page Boy was later acquired by a company called Mother's Work, which eventually became known as Destination Maternity, which was folded into the Hatch Collective in 2023.

Then there were the clothes themselves, which seemed designed to yank the pregnant body back into a previous century. I had heard pregnant women grumble about how maternity wear was infantilizing, but by the time I got pregnant, infantilization was on trend: everything was pocked with eyelets and finished with pie-crust hems. Many of the styles would not have been out of place in a prairie schooner or on a plantation tour. In her skeptical take on the prairie dress trend, the writer Molly Fischer speculated that dressing like a frontierswoman evoked a childish nostalgia: In a feminine old-time dress, "you are your own American Girl doll, trying on the strictures of another time or place for fun," she wrote. "You inhabit a fantasy past, a world where you can always be the spunky heroine—the one to whom the rules don't apply."

But a pregnant belly smothered any parodic spirit in the clothes. They just made a maternity model look like she was committed to producing the future of the race. Pulling maternity looks from America's beginnings only emphasized the fact that the maternal ideal has long promoted the white mother as the standard of delicacy, purity, and virtue, while the Black mother has been smeared as her demonized other. As Kimberly C. Harper writes in her 2020 book, *The Ethos of Black Motherhood in America: Only White Women Get Pregnant*, it was the work of enslaved Black women, raising and wet-nursing white children, that enabled wealthy white women to spend their time cultivating the image of the ideal mother. "The valorization of White motherhood is reproduced for every generation and taught through television, movies, magazines, websites, Internet searches, and pregnancy literature," Harper writes. She argues that the vaunted image of the ethereal white mother—"thin, beautiful, well dressed, and middle class"—has had devastating, even lethal, effects for mothers who stand outside her narrow spotlight.

Harper is a professor of English, and before she became pregnant, she had not thought much about the inequities of maternal care. "I just thought people got pregnant, had babies, and went home with them," she told me over Zoom. But in interactions with pediatricians, obstetricians, and labor-and-delivery nurses, medical cultures rooted in the white middle class, she was viewed with suspicion and neglect. She was assumed to be uninsured and ignorant of prenatal care. She told an obstetrician that she was eating avocado because she learned it was good for pregnancy, and the doctor replied with surprise—"Who told you that?"—before admitting that Harper was correct. At the hospital, nurses induced her labor without her consent. After Harper barely avoided a postpartum hemorrhage during her daughter's birth, she started investigating the cultural backdrop that had informed her treatment in the medical system.

I had seen maternity ads' denial of death as a delusion. But being in a white body, and dressing it in expensive clothes, could indeed confer protection from death. I did not follow the internet's maternal wellness instructions—I did not ingest optimized pill packs or oil my stomach like antique wood—but I still accrued value and goodwill from its system. I was small and white and had a wedding band lodged on my bloated ring finger.

At week twenty *(your baby is the size of a green juice)*, I pulled the trigger on Hatch's most funereal offering, a long black dress with a scoop neck, an empire waist, and a reduced price. *Think '90's cool girl*, Hatch assured me, but as soon as the order was processed, her voice stiffened. *This item is final sale,* she warned. *Shipping may be delayed due to Covid-19.*

At week twenty-three *(the size of a loofah)*, I pulled the dress on and swanned into the summer heat. I adopted an exaggerated backward lean, jutting my hips to juice the bump. I toggled Marc's iPhone camera to portrait mode, sat cross-legged on a slope of grass, and posed for the photo that would announce the pregnancy to my friends, my family, my haters, and the wider Instagram community. My palms gravitated unthinkingly to my stomach. I held the bump with one hand and then with both hands, trying to smooth its severe proportions. I coached Marc on angles and instructed him to take several dozen shots. Then I sat in the grass and silently paged through the results. I chose one where I was smiling in a way that I recognized from photographs of myself as a child: a fat-cheeked imp, mouth bent into a crescent moon. I posted it to Instagram with a caption referencing a meme about the amount of salami you were allowed to feed a cat: *amanda and marc can have a little baby as a treat,* it said.

The comments came in: my baby was *lucky, cool,* a *gift from heaven.* For the rest of the day, I slid my finger down the face of my phone, refreshing the post to watch the like count increase like tokens pouring into the tray of a slot machine. Like it was funny money.

I tap into your blessing, the ladies on Flo said.

Chapter 3

Life

In the summer of 2020, California burned with a wildfire sparked by a gender-reveal party. A "smoke-generating pyrotechnic device," designed to release a signal plume of blue smoke, sparked grass and burned through twenty-two thousand acres of forest. The last time a gender smoke bomb started a wildfire—in 2017, in the Arizona desert, not far from where I grew up—I tweeted a photograph of black hills with a sick joke: *Boy or girl?* Now I read the news reports silently, thinking about the person whose pregnancy has become a disaster.

When my grandmother was pregnant with her first child in 1951, her baby's sex was revealed when it was born—a girl, my mother. When my mom was pregnant with me, in 1985, an amniocentesis or ultrasound examination conducted several months into a pregnancy could be used to determine the baby's sex, but my mother, too, did not learn my sex until I was born. When I was thirteen weeks pregnant—Hatch reported that my baby was *the size of a friendship bracelet*—blood drawn from the crook of my arm was shipped to a lab, which analyzed it for traces of fetal DNA. I could assign my child a sex before it had knees.

As that process grew easier, some parents devised complex

mechanisms for spreading the news. They colluded with a doctor, sealed the sex report in an envelope, and arranged for the message to be delivered to a baker, a party outfitter, or a novelty arms dealer. At a party held to announce the findings, a knife sliced through a layer of frosting to reveal the fleshy gender inside. A pregnant woman beat a piñata until its gender spilled out. A father-to-be pulled the trigger and rained gender across the range.

The "gender reveal" animated a lonely bit of genetic data into a scene. The fetus did not have a body of its own, but it already had an outfit. Once this was a feminized practice, a baby shower activity styled for Pinterest. But then it became a guy thing: there were gender cannons, gender pipe bombs, gender tire burnouts primed for TikTok and YouTube. The aesthetic was *America's Funniest Home Videos* meets terrorist beheading: a fixed camera recorded an anonymized landscape crawling with a support crew of undifferentiated men. Men who could not get pregnant could seize information about the pregnancy and explode their claim across the sky. Across the internet, too. Videos of gender reveals racked up millions of views if they were sufficiently dramatic, chaotic, and perverse.

Some of the most popular gender reveals unveiled emotional catastrophes. On TikTok, a spritz of pink confetti fell atop a pregnant woman and her thick husband. He swore and stormed out of the frame, leaving their two existing daughters to splash in the puddle of tissue paper. Other videos offered the cruel release of the reveal *gone wrong*. In one, a sedan belched blue smoke from its back tires, coughed out its driver, and burned to a crisp. These videos supplied the spectacle of man battling nature, and his comeuppance. Which, occasionally, was death. The California blaze killed a firefighter sent to extinguish it. In Iowa, shrapnel from a gender pipe bomb struck the skull of a grandmother-to-be, killing her instantly.

In the years before I got pregnant, these videos appeared on my feeds in flashes of ironic disaster. I casually delighted in the smitings, rewatching the moment a dad's face shaded with displeasure or a bro hopped away from a licking flame. It was easy to diagnose their politics and dissect their mistakes. Who cared so much about the sex of a fetus that they were moved to show their ass on TikTok or cause mass environmental devastation throughout the American West? In my own social circle, gendering unborn children had become an uncomfortable idea. Some expectant parents announced that they would not be announcing. Others disclosed apologetically, couching the announcement in qualifiers about how they planned to dress the child in neutrals, offer them trucks alongside toy strollers, wait and see how the baby identified. The Chicago woman credited with popularizing the gender-reveal party, which she detailed on her blog *High Gloss and Sauce* in 2008, later called her legacy a "nightmare" and begged parents to stop. Her kid, introduced to the world in a glob of pink icing, was now dressing in smart little suits. Gender was a construct, she said, the job of children to build or dismantle for themselves.

In 2018, the year before Marc and I got married, we squeezed into a banquette at a restaurant down the block with our friend Martha, who was visiting from Texas. She was newly pregnant, and she told us over dinner that it was a girl. I asked her why she had wanted to know. The information was not so important on its own, she said, but it arrived amid a crush of genetic information—all of it possibly frightening, some of it potentially catastrophic, none of it fun, except for this little puzzle piece, which felt neutral, which meant it felt interesting, tantalizing, hopeful. So, not neutral at all. Our knees knocked against hers beneath the table, but it was as if she were speaking from across a great distance.

Years later, her message made its way to me. I was pushing a shopping cart down a grocery aisle, a medical mask sealed to my face, when my phone lit up with the number of my obstetrician's office. The cart drifted from my hands and into a tower of cereal. I whipped the phone to my ear. I had not cared, and then I cared so much, it spooked me. When the doctor said, "It's a boy," I hissed three words back at her: "I knew it." But I hadn't known. Actually, when I imagined a child, I envisioned a girl. The moment the information hit me, I felt the urge to reclaim it, to internalize and embody it, to act as if the boy DNA were so potent in my blood that it pulsed a message directly to my brain.

In the beginning, I was the only one who knew that the pregnancy existed. But now, the details of my child's future life were arranged from afar. His genetic information had been extracted from my body, shipped to a lab, analyzed by a technician, printed on a PDF, read by a doctor, and transmitted back to me through the phone. When I said, "I knew it," I meant, *I am the keeper of my body's secrets.* Just like the parents staging their gender reveals, I wanted the information. And like them, too, I wanted the information to feel like an experience.

One year later, I would read a news story about a man who died preparing for a gender-reveal party in upstate New York, a few hours from where I lived. He made a bomb, and it blew up. I paged through his photographs on Google and found his obituary. He had worked in a diner and fixed old cars. On Facebook, I slinked to his widow's profile and scrolled back. I watched her trauma wind slowly in reverse, my nerves tightening as her posts drew nearer to the event. Her baby was a boy too, named for his daddy. I watched her son tear across the living room carpet on a toy backhoe, then romp with the family dog, then crawl. I watched him shrink from a toddler to a baby. I saw him disappear, drawn back into his mother, who was pregnant and alone. I flicked the browser window away with my finger, as if the force of it could delete the image from my memory. I knew what it felt like, then, to take a genetic signal, arouse it into a spectacle, and watch it tear through my life.

There was no such thing as neutral information.

One night, lying in bed, Marc and I swiped all the way through Flo's pregnancy calendar, watching the cartoon fetus grow to full term. It sprouted gangly limbs and a face with a button nose and a tranquil smile. *This app is insane,* I thought. And also: *Look at my baaaaaaby.*

A fetus was not a person—this I knew. But the culture of pregnancy styled it that way. It was always prompting me to swipe forward to imagine its future self. In test results, sonograms, and apps, the fetus was staged and ventriloquized. Its image could be pasted inside a baby book, or it could be replicated on social media, building an audience before birth. On Instagram, a couple announced a pregnancy by lifting a picture of their sonogram to the camera, each pinching a corner of the square, their fingers tense and white with effort. A pregnant influencer created an account for her unborn child, posted the sonogram, and said, *Let's get her to 100k before she arrives.* An ultrasound retouching company posted the faces of fetuses that it had scanned and edited into smooth-skinned, pink-lipped pre-babies. It called this offering *8K Ultrasound Enhanced Imaging,* as if it were a technological breakthrough. *It's hard to believe you're not staring at a real person,* the company said.

The first time I saw my baby—the thing that would become my baby—I was pantsless on an exam table, a lubricated wand stuck up my vagina. On a dinky screen, a black blob shifted inside a fan of white static. Was I *staring at a real person?* The monitor was positioned so that I could see, but the image was dense and inscrutable. I needed a doctor to tell me whether I was looking at a head or a tail. And then how I ought to feel about it. She gestured to a pointillist bean and assured me that everything looked as it should. Then she triggered an urgent scrunching noise—an electrical signal converted into a simulated heartbeat for a heart that was not yet formed. When she was finished, she printed out a snapshot of the abscess overlaid with a string of unexplained markings and the Samsung logo. I couldn't exactly see a baby, but its presentation made it seem sciency and real. I stuck the picture to the refrigerator door.

My pregnancy produced hours of ultrasound sessions and dozens of glossy sonogram images. I accumulated so many of them, they billowed from my purse and burped out of my desk drawers. Recently, I circled our apartment and scooped up the ones I could find. When I first received them, I was dazzled, like I had seen Jesus's face in a pierogi. Now I recognized how comically ghastly they always were. The baby appeared as a spray of fleshy globs, a leering skull, a face melting and fusing into a wall. In one, he surfaced from the static of my uterus like a ghoul crawling out of the TV. In another, which used a technology called "3D ultrasound" that was supposed to reveal a fetus in lifelike form, he resembled a creature caught by a flashlight in a dank cave. When the German physicist William Roentgen invented the X-ray machine in 1895, he slipped his wife's hand under the device and she said, "I have seen my death!" The sonograms looked deathly, too, but everybody talked about them like they were the opposite. They were proof of life.

The ultrasound was a diagnostic tool, but from its beginnings, it was also a narrative device. Fetal ultrasound developed under the eye of a British professor, Ian Donald, in the 1950s and 1960s. I found a black and white photograph of Donald online. He appeared like an old-time TV doctor—square jaw, rumpled brow, smug look. In 1958, he scanned a woman's torso using a naval tool for inspecting metal ships. The tool was called *the flaw detector*. At one demonstration, in 1978, he narrated the tape of an ultrasound of a twelve-week pregnancy as if watching a child at play. "Here's the baby, see how he jumps," Donald said. "It is rather like a child on a trampoline, tremendous strength, energy, and vitality." Donald emphasized the obliviousness of the mother, the untrustworthiness of her experience compared to the findings of his machine: "She does not even know she is pregnant." He continued: "One of the things that this film has done, if it has done nothing else, is to kill forever the lie of the pro-abortion lobby that there's nothing there, just a 'potential' human being, just—oh, look at that jump, he bumps his head against the roof nearly, doesn't he—this lie that he is just a 'potential' human being when in fact that baby is as human as an old man."

A woman had once been the narrator of her own pregnancy. Several months in, she felt fetal movement, called quickening, and she relayed that information to other people, or she did not. Now the ultrasound had intercepted the fetus and dragged it into public view. Doctors and activists could claim it with their eyes before she felt it in her body. Donald told his audiences that "seeing is believing," but his flaw detector required an interlocutor to turn the fetus into a little boy, bouncing in his mother's house. A fetus became a person, and a woman became a roof.

In the 1960s, as Donald was developing his flaw detector, a Swedish photographer named Lennart Nilsson was also laboring to peer inside the womb. In 1965, a series of his photographs revealing the "drama of life before birth" was published in *Life* magazine. I bid on the issue on eBay, and when I ripped it from its packaging a couple of weeks later, I was impressed by its gargantuan size. The fetus on the cover was bigger than my head. Its body was suspended in a white-flecked blackness, like it was drifting in space. It was described as a "living 18-week-old fetus shown inside its amniotic sac." I was confused. I had a fetus inside me at that moment, at a similar developmental stage. You couldn't take a full-color picture of it, head to toe, because there was something in the way: me.

Inside the magazine, I found a note from the editor praising Nilsson's "unprecedented photographic feat," which was "not only photographically exciting but scientifically valid." On the opposite page, a less conspicuous text box clarified the cover model's status. "This embryo was photographed just after it had to be surgically removed from its mother's womb at the age of 4½ months," it said. "Though scientists hope someday to be able to keep such early babies alive, this one did not survive." I flipped back to the cover. It didn't show "life before birth." The fetus was not alive, and it would never be born. It was a picture of an abortion.

Life had pitched Nilsson as a prenatal nature photographer, but he was a puppeteer. He had secured abortion or miscarriage tissues from surgeons in Stockholm, posed them tenderly, and illuminated them from within. He submerged them in aquariums, cased them in gauzy tissues, and floated them in bubbly fluid that masqueraded as a starry sky. He shot them so close that they appeared epic, planetary. He called one of his specimens *Rymdfararen*, Swedish for "The Spaceman." *Life* quoted an anonymous gynecologist who said, "This is like the first look at the back side of the moon." Stanley Kubrick's Star Child from *2001* was created downstream of Nilsson's image. NASA sealed Nilsson's photo inside the Voyager probes and blasted it to interstellar space.

When I opened Flo again, I was confronted by a smiling, peachy sylph suspended in a misty orb. I knew that Flo's digital fetus wasn't modeled after my own baby. Now it was clear that it was informed by Nilsson's specimen, or its many cultural derivatives. Styling the fetus as a celestial creature made it seem more than just human. It was made to seem better than we were. More advanced. As the fetus drifted through the cosmos, it became a mascot of both natural and supernatural wonder. It was an astronaut, or an alien, or a god. And then there was me. If my fetus was a spaceman, I was his airless terrain. I was the vacuum of space.

In "The Politics of Abortion and the Commodification of the Fetus," the political scientist Joanne Boucher writes that the fetus's public persona relies on "a double suppression." It obscures the body in which it grows and denies the technological artifice through which it appears. Only then is it freed to circulate as a political symbol—a mirage of life before birth.

Prenatal technologies—Donald's sonogram, Nilsson's photographs—helped animate the political movement to establish a legal claim to "fetal personhood" from conception. Nilsson's pictures were printed in antiabortion pamphlets and plastered on placards. When the Supreme Court overturned *Roe v. Wade* in 2022, revoking the constitutional right to abortion, it used prenatal imaging as one rationale. The technology has ushered in "a new appreciation of fetal life," Samuel Alito's opinion said, because "when prospective parents who want to have a child view a sonogram, they typically have no doubt that what they see is their daughter or son."

Now Flo was borrowing the same aesthetics for its own interface. Each week, she delivered a dispatch on what my blastocyst or embryo or fetus "looked" like. The entries zoomed in on prenatal clumps and clods and narrated them as if they were gurgling tots. On week four—just two weeks after ovulation—Flo called the embryo *the baby* and my *little one*. It was the size of a poppy seed, two millimeters long, but it appeared in the app as a fat pearl earring. On week six, Flo told me, *The folds in its head have started to form a little face.* And: *It's already getting ready to meet you in a few months!*

I stared at the lump on the screen. My *little one* looked like a bedbug-sized shrimp with a vestigial tail. If it had gotten stuck to the bottom of my shoe, I would have thought, *Eww, eww, what the fuck.* But inside Flo's portal, I was led to visualize it as my *future baby.* I wanted a future baby, but I was not so presumptuous as Flo. Protecting myself required adopting a measure of ambivalence about the pregnancy. I was not sure that it would be carried to term, that it would not end by miscarriage or termination. But even as Flo conjured images of my child's future, she made me disappear. She served up images of pregnant people who resembled disembodied torsos, sliced off at the neck and limbs—the kind of thing you heard about washing ashore in a trash bag and sparking a manhunt for an estranged husband.

A few years after Flo tracked my first pregnancy, as I researched this book, I downloaded a suite of other period apps, plugged fake due dates into each of them, and started messing around. Many of Flo's competitors—Ovia, Glow, BabyCenter—shared Flo's look and her vibe, with a few distinguishing tweaks. Inside the Glow interface, I could press the screen and make its fetus squirm. Every time I logged in, it confronted me with data about the daily routines of other *Glow Mamas,* informing me of the high percentage of them who had exercised their bodies or contracted the muscles of their pelvic floors. When I signed up for an app called Ovia, it started emailing me a pregnancy update every twenty-four hours, and its daily reports described the fetus as if it were already a child toddling about. *Baby has developed eyelashes on her adorable face,* it said. *Baby has gotten so smart and coordinated.*

Then I downloaded Clue, the menstrual tracker that started

them all. Its aesthetic was clean and white and accented with primary colors. It looked more like a sketchpad than a diary. It had a visual representation of the growing fetus, too, but it was rendered in the style of a wobbly drawing, not a photorealistic doll. Its weekly updates were straightforward, but they presumed nothing. Inside Clue, my pregnancy was not necessarily a mystical period of boundless joy and self-transformation. *It's normal to feel ambivalent about pregnancy and common to consider abortion,* Clue told me in week five. *Not feeling excited 100% of the time? You're not alone,* it counseled in week seven. Instead of serving me relentless information about what constituted a "normal" pregnancy and a "normal" pregnant person, Clue anticipated that some of its users would have unplanned pregnancies, mood disorders, herpes outbreaks, abnormal genetic testing results, preeclampsia, C-sections, and feelings of sadness, confusion, or despair. It expected that some of its users would be trans men, or partnered with women, or not partnered at all.

In 2023, I summoned Ida Tin, Clue's creator, over Zoom. When I first reached out to the company, I received a bounce-back email from its executive chief of staff indicating that she would be out on maternity leave for the next thirteen months. I connected with Tin a few weeks later, me beaming in from Brooklyn at sunrise, she from the afternoon in Berlin. She sat in a sunny flat, a child's drawing of a fire-breathing dragon snaking across the white wall behind her.

My meeting with Tin was well timed. She had just returned from a tech conference in Cyprus, where she encountered a Flo founder for the very first time—"a surreal experience," she said. For years she had watched the Flo guys rack up investments with their bubblegum pink spin on the menstruation app, and now she was finally meeting one of them face-to-face. "I understood that they had started this company because they were app builders. They could see a market opportunity and they wanted to make money," she said. "What I also saw was that over the years, they really had educated themselves to be like, 'Oh, it's actually something kind of important we're building.'" They had learned from the women in their lives and their offices. "So that was the silver lining," she said.

Still: "It matters who builds technology and why we build it," Tin said. It matters if a period app is built by people who experience periods, and if a pregnancy module is designed by people who understand the tremendous range of implications and outcomes of that event. "A pregnancy might not be wanted. You might lose it. And when you are living it, you know these things," she said. For all that Flo had done to tune the app to the lives of its users (a practice that would of course only improve its market position), Tin still could not bring herself to entrust Flo with her data, or the narrative of her reproductive life.

It wasn't that the founders were men, exactly. "I want men to be participating in femtech. I think that's a good thing," she clarified. It's part of the reason she made Clue red instead of pink—to release the body's information from the trap of gender. She has heard people describe her product as "by women, for women," but she rejects that framing as binary and exclusive. "But I mean, if you have 'by women, for women,' that's definitely better than 'by men, for women,'" she said. "Right?"

Within a decade, public perception of the period app swiveled. Once, the lack of menstrual-tracking technology was a signal of tech-bro neglect. Now that same technology was identified as a locus of patriarchal control. In 2021, the Federal Trade Commission filed a complaint against Flo, claiming that the company had shared sensitive health information with "outside data analytics providers," like Facebook, "after promising such information would be kept private." Flo settled the complaint without admitting wrongdoing, but later that year, users filed a class-action suit against the company in the state of California. ("Our stance on this matter is firm—Flo has never sold user information or shared user information with third parties for the purposes of advertising. We are vigorously defending against allegations stipulated in the case for this reason," a company representative said. The case was ongoing as of January 2025.) Were the suit to succeed, I would be included as a member of its class.

When the Supreme Court overturned *Roe v. Wade* the next year, brewing privacy concerns boiled over. The squishy data policies of some menstruation apps contributed to the prevailing sense that our bodies were not our own. Some commentators urged users to delete their period apps immediately, in the fear that they could be weaponized by the state to prove that users had lost or terminated their pregnancies. "If I had a chance of getting pregnant, there's no way in hell that I would put it in an app," Jen Golbeck, the computer science professor, told me, though she emphasized that this would not be sufficient. "We've gotten to the point where there is only a legislative solution," Golbeck said. "There are no individual solutions."

Pregnancy has long been a site of state surveillance, an American tradition that Michele Goodwin, in her 2020 book, *Policing the Womb*, traces to slavery and eugenics. After *Roe* established a right to abortion in 1973, a countermovement arose to establish what it called "fetal rights." A web of "fetal endangerment" laws stretched across the United States, ensnaring pregnant women who fell down the stairs, experienced a stillbirth, refused a cesarean section, or tested positive for drugs. Prenatal care facilities doubled as police nets, with seemingly routine blood and urine tests used to screen pregnant patients for drugs without their consent. Those punished by these laws have been jailed in pregnancy, shackled on the postpartum hospital bed, separated from their children, or conscripted into a child welfare system that holds them under the thumb of state control—even when, as is often the case, the child is born healthy and wanted.

Goodwin calls the disproportionately poor and Black targets of state surveillance "canaries in the coalmine"—harbingers of a criminalization movement that is expanding to control all pregnancies. In 2022, the American Association of Pro-Life Obstetricians and Gynecologists said that patients suffering from miscarriages or life-threatening complications ought to be compelled to deliver an "intact fetal body," regardless of its viability. In 2024, the Alabama Supreme Court decided that even embryos in an IVF lab enjoy the status of "extrauterine children," frozen in what it called a "cryogenic nursery." When the state of Texas passed its abortion "bounty-hunter law," in 2021, it felt like a consummation between the ideologies of state and commercial surveillance. The state invited its citizens to sue anyone they suspected of performing or aiding an abortion, with the abortion hunter receiving a $10,000 prize for proving the case. The law functioned like a high-stakes version of an ad exchange: information about a citizen's pregnancy may only be valued at a fraction of a cent, but information about her ending her pregnancy—that was now worth a small fortune.

And yet the relationship between these various surveillance mechanisms was complex. "There's been so much focus on period trackers, but we've never actually seen a law enforcement official rely upon a period tracker," said Emma Roth, an attorney with Pregnancy Justice who defends women in pregnancy criminalization cases. The focus on this theoretical threat has had the effect of overshadowing the established threat. "Far and away, the most common way that one of these cases begins is through a medical provider sharing a pregnant or postpartum person's medical information," she said.

In her book, Goodwin notes that poor women's pregnancies are criminalized even as affluent women avail themselves of reproductive technologies, welcoming the monitoring of their bodies and paying for the privilege. When the eye of the pregnancy surveillance state scans these bodies, it deems them worthy. Playing along confers an advantage, a glow of approval. One day, on a Reddit pregnancy forum, I watched a woman complain that she had been tested for drugs without her consent. Commenters piled in to tell her she was overreacting. They seemed pleased for the opportunity to prove how good they had been during their own pregnancies, so good that they welcomed doctors secretly testing their piss. Ending pregnancy criminalization, Goodwin says, requires reckoning with "mass incarceration, the US drug war, welfare reform, and even our nation's notorious, but largely hidden, history of eugenics." It cannot be resolved through consumer choice. Even as a woman deletes her pregnancy app, she enacts an individual solution to a social problem.

At my first prenatal appointment, a nurse led me to a corner of the office to take my blood pressure. As the band squeezed my arm, my attention drifted to a cabinet stacked with glossy test boxes. Each was stamped with a logo for Natera, a biotech company, and inscribed with cheery clinical gibberish. The tests were named Anora, Panorama, and Empower. They sounded like figures from Greek myth: a trio of nymphs who would decide the fate of my pregnancy. As the weeks passed, my doctors proffered various methods for screening and diagnosing my pregnancy, and I picked some and declined others as if choosing from a menu of information. I would start with the carrier screening, and then I'd have the NIPT but not the CVS. I'd take the sequential and pass on the amnio.

Each of the results was reassuring except for one. Just after my thirty-fifth birthday, in June of 2020, my doctor called to say that one of the proteins had been detected at a slight elevation from normal levels. Also, my pregnancy had just crossed the line into a "geriatric pregnancy." The combination of the hormone reading and my advanced maternal age was enough to trigger a precautionary protocol, the doctor said: I should chew a sugary baby aspirin tablet each day and submit to regular ultrasound examinations. She wanted to ensure that my blood pressure remained stable and that my placenta grew however a placenta was supposed to grow.

With its lights dimmed, the ultrasound exam room revealed itself as a theater of my body. As the weeks passed, I became versed in its dramas and clichés. The technician described the baby's movements as if sportscasting a playdate. No matter the stage of my pregnancy, she referred to the figure on the screen as *baby*—just *baby*, no *the*, as if that were his proper name. *Baby is cooperating today*, she would say, or *Baby is being shy*. When it was over, she typed silently into the machine for several minutes. Her findings were transmitted remotely to a doctor, who reviewed them in an undisclosed location before appearing in the ultrasound room and delivering his opinion, like a god lowered by a crane to resolve the action on the stage.

I sensed I had a role to play, too. The thrilled mother-to-be. Entering the exam room felt like stepping into a stress dream, one where it was opening night and I had never learned my lines. I was in a hospital, receiving an examination developed to detect a condition that kills women. The ultrasound machine was designed to hunt my pregnancy for abnormalities and flaws. But I was supposed to be grateful for the opportunity to watch the fetus swim inside me. I thought of all the prenatal care instructions laid out by my doctors, by Google, by Flo, and I wondered if my failure to perfectly comply would manifest itself on the ultrasound screen, in a form that I could not perceive. I sweated on the table under my mask of enthusiasm.

Covid rules barred Marc from my appointments, so after each visit, I carried the doctor's findings out of the room and relayed them to him. I emerged with a glossy roll of sonogram images, found Marc waiting in the car outside, and shouted something insufferable to assure him everything was fine, like: *Perfect baby!* Then I maneuvered my body into the passenger seat and interpreted the shapes on the sonograms like I was reading the leaves at the bottom of a teacup. I repeated the doctor's commentary about the successful fusion of the neural tube or the penis emerging between his legs. I recounted these findings with assurance, as if I knew what I was talking about. Only after I related the information to Marc did it feel final.

One day, before an ultrasound appointment, I tried to call up the location of the clinic on Google and instead ended up on the website of a private center a few blocks away, proffering "elective ultrasounds." I poked around the site, drifting past images of plush bears and vacant-eyed pregnant women until I reached the center's menu of recreational jabs and scans. I googled on, touring an international network of elective ultrasound centers. They styled themselves as *baby studios* or *ultrasound spas* and had names like Cherished Memories and You Kiss We Tell. Inside them, prenatal imaging was cleansed of its medical baggage and elevated into a pure commercial offering. *See baby on your own agenda,* the You Kiss We Tell website instructed me. It offered an exam with *NO medical purpose* that would yield *no medical reports*. Instead, I would receive a *cherished experience*. In fact, if my ultrasound did unexpectedly veer into diagnostic territory, I could get my money back. *In the unfortunate circumstance that we find a fetus without a beating heart,* the website said, *you will be refunded in full no questions asked.*

Something felt off-label about the enterprise. The FDA agreed. The agency discouraged the use of ultrasound for nonmedical purposes, "such as obtaining fetal 'keepsake' videos." But it also said that keepsake images were "reasonable if they are produced during a medically indicated exam, and if no additional exposure is required." Ultrasound was "generally considered to be safe," the FDA said, but it held theoretical risks, so it should only be used when the pregnancy presented other risks, risks that required ultrasonic investigation. This meant that the riskier my pregnancy became—the more medical monitoring it required—the more cherished experiences I could access, the more keepsakes I could claim.

I had learned that a good mother protects her unborn child from unnecessary dangers, even theoretical ones. But I had also learned that a good mother longed to see her baby. In 2006, the obstetrician and founding editor of *Ultrasound in Obstetrics and Gynecology,* Stuart Campbell, argued that mothers who failed to delight in the image of their fetus on the screen ought to be tagged as "sub-optimal bonders" and treated with more intensive ultrasound technologies. The styling of the ultrasound as an affective technology, the feminist theorist Jennifer Denbow writes, has escalated the standard for "good mothering before birth." Now spas were capitalizing on this expectation, marketing elective ultrasounds to women whose doctors had not ordered many scans or whose insurance companies had not covered their costs. Their ad copy also seemed tuned to reach women like me—women who had seen their babies through a medical lens and who wanted instead to see them through a consumer one.

You Kiss We Tell described its elective ultrasound as a therapy for the stress incurred by the medical gaze. *If you are feeling anxious about your baby,* its website said, *an elective pregnancy ultrasound will surely ease your mind with the sole purpose being to adore your new bundle of joy.* In the ultrasound spa, you could perform the fantasy of uncomplicated maternal attachment, in a place where the only thing revealed by the machine was the mother's appropriately happy affect. One center called its offering *the Reassurance Package.*

In the twenty-ninth week of my pregnancy, I reported to the hospital for my last scheduled ultrasound before the birth. Hatch told me that the baby was *the size of a size 9 Birkenstock.* Flo showed him smiling, tumbling through an ethereal mist. *This week your baby can cry,* Flo said. *Yes, in the uterus!* I wore the black dress to the ultrasound appointment, pooled it on a chair atop my phone, and smiled at the screen.

The hour passed.

The doctor opened the door. He had what Marc and I referred to as *surgeon energy,* a blunt, unnerving confidence earned through repetitive high-stakes decision-making and superior hand-eye coordination. When I'd first met him, many checkups ago, he'd lowered his mask to smile, presenting his teeth to signal that he was not a threat. But now he was again obscured behind the crimped blue fabric.

The doctor told me that he saw something he did not like. He wondered if it could be a case of—he said a strange word, then another one, then the word "syndrome." He carved into my baby with his professional opinion, dissecting him into abnormal measurements and cardinal features. The kidneys and torso were very large. The baby was growing very fast. The tongue was protruding from the mouth. It's not supposed to do that. "This happens, like, once a year," the doctor said.

The information passed uncomprehendingly through me. I would be assigned a genetic counselor, a prenatal psychologist, an obstetrician who specialized in high-risk pregnancies. I would return the next day for an amniocentesis. Fluid would be extracted from my uterus with a long needle and submitted for testing. I asked the doctor to write the name of the syndrome on a slip of paper so I would not forget. "Don't google it," he said.

A trapdoor opened in the floor of the basement exam room, revealing hidden lower levels—*Pregnancy mode, Complication mode, Fetal Abnormality mode.* My memory looped through the weeks of my pregnancy. My reason dialed back centuries. Even as I submitted my body to advanced scientific protocols, my mind belonged now to the realm of judgment, superstition, and myth. Soon the internet would feed me from its bank of dark materials. Coincidences would string together to form patterns and theories. With the light of my phone to guide me, I descended into the pregnant underworld.

God is always in complete control! let him decide! a Flo user said. *See that?* Hatch said. *That's the light at the end of the tunnel.*

Chapter 4

Risk

When I seized my phone, I texted Marc the euphemism scraped from my short-term memory: *The doctor saw something he didn't like.* I exited the exam room as an avatar in a game, programmed to move through the hallway, wait for the elevator, enter it, wait, leave the elevator, open the door, turn left down the sidewalk, stop at the car. When I arrived, I was surprised to discover that my dress was waterlogged from rain and dragging on the ground. I wrung it savagely onto the street and lowered myself in. The storm fogged the windows and hushed the city. The wet doctor's note fell apart as I unrolled it. We pulled out our phones and googled *Beckwith-Wiedemann syndrome* side by side.

Even the length of the name was unsettling. I pressed on an officious website and thumbed down a long list of potential symptoms. Babies could grow very quickly, it said. Tongues could grow very large. There could be problems eating, speaking, breathing. Intestines could grow too big for little abdomens, protrude outside the belly through the button. One side of the body could grow faster than the other side. There could be red facial birthmarks, creased ears. In some cases, cancerous tumors could rout little kidneys and little livers.

The material quickly exceeded my vocabulary. The internet referred to *genomic imprinting, abnormal regulation, methylation.* The symptom list bottomed into a caveat about how not every child exhibited every trait, but my screen was wet with rain and tears that confused the phone's sensors, so the web page kept jumping back to the middle of the list: baby cancer, baby cancer, baby cancer.

My memory of the next hours and weeks bumps between dioramas of medical scenes. I am pregnant on an exam table, slathered in gel. I am pregnant in a consultation chair, receiving a genetic forecast. I am pregnant inside the tube of an MRI, counting to twenty and holding my breath. My phone kept the score, a record of the fears that I dumped inside.

For seven months, my search history was a map of anxieties I never articulated aloud—not to my doctors or to Marc. I searched for problems—*hot bath neural tube, first trimester benzodiazepine, preeclampsia symptoms.* I daydreamed about a complication, playing it out like a medical drama. Worse, I fantasized about not being pregnant at all. In the exorcism of my anxiety, I gained a sense of control that shaded into pleasure.

At home, I searched my email for the results of all the tests I had undergone during the pregnancy. I read them again, not with new wisdom but with ignorance freshly revealed. Wait—what was a *sequential?* What was a *quad screen?* What was a *CVS?* I looked it up—*chorionic villus sampling.* Okay, what was *chorionic* and what the fuck was *villus* and what were they *sampling* it for!!! I tore back through the findings, furiously googling the definitions—what-the-fuck-was-an-*AFP*, what-the-fuck-was-*nuchal*, what-the-fuck-was-*translucency.* I learned that *AFP* was a protein and a serum. And what the fuck was a serum.

The thumbnails of my medical documents fanned across my laptop screen as if arranged by a magician's hand. One PDF featured a series of impenetrable bar graphs charting my pregnancy's risks. At the time I received it, it had felt so reassuring, so precious in my inbox. I did not consider that it only ran the odds on a small band of conditions and that it had nothing to say about an obscure genetic disorder with a name I had already forgotten how to spell. Now my position had been reevaluated, my pregnancy recoded as *high-risk*. High risk of what, nobody said.

When I closed the PDF, a new email awaited me. It was an automatically generated message from a genetic counseling company called Integrated Genetics. Inside the email, the tail of the G in *counseling* snaked back under the word, mingling with another line to form a double-helix logo. Integrated Genetics was an arm of Labcorp, a company that sounded like a villainous conglomerate in a Batman movie. I had never considered that Labcorp employed human beings, but now I was instructed to report to a virtual appointment with one of them the next morning. *Genetic counselor subject to change based on availability,* the email said. *Thank you again for choosing Integrated Genetics.* And I thought, *I did not choose you.*

That night, I crept into the recesses of my phone, crawling through medical journal stubs and old mom-group threads. I uncovered a long-dormant pregnancy message board and blew off the dust. The messages were from two, six, ten years ago. The pregnant women of the past tossed their fetuses' symptoms onto the board. *Is this normal,* one of them typed into the void. *Anyone else's LO sticking their tongue out, I wish that I could unread what I read. The internet is a blessing and a curse sometimes.* None of them had returned to the thread to report the outcomes of their crises, to say whether their babies turned out okay. I wondered if that was because their babies were fine, or if it was because they were not fine.

On the *Daily Mail* website, I raced through an article that pitched the birth of a little boy in Oklahoma as a news-of-the-weird–style report. *Cancer-surviving toddler born with a tongue "DOUBLE the size it should be,"* it said. *His parents initially believed he was poking his tongue out to be "cute."* A photo spread featured a bald baby, his eyes smiling, his pink tongue reaching past his chin. Tubes cased his body from groin to neck. At the end of the article was a link to a GoFundMe account to cover the cost of his surgeries. *It will be exciting to explain to him where his scars came from when he gets older,* the mother said.

I dropped all my coins into the well of the internet, waiting to hear how far they fell. On Reddit, in a sub called Thanks I Hate It, I found a comment under a picture of another baby born with BWS and a very large tongue: *What could they do? Cut it off? I don't think that's a solution.* In a study from 1970, six Jamaican infants with signs of the syndrome were described. Their condition was associated with *early failure to thrive;* three of the babies died. Inside a database of digitized medical journals, I found a scan of a yellowed letter published in 1801. In old-time script that made the S's look like F's, the writer told of infants discovered with *an incurable monſtroſity, diſguſting to all who ſaw,* with *the tongue out of the mouth, and hanging on the chin, like that of a calf recently ſlain.* Of one case, the writer continued: *Nevertheleſs, it fucked pretty well, provided the nurſe's nipple was large and elongated.* At fourteen months, the child died of an unknown cause.

The article proposed several treatments for children with the condition. Enclosing the tongue in a bag of fine cloth. Rinsing the child's mouth with wine. Covering the tongue in pepper, ginger, mustard, and salt. Leeches.

In the scanned collection of the British Museum I found a series of stone tablets, sourced to an ancient Mesopotamian library and dated to 650 BC. The tablets, known as *Šumma iʒbu*, or "If a reject," contained a list of ominous birth defects, imprinted in an alphabet of wedgelike signs. One entry translated to: *If the tongue of the reject is wide on its throat and hangs down from its mouth, an enemy will seiʒe my border city through revolt.*

I searched all the way back to the ancient world, and there was my baby.

When my phone rang the next morning, signaling a private number, I steadied the device in one hand and slid my fingertip slowly across the screen. It was the counselor dispatched by Labcorp. I put her on speakerphone. She asked me and Marc questions about our family medical histories, extracted the mistakes I had made during my pregnancy, and offered various facts about genetic tests. At the amniocentesis appointment, she said, the doctor would use a needle to retrieve a vial of amniotic fluid from inside my uterus. In a laboratory, cells that had sloughed off my baby's body would be made to multiply so they could be tested again and again.

The tests would take an estimated seven days to complete, or three weeks, or five weeks. Something called a *fluorescence in situ hybridiʒation (FISH) test* could check for deleted chromosomes quickly, but it was sometimes wrong. More definitive results would appear in something called a *microarray;* something called a *karyotype;* an extra-special test for Beckwith-Wiedemann syndrome; and something called *whole exome sequencing*—a thorough map of the baby's genes that promised a near-comprehensive report of all potential abnormalities encoded in his DNA, even ones that might never manifest during his lifetime. I learned that the doctor could only withdraw a limited amount of fluid, and each test would deplete its store of baby cells. The more tests we chose, the longer it would take to grow more cells. If the tests were completed as quickly as possible, we would have all the results by the time the baby was *the size of a fanny pack*. But if they took more time, he would be bigger, *the size of a large bag of Cheetos*.

I asked the genetic counselor to send me a list of all the things that the tests would test for and she said that she could not because the tests would test for too many things.

When I was the only one who knew that he existed, I knew him through direct observation. He was the orange vomit rising in my throat at breakfast. Later he was wandering bubbles in my stomach, then athletic jabs, then squirming rolls that made me feel like I was falling in love. He was still in there, but he felt outside of me now. I bundled him up and handed him over to the realm of information. His cells would soon be on their way to a medical campus in Minnesota, where scientists would make them multiply. The information that Labcorp would glean from those samples, the genetic counselor would not even try to explain. All the things they would know, that I could not possibly imagine.

When we returned to the imaging center for the amniocentesis appointment, I waited in the lobby as other pregnant women filtered in and out, lugging heavy water bottles and scrolling lazily through their phones. I felt costumed as them, squeezed into the bulky padding of a normal pregnancy. Marc sat at my side, a rare exception to the Covid rules. When a nurse called us inside the exam room, Marc was instructed to remain seated in a chair against the wall, where my phone had sat mutely the day before.

The ultrasound technician burned a hole in my body with her

wand. The baby surfaced on the screen and Marc called out with urgent delight. He had not seen him for many months. The baby moved, and Marc called out again. I was afraid to look and guilty for being afraid. I tried to borrow Marc's happiness like one of his dress shirts. I watched the nurse drag her cursor across the image of his belly, measuring its circumference. "Wider," the doctor said, and she pulled the cursor a little more. "Wider, wider," he goaded. She pulled the cursor more. She did not stop until the doctor was satisfied that she had encircled my son completely, that the measurements of his midsection had climbed to suitably alarming heights.

Then the technician found his little face. "See, the tongue is all the way out of the mouth," the doctor said. "See the tongue there," he said. I nodded vigorously, praying for him to stop.

"It's like this," the technician said. She lowered her surgical mask, placed her tongue between her lips, and said: "Pffft." She replaced the mask.

"See the tongue," the doctor said.

The technician lowered the mask again: "Pffffffffffft."

The doctor presented the amniocentesis needle, a horror movie prop. He instructed me to thread my fingers together and place them under my head so that I would not flail my arms in distress and disrupt the procedure. I did not know what that meant, but my imagination supplied the answer: if I moved a muscle, he'd spear the baby like a fish. This was a scenario where you did, in fact, want your doctor to radiate surgeon energy. He plunged the needle capably into my stomach, removed three vials of yellow fluid, then left me lying there like a deflated basketball. Marc told me that I did a good job. But all I did was nothing.

When it was over, it was late in the afternoon. The receptionist informed us that we would need to mail the samples ourselves. She handed me a padded envelope closed with medical badges and tapes.

I had not known how baby cells made their way from a body to a lab. I could imagine it as a frictionless and mystical process. Now the baby's DNA was revealed as an object like any other. We raced to an open FedEx Office Print & Ship Center and slid his cells across the countertop. The point of the amniocentesis, the doctor explained, was to acquire more information. These doctors, they could never get enough. When we told the doctor that we wanted the lab to run the karyotype and the microarray and the BWS-specific test but that we did not want to map our baby's entire genome before he was born, he shook his head ruefully. "Soon this will be the standard for prenatal testing," he said. Information about my son's body could not terrorize him. It could only enrich and satisfy him. "This only happens once a year," he had said, as if remarking on a comet burning through the sky. He had done nothing wrong, only his job. Really, he had done a wonderful job. But his job was to look at my son and see things he did not like, and for that reason I never wanted to see him again.

As the cells made their way to the lab, Marc and I visited another doctor, a specialist in medically complex pregnancies, to get a second opinion. The walls of her exam room were papered in postcards of tiny babies with closed eyes. They wore fuzzy pink headbands or yarn knitted to resemble cabbage. When the ultrasound technician turned the lights down, the glow of the monitor lit the room, and the postcard babies seemed to bob peacefully at the border between darkness and light. This technician kept her tube of ultrasound gel in a pocket warming device so that when she smoothed it on it felt like wading nervily into the ocean and discovering that the water was the temperature of air.

As she conducted her business, she told us that she had a daughter who lived in Ireland whom she could not see very often. She missed her daughter very much. With her, I felt safe imagining that I had a child, too, one I wanted to see more. He could be here soon, styled adorably and pinned to her wall. I watched my baby hiccup, extend a foot, hold his hands over his face like a troubled celebrity hiding from the paparazzi. I tensed my legs and opened and closed my hands and willed his tongue to stay inside of his mouth. Marc asked the technician if she saw anything out of the ordinary and I flushed in embarrassment at his violation of the procedure's norms. "I just take the pictures," the technician gently replied.

When the doctor arrived, I looked away. I did not want to see the baby through her knowledgeable eyes. She assumed control of the wand and moved it efficiently about my belly, her eyes focused on the screen. Afterward we walked a cramped hallway to her office. It was bare, like an undressed set. On a shelf sat a mug stamped with a cartoon uterus that said "AT YOUR CERVIX." The doctor gestured for us to sit in two chairs facing a desk. She asked if we preferred she use the term *baby* or *fetus*. I recognized the look on her face, the effort and deliberation behind her steady eye contact. It was how I imagined myself to look when I had to ask a question in an interview that I did not want to ask.

I don't know the sequence in which she revealed her findings. Every time I scrounge for them in my memory they come out in a new order: The tongue did not actually seem so big. The torso did not actually appear so big. The kidneys appeared a little big but sometimes people have kidneys that are a little big. The baby's ultrasound images had been reviewed by a doctor in the practice who was an expert in fetal brains. Something in the baby's brain caught her eye. The folds of the baby's brain did not appear as folded as they should. The folds of the baby's brain appeared as smooth as the folds of a much younger baby.

Something was wrong with the chair. I rocked in the seat, butt cheek to butt cheek, a kid bouncing on the hot lip of the pool. When sitting became impossible I crouched low over the chair, hovering just above the seat. If my body was not in contact with any other object in the room, then maybe it could not be said to be in the room at all. It could go completely undetected. It could disappear.

The doctor said that the tongue could be sticking out for a "neurological" reason, and I asked what "neurological" meant, and she said that it meant that it could be related to the brain, and I asked why that would be, and she said that there might be no genetic explanation, that it could be an isolated abnormality, and I protested that the brain would be the worst place for an abnormality to be isolated, and she nodded with sympathy, or agreement. The first doctor's suspicion of Beckwith-Wiedemann syndrome was alarming, but the second doctor's brain theory was catastrophic. Now I spoke to her like she was an attorney and not a physician. Like I could negotiate the diagnosis and angle for a better offer.

Marc went ahead to fetch the car so that I would not have to walk all the way there. I rode down the elevator and into the heat like a gumball rolling into a sweaty hand. The city slid past as I stood on the sidewalk, looking like a woman who was going to have a baby.

The second doctor referred me to a third doctor, one with an MRI machine. An MRI would provide a clearer picture than an ultrasound, and it could determine whether the baby's possible brain abnormality was a probable brain abnormality. His office scheduled me for an appointment one week away. For seven days I opened my mouth and swallowed my prenatal vitamin like it was a placebo in a clinical trial. For seven nights I hid beneath the covers and stared into my phone. Pallets of unopened nursery furniture accumulated in the hall. Stroller ads stalked me around the internet, images of babyless carriages rolling behind me wherever I went. As much as the internet pretended to know me, it did not know when to shut the fuck up.

In that week a dense underbrush of online content grew up around me. I googled foreign words from my doctors' notes—*macroglossia, trisomy, lissencephaly*—and conjured medical images attached to scientific journals: a red fetus on a specimen plate; a jarred human brain that resembled a chicken cutlet. *Lissencephaly* meant, literally, "smooth brain." In the summer of 2020, my baby's possible diagnosis became a meme, a term for minds that had been so dulled by repeated internet exposure that they had lost the ability to absorb information. People on Twitter wrote of their *incredibly smooth brain* and their *silky smooth pandemic brain* as if describing an aspirational state.

I searched and searched online, remixing the ultrasound findings—tongue and brain, brain and kidney, kidney and tongue. I hunted for meta-commentary on my situation—the ethics of prenatal diagnosis, the parents cast as humanity's *moral pioneers.* There were specific chromosomal abnormalities I wanted to investigate—trisomy 18, trisomy 21—and I found that Google had commissioned portraits of imaginary children affected by those conditions, sketching them in colored pencil. Google did not supply a portrait of a child for one syndrome associated with lissencephaly; instead, it gestured at *severe* defects, reported that most babies *don't live past their first week of life,* and presented a drawing of a pregnant woman reclined on an exam chair, her shirt pulled up to expose her stomach.

A doctor performed an ultrasound as they both gazed at the fetus on the screen. The doctor looked grim, but the woman was smiling.

My thoughts wandered to the lost Malaysia Airlines plane, the disaster that had resisted explanation. In 2014, a few weeks after the plane disappeared, a commercial vendor of satellite imagery tried to crowdsource the search, inviting anyone to page through images of the open ocean and flag signs of wreckage. On Twitter, the rock star Courtney Love posted a screenshot of white waves on blue water marked up in childlike red digital finger paint. *Oil,* she scrawled. *Plane?* She signed the image *C-L.* I was about as likely to diagnose my son on Google as Courtney Love was to find the missing plane on her phone. But my pregnancy had trained me to shop online for all of the answers: who to wear, what to eat, when to announce. Now I charged through the internet's picked-over aisles. My lazy phone habits sped up into stress responses. When I pressed on the Flo icon, I found a cartoon of someone else's baby, smiling like the smug emoji.

Your baby is the size of a bag of Trader Joe's Cauliflower Rice, Hatch said.

A medical journal article described what I was experiencing as *the diagnostic odyssey.* I had never absorbed the details of Greek mythology, but now I was assigned a lead role in an epic. Everywhere, I was confronted by classical symbols and signs. When I called my obstetrician's office, the receptionist put me on hold, transferring me to a fuzzy musical recording that I thought of as "the can-can song." The made-up lyrics bounced in my head: *Can, can you do the can-can, can you do the can-can.* One day I googled the song, trying to understand why a doctor would choose to play it for her patients, and I learned that its true title was "Galop Infernal," and it had been composed for the comic opera *Orpheus in the Underworld.* The song played as the Greek gods threw a party on the banks of the river Styx. I searched *river Styx* and found an explainer on a fan site for Hades, a myth-based role-playing computer game released in 2020. Styx, it said, was *the barrier between the surface world and the land of the dead.*

Odysseus roamed in search of his home for ten years, going to Hades and back, but I did not have that kind of time. The point of the tests was to acquire information, and I knew more information about the information now. I knew all its secret uses. If you had information, it could be used to prepare to treat the baby's condition after its birth. Or it could be used to prevent its birth, to secure what was euphemistically called a therapeutic termination. I pulled out Flo's calendar and marked out the weeks. I was twenty-eight weeks pregnant now. When the MRI was scheduled and the first test on the fetal cells was due to be completed, I would be twenty-nine weeks pregnant. When the second test was done, I would be thirty-one weeks pregnant. When the last test was done, I would be thirty-three to thirty-five weeks pregnant.

In New York, I was told, doctors typically stopped performing abortions at twenty-four weeks, but I learned that a handful of American doctors were known to perform them later than that. One at a clinic in Maryland, one in New Mexico, one in Colorado. There used to be one in Kansas, until Dr. George Tiller was assassinated, and then there was not one in Kansas anymore. When I searched the names of these clinics, Google produced starred user reviews where real patients competed with antiabortion activists hoping to drive down their rank.

Run down outside, a review of one clinic said. *Heavy security with video and audio. Makes me feel like they're doing something wrong.* One star.

I was provided no feminine care products. Just some crackers and apple juice. Three stars.

Visiting this clinic was the hardest thing I have ever had to do. If it wasn't for [doctor's] care, I would have killed myself. Five stars.

The day before the MRI appointment, nearly a week after the amniocentesis, one page of test results fluttered back to us. The genetic counselor called to explain the findings, and my doctor dropped a scanned PDF into my email. The test was called the Labcorp Reveal® SNP Microarray. The Labcorp website explained that it was designed to scan *more than 2.6 million genomic markers,* including some of the genetic causes of Beckwith-Wiedemann syndrome. The report included a picture of my baby's actual chromosomes, presented in pairs like pretty worms pinned to a collector's board. I didn't know what a chromosome was supposed to look like, but the report assured me that my baby's appeared perfectly ordinary. In thick black letters, it announced: *NORMAL MALE.*

It was the result I had hoped for, but the words hung uncomfortably on the page. If you had asked me of my dreams for my child, I would not have said that I wished to produce a "normal male." The report exposed this desire and bolded it for emphasis. But it also said: *This result does not exclude the possibility of congenital anomalies due to other etiologies.* I looked up the word *etiology* and found that it could refer to *the cause of a disease or condition,* but also to an *origin story.* A *mythical explanation.*

The microarray was good news: it had not produced a diagnosis. But it was also bad news: it had not produced a diagnosis. The more comprehensive Beckwith-Wiedemann test, the one that would analyze my baby's cells for each of the syndrome's causes, was weeks away from completion. If the condition had no genetic cause, it could point to an environmental explanation. As the baby's cells grew in the lab, I roved from doctor to doctor, confessing my sins. I had taken the bath, drunk the wine, swallowed the Ativan.

One geneticist told us that the baby's condition, whatever it was, did not suggest a prenatal exposure. But when her office uploaded my chart to an internet portal, it said:

Fetal anomaly
Teratogen exposure in current pregnancy, single gestation
Advanced maternal age (AMA) in pregnancy
Anxiety during pregnancy, antepartum
Other

I felt sad for the person the chart described. Here was an official list of all her failures, plus a bonus failure. *(Other.)* When I searched for *teratogen* I found clip art of a bald fetus. Red arrows prodded at its body, leading to a hovering cluster of threats: a neon radiation sign, an orange pill bottle, a beer. Deep down, I did not believe that my baby's condition, whatever it was, was caused by something I did. I believed that it was caused by something that I was. I dreaded what the baby would do to my body. I grieved for my vanishing life. I thrashed and sobbed in bed one afternoon, acting like a dying animal. I should have become a better person before making a copy of me.

The doctor's opinion, that the baby's abnormality did not seem teratogenic, was a comment floated over Zoom. As soon as she delivered it, it self-destructed. But the entry in the medical portal would stick to my chart forever. The orange pill bottle rattled in my head. Medically, the Ativan seemed to be a small thing, but it grew to represent all the judgments stalking my pregnancy. My mind sketched them out for me: I had not capably disciplined my body; I had failed to control my mind; I had chosen my work over my baby. Also, the work had not been particularly meaningful: I had taken the Ativan to prepare for interviewing a celebrity. The words *teratogen exposure in current pregnancy* sat in an open tab on my computer, marking me as a bad pre-mother.

Before I was pregnant, I was a person. I had stressors and obligations. The Ativan posed a danger to my body, but I had started taking it because my body had been exposed to other dangers. In the summer of 2018, when Flo was just my period tracker, *The New York Times* assigned me to write a story about a forthcoming podcast, an interview show hosted by John Cleese. Cleese was the most recognizable member of Monty Python, and now he was in his seventies, coasting on his status as a comedy legend and general sage. I arranged to watch Cleese interviewing one of his guests, a self-help guru who coached people on how to be happier, and then interview Cleese myself.

When I arrived at the recording studio, I sat in a round of couches in the lobby, which were soon filled with people also there to meet Cleese—producers, flacks, and the happiness guru, who sat across from me, looking unhappy. We spoke quietly, frozen in place, our bodies braced for the famous person to arrive. He burst in and swiveled our necks. Cleese was huge and barreling toward us at speed. I stood from the couch, stuck out my hand, and explained that I was the reporter who would be interviewing him that day.

He laughed at me. *Ho-ho-ho,* he said. With both hands, he grabbed my stomach fat through my dress and squeezed it hard. Then he leaned his body into me. I dug my feet into the floor, resisting his weight, and we grappled for a few seconds until he removed his hands from my stomach, placed them on my shoulders, and easily shoved me back onto the couch. I squirmed like a bug flipped on its slick back. Then he said, "I've always wanted to do that to a *New York Times* reporter."

I pulled myself up and scanned the room, looking for a clue. A man I did not know met my eyes with an outraged, sympathetic expression. One of the publicists drew close and wrapped an arm around my shoulder, and Cleese crowded in. He squeezed me to his chest and kissed me atop the head. The crowd moved toward the recording booth, where he and the happiness guru launched into an ingratiating hour-long conversation as if nothing had happened. I watched them through a soundproof window as they laughed and laughed, a pillowy headphone set piping their voices into my ears.

I turned the volume down and studied Cleese. As if he were sitting behind police glass. My anger and my doubt bickered with each other in my head. When the hour was up, I entered the podcasting booth and sat in the guru's place. I switched on my recorder and asked several generic questions about the podcast. Then I described the moment we met.

"Oh, yes," Cleese said. "I did push you a couple of times, that's right."

He noted that a lot of people would be offended by that greeting, and he hoped that I was not among them. When I indicated that I was, he said: "But you're quite uptight, aren't you?"

The politically correct, he went on, have no sense of relaxation or play. Cleese's comedy was spontaneous and naughty and disrespectful. Political correctness ruined the party. "It's a bit like having a sort of elderly maiden aunt come in the room," he said. "And everyone has to stop having fun until she leaves."

"So, that's me?" I said.

On the recording I sound like I am about to cry. I had remembered the encounter ending quickly after that, but when I played the tape back to relay the incident here, I found that it continued for nine more minutes. I lobbed Cleese more softballs. I laughed at his jokes. I agreed to accept a copy of his latest book. He led me into saying that I was offended—as if the problem were not how he touched my body but how I interpreted the touch—and now my tight voice strained to prove just how unoffended I could be. I was highly reasonable and sooo relaxed. Cleese told me that I was naughtier than I looked. I laughed at that, too. Then the recording stopped. I remember that as I left, he said he was sorry.

After the interview, I walked the plaza below in dazed circles. What had just happened? He had not sexually assaulted me. He had, I guess, sexistly assaulted me. I wondered if he had done it because I was a woman, a young woman, a young woman with fat in a nonsexual place that seemed available for squeezing. He said he did it because I was such an important person, working for *The New York Times*. It was my first celebrity interview for the newspaper. I faked my confidence the way young women are instructed to do, and he easily sensed my weakness. He put his hands on me and tipped me right over.

The incident slid back through my memory, reactivating past physical intrusions and professional humiliations. Even as I walked away from the podcast studio, my brain started working to contain the incident, to make sure it didn't claim too much mental space. I thought about the article I had been assigned, how I could possibly write it without describing the subject's behavior. I imagined the encounter aggregated by the *Daily Mail*, my severe and unflattering photograph stitched to his jovial headshot and splashed across Twitter. I imagined his face looming forever above the internet's idea of me. I killed the story.

In the coming months, I did two things. I downloaded a weight-loss app called Lose It!. And I made an appointment with

a psychiatrist. When I descended into her office and described my work-related anxiety, it did not occur to me to mention John Cleese. I had already capably metabolized the whole thing. I needed to interview celebrities for my job, I told the psychiatrist, but they scared me. My social anxiety dated to childhood, I explained. I'd been like this since I was a little kid. The psychiatrist prescribed me a benzodiazepine called Ativan, and now I took five milligrams of it an hour before I interviewed anybody famous.

In January of 2020, when I was six weeks pregnant, I swallowed a pill before meeting Sarah Jessica Parker and her husband, Matthew Broderick, at an Italian restaurant in midtown Manhattan to interview them about a play. When Parker slid her cosmopolitan toward me, insisting I take a sip, I declined. She teased, "I think you're more sophisticated. I think you're above this," and so I said, "I'm pregnant," and she was so, so excited for me.

Before I got pregnant, I asked the psychiatrist about the risks of my medications. Use of Ativan late in pregnancy might make a baby floppy after birth, she said as she extended her arms languidly in front of her, but it was otherwise not associated with negative outcomes. She would, she said, send me a full medical review of the medication to read. When I told my obstetrician this, at our first prenatal appointment, she was alarmed. I should, in her opinion, definitely not take the Ativan. Worry squeezed into my chest and made itself at home in there. I did not take the pill again.

Now, months later, I searched back through my email for the psychiatrist's report. Its subject line was bolded accusatorially—the email was unread. I had never opened it. I clicked to reveal a wall of text. The first sentence said, *Quick take: Experimental animal studies do not suggest that clinical use of lorazepam increases the risk of congenital malformations.* But the report went on and on and on, noting a *mouse study* with *400 times the human dose* that caused *increased incidence of cleft palate*, and an *exploratory study* in a *French registry* that *identified an association* between prenatal Ativan exposure and *anal atresia*.

That image lived somewhere in my body now, next to John Cleese's hands.

In 1575, in France, a barber-surgeon named Ambroise Paré published an influential volume on the causes of birth defects. During the Renaissance, the same guy who gave you a shave could also amputate your leg, and Paré was the most famous of these guys. In a modern publication of his work, *On Monsters and Marvels*, his translator praised his "poetry" and "attention to detail" and concurred with another reader's assessment that he was "a true literary genius." Nearly everything he said would eventually be proven wrong, but if you were a guy during the Renaissance, you could be wrong about everything and still be celebrated as a genius several hundred years later.

This is where he said birth defects come from:

There are several things that cause monsters.

The first is the glory of God.

The second, his wrath.

The third, too great a quantity of seed.

The fourth, too little.

The fifth, the imagination.

The theory of *maternal imagination*, or *maternal impression*, suggested that a fetus could transform into the things its mother saw.

It could even change into the things she imagined. The idea dated back to antiquity. "Various states of the soul," the Greek physician Soranus wrote sometime in the second century, "produce certain changes in the mold of the fetus." The idea pitched forward through the centuries until it made its way to me. In 1733, the midwife Catharina Schrader wrote in her diary of a son delivered to a mother who "had seen apes dancing. It did not live long. Oh Lord, save us from such monsters." In another entry, on another birth, she wrote: "How careful the pregnant woman must be in all she does and thinks." In 1920, in *Radiant Motherhood*, Marie Stopes relayed a story about Oscar Wilde's mother. While pregnant, she was "intensely and passionately desiring a daughter, visualizing a girl," Stopes claimed. And now Oscar was "known to all the world as a type whose distressing perversion is a racial loss."

By the time I got pregnant, theories of maternal imaginations and impressions had dissolved into explanations of genetics and teratogens. But they still bubbled under the surface of these rational pursuits. One medical journal pointed me to the Maternal-Fetal Attachment Scale, an assessment created by a nurse in the 1980s to rate a pregnant woman's emotional fitness for motherhood. Its prompts quizzed her on the strength of her maternal imagination: "I wonder if the baby thinks and feels 'things' inside me, one prompt said. I can almost guess what my baby's personality is going to be by the way he moves," said another.

My medical chart said that I had *teratogen exposure in current pregnancy*. But it also noted that I had *anxiety during pregnancy*. Was my antianxiety medication to blame, or was it the anxiety that I experienced when I stopped taking it? And what about the anxiety I had thinking about the potential effects of my antianxiety medication (and/or anxiety) on my unborn child? The Online Etymology Dictionary told me that the word *teratogen* came from the root *terato—*

"marvel, monster." The suffix -*gen* meant "thing that produces or causes." The online medical chart was supposed to be modern and scientific. But when I decoded its medical terminology, it said that I had created a monster.

During our diagnostic odyssey, Marc bought me a workbook of cognitive behavioral approaches for pregnancy and postpartum anxiety. The cover featured another headless white woman. The book detailed all the difficulties visited upon "babies of moms who suffer from anxiety during pregnancy," and then it apologized: "Having read the above information, you may be feeling even more anxious than you were before," it said. The workbook supplied the example of Marcy, a woman who was six months pregnant with her first child. Despite "reassuring prenatal test results, Marcy could not stop thinking about the possibility that her baby might have a congenital defect," the workbook said. "She often found herself worrying and pacing in the kitchen at three o'clock in the morning or searching the Internet for information." Marcy had taken a "situation that involves slight or no risk" and "made it seem threatening and dangerous," the book said, and she needed to use the strategies of cognitive behavioral therapy to assure herself that nothing was wrong.

As I read the workbook, I realized that I was not Marcy. I was her nightmare. My pregnancy was the idea from which other, normal pregnant women needed to be shielded. I had already been corralled into the maternity section of the internet, and now I was being led into a back room. The internet finally had nothing left to sell me. A confused Google offered me ads for lifelike simulated body parts from a website called Anatomy Warehouse. When I searched Flo's Secret Chats for *fetal abnormality* and *birth defect* and *stillbirth*, she said: *Please try searching for something else.*

"We will note in passing how dangerous it is to disturb a preg-

nant woman," wrote Ambroise Paré, the barber-surgeon. Paré
anticipated a critic who would censure him for even articulating
this idea in writing. What if a pregnant woman were to read his
descriptions of "deformed and monstrous" beings? Would she not
risk birthing a monster herself? "I will answer him in a word," Paré
wrote. "I do not write for women at all."

In the morning, Marc and I drove an hour north of the city to the
imaging center where I would have the MRI. A receptionist had
versed me in the rituals of the place. I was to enter the building
alone. A technician would perform the scan. I would wait for the
doctor to review the images, and then he would call me to relay
his findings. I would never see him. In the week since Marc and I
learned about the existence of a fetal MRI specialist, he had grown
into a mythic figure in our minds. Only he could look into our
baby's brain. Now I prepared for his omniscient voice to deliver
its final judgment.

Marc parked us at the edge of the lot, under a canopy of trees. I
opened the door to screaming birds. "Say hi for me," Marc said. I
left him to pace the parking lot, a nonplayer character in the MRI
video game.

Inside the center was a scratchy carpet strewn with sagging
chairs. I approached a clear plastic partition and filled out an intake
form. Anxiety shook my fingers as I wrote it out, in my own hand:
fetal abnormality. I traded the paperwork for a kid-sized carton of
apple juice. The sugar was to enter my bloodstream, cross the placenta and excite the baby, then tire him out. When he had grown
sluggish inside of me, the MRI technician would attempt to get a
clear look at his brain.

The MRI machine made the ultrasound look like an Easy-Bake

Oven. It was a glowing white donut, a sci-fi movie portal to another dimension. I lay in a human trough at its entrance. The technician covered my ears with headphones, handed me a remote control covered in a latex glove, and instructed me to hold my breath on command. Then she entered a glass control booth behind my head and initiated the sequence. My rigid body slid into the tube. The machine bleated in alarm. Some force pounded furiously at its walls. *My baby is trying to sleep*, I thought. The technician's voice counted in my ear. The baby kicked inside. I held my breath until my lungs whined. At the end the technician pressed a DVD of images into my hands and said, "Enjoy your pregnancy."

I returned to the waiting room, holding the crystal case. The answer was inside, unplayable. Finally the receptionist called my name and informed me that there had been a change in protocol. The doctor would like to speak to me in person. I called Marc and swept him inside. A nurse left us alone in a tiny square room with no door. The space felt styled as if preserved from my childhood: cream padded chairs, pink-flecked side table, phone with a curly cord. A brittle copy of *Good Housekeeping* advertised cookie recipes from a lost Halloween. I wrapped the phone's cord around my pointer finger like I did when I was a little girl.

The doctor's figure suddenly loomed in the doorframe. Like a comic-book character who appears in a flash of lightning. He lowered himself into the room's empty chair and regarded us both. Then he said: "I got a pretty good look at a pretty good brain." Nothing appeared abnormal about it at all. We thanked him, as if he had cured our baby, and he looked at us with some bemusement and said: "First-time parents?"

Marc and I escaped into the parking lot to a high sun. I took his hand and stepped toward the car until my arm pulled taut. I looked up to see that he was crying. For a week I was a pair of swollen eyes, a mouth drawn on with a shaky hand. Marc was Marc, firm and optimistic. Now I wrapped my arms around him as he blubbered into my neck. Across the lot, a woman turned her face to watch us. I wondered what tragedy she thought had befallen us, the man sobbing outside the MRI center with his hugely pregnant wife. She did not know what we knew—that all images had been reversed.

Chapter 5

Nature

It felt like a miracle, but really it was nothing. The woman with the ultrasonic waves saw something, but the man with the magnet saw nothing, and his nothing beat her something. With one diagnostic instrument, my baby was condemned. With another, he was saved. The thirtieth week of my pregnancy was a scary movie and my body was the set. An imperfect medical tool glitched in the conversion of sound into light. Google interpreted the findings and sketched them out in colored pencil. When it was over, I floated across the imaging center parking lot, clutching my proof of nothing.

The MRI machine created a temporary magnetic field inside my body. It realigned my atoms, his atoms, then set them back into place. But I still felt different, oddly charged. I was tuned to a higher frequency. Also, a lower frequency. I cried listening to Eric Clapton ballads from the 1990s. The opening plinks of "Fight Song," the Rachel Platten anthem that became Hillary Clinton's banal campaign song, made my arm hairs rise. I watched a fleet of little turtles swim in a Central Park pond, and when I noticed a very large turtle surfacing undetected beneath them, it felt like an omen. *So big*, I emailed to myself. *Alarming*. I started seeing birds every-where, and of course birds were always everywhere, but now my brain was scanning for patterns, and their habits and movements acquired great personal meaning. One day Marc ordered a bird feeder online, filled it with black-oil sunflower seed, and secured it to our fire escape. But the weeks passed and no birds came to visit. I marked it in my ledger: sign, meaning unknown.

I was not religious, and I was not spiritual-but-not-religious. I was a newspaper writer. I believed in the scientific method. But now I had entered a world beyond information. Eric Clapton, Rachel Platten, big turtle, no birds. These experiences felt no less significant to the course of my pregnancy than the picture on the ultrasound machine. If this was really a diagnostic odyssey, the machine was a trickster god. It lured me into imagining my child in a certain way—as a *teratogenic exposure,* a *fetal anomaly,* a *potential etiology.* Its words flew from its medical portal and into my brain. It pulled off its mask and said, *Pffffffffft!*

A new ultrasound was scheduled every week, until the doctors reached a diagnosis, or until they didn't. I reported to all my appointments, peeled off my shirt, smiled at the screen. The baby was Alice now, measuring big, then small, then regular sized, which meant that my body was the rabbit hole, or my body was a Wonderland. (I was also tuned to the "John Mayer frequency," where girls become lovers who turn into mothers.) I liked my doctors more now that their infallibility was revealed. We were fellow travelers, roving in circles. They created their glossy sonogram squares, and I collected them to toss into the wind. When I visited their offices, I took notes inside, like: *Baby's kidneys measuring large today.* And I took notes outside, like: *Three crows pecking at a rotten apple.*

The clinical euphemism was that my pregnancy was *high-risk.* But years later, as I searched for an easy gloss on my experience, I would instead say that my pregnancy had been *highly medicalized.* I would say those words to Emma, a new friend, as we traded birth stories between bites of cheese sandwiches. "I'm not even sure that *medicalized* is a real word," I said. Then I paused and whispered: "I think it's a word that I got from *them*."

Them. When I first heard about them, I was sitting on a grassy knoll. It was springtime, before the pregnancy's complexities were known. Our friends Laura and David sat uphill from me and Marc, and Laura told me about an article she had read, her words drifting down to me from above. The article was about women who gave birth with no medical assistance. No hospitals, no doctors, no midwives. The women birthed the babies and caught them themselves. On purpose. Some of these women refused pregnancy tests, blood draws, and ultrasounds. They called it *freebirth*, and the article was published after one of their babies died. "Actually," Laura said, "maybe you don't want to read that article right now." I pulled it up as soon as we parted, blades of grass still imprinted on my thighs.

The article, by NBC News misinformation reporter Brandy Zadrozny, was about a twenty-eight-year-old woman named Judith who had been pregnant for the first time. Judith carried the baby well past her due date, until she was nearly forty-five weeks along. She ignored a doctor's recommendation that she induce labor in a hospital. Instead she said she consulted strangers who hung out on Facebook groups dedicated to "unassisted birth" and steeled herself by mainlining episodes of a podcast produced by the Free Birth Society. She loved one episode where a woman birthed a baby in a yurt with only her dog acting as what she called a *midwolf*. "I became obsessed," Judith said. "I would just wonder, 'What's my story going to be like?' and think, 'I want my story to be as badass as their stories.'" When Judith finally went into labor, her baby's movements stalled. When her water broke, it was stained brown. By the time she made it to the hospital, the baby was dead. "Your whole responsibility is to protect your child, and I didn't before he even had a chance to breathe," Judith told NBC. "I think I brainwashed myself with the internet."

I promptly bleached Judith and her baby from my memory. But after the MRI, as I trudged around the perimeter of the park, trying to make up for the flood of stress hormones by bathing the baby with endorphins, I called up *The Free Birth Society Podcast* on my phone. The thumbnail featured a picture of a white woman sitting cross-legged at the water's edge, pregnant in a bikini, her arms lifted exultantly above her head. She was the podcast's host, Emilee Saldaya, a former doula in Los Angeles who had since rejected *the medical model* of birth, founded her society, and built a homestead in North Carolina that became the home base for its work. She launched the podcast in 2017, in anticipation of her own motherhood journey. "I wanted to absorb as many stories of women birthing in their power that I could as I prepared for my own birth," she said.

I selected an episode from March and listened at 2x speed. A cabasa rustled. A drum bonged. A woman sang: *Into the wild I go, into the wild I am. It's been a while, freedom chiiiiiiiiiild—since I left my roots back home.* The theme was a woo-woo hymnal, but when Saldaya started talking, she had a wry millennial podcast voice, like she was there to dish on the pitfalls of modern dating or recap a sexy true crime. She sounded like a friend, or the kind of internet personality I could pretend was my friend. "Today I have my friend Simone," Saldaya said. "Simone came to choose freebirth from watching her own cat give birth and tells us how it all began with the thought, *If a cat can do it, I can too.* And so she did."

Simone and her housecat were pregnant at the same time, and one day Simone came upon her pet mid-delivery. She said, "The cat had seven kittens by herself. And that totally inspired me." Simone watched YouTube videos about potential birth complications and decided that they were rare, "unless you're, you know, completely unhealthy and not in tune with your body." After all, "we as a society wouldn't be here without this instinct of birthing." She added, "I'm a woman, I know that this is what I'm supposed to do." Her prenatal care consisted of brewing herbal teas, practicing yoga, and sunbathing. When her water broke, she labored under a tree as her partner played the didgeridoo and watched cord-cutting tutorials on YouTube. She called her contractions "waves." When the baby arrived, "I was completely at bliss. I didn't know anything else," Simone said. "We were all bloody and all juicy with womb juice all over us." And Saldaya said: "It's just such a beautiful image."

I debated the freebirthers in my head. *A cat is not even a primate,* I thought. And, *What would a cat midwife even do in an "assisted" cat birth? Claw the baby out? By the way, the mere fact that human life persists on Earth is not helpful in calculating my personal risk in childbirth, because regardless of the persistence of "we as a society," I, specifically, wish to live.* And yet, Simone had just produced a baby with the help of only a video-sharing platform. I could sense my reasoned arguments begin to crumple under the intensity of her physical achievement. It was Simone's commentary on birth complications—they do not occur *unless you're, you know, completely unhealthy and not in tune with your body*—that really irritated me. I had been haunted by the idea that my pregnancy would reveal all my failures and weaknesses—nature's flaw detector. When Simone articulated my paranoia, she cut it loose and handed it to me to inspect more closely. It sounded so mean when she said it out loud.

As I waited for the call from Integrated Genetics (an arm of Labcorp), I searched the internet for more stories of unassisted births. I followed witchy Instagram accounts and requested access to locked Facebook communities. I agreed to their demands: *No induction discussion. No assistance talk. Don't use words like hospital, OB, birth center, midwife, induce etc. Don't talk about birth related medical professionals or their opinions.* When one group said, *This is a biblically based group that openly talks about Jesus . . . Is that ok with you?*, I pressed the "yes" button. Inside the groups, I found messages like: *Are there any Christ faith mamas who consume the placenta?* And: *What are the unnecessary vaccines we feel are just for pharmaceutical gain?* I knew that the percentage of people who delivered babies without assistance was just a sliver in the pie chart of humanity, but inside my phone they grew to populate an entire world.

The freebirthers had their own vocabulary: They spoke of *physiological birth, ecstatic birth,* and *pain-free supernatural childbirth.* Getting pregnant was *calling in their spirit babies,* labor was *the birth dance,* delivery was *bringing their babies earthside,* and becoming a parent was *entering the portal* to receive their children. They prepared for birth with *wild pregnancies, deprogramming, plant medicine,* and *energy work.* They gave birth in a cabin, or a teepee, or a stream. They had a name for my pregnancy, too: I was *birthing in captivity.* Inside my doctor's office, I stared at my own window to nature: a framed stock image of dewdrops suspended on a leaf.

Emilee Saldaya was right about this: the stories of the births on her podcast of steel-willed women birthing in nature were compelling and dramatic. "I love the image of you outside," Saldaya told Simone, "all bloody on the grass on a blanket with your baby and your man." Simone's partner had filmed the whole thing.

I knew that this was not for me. I did not want Marc to play a wind instrument like some storybook imp, nor did I want sand anywhere near my dilating cervix. But when I tried to envision my own birth, nothing came up. My future hid behind a hospital curtain. The medical system had its own obscure birthing vocabulary, too, terms I had to look up: *induction, Pitocin, episiotomy, Foley balloon.*

The freebirth stories smudged out my mental images of hospitals and machines. There were no forceps or scalpels to hasten their childbirth plots. I wanted access to these technologies to get my baby out safely, but clearly, I did not want to have to think about them. I could not even imagine how they might be deployed. These women had crafted their pregnancies into epics and cast themselves as conquering heroes, and I consumed their stories like they were streaming on Bravo.

Judith had come to the Free Birth Society for inspiration as she tried to create her own badass unassisted-birth story. And I was there because—why? I wasn't listening to a podcast about birthing in the hospital, preparing to bring my own child into the world. My baby's complication remained mysterious, and I was newly skeptical of the system that I had trusted with diagnosing it. The freebirthers, who sounded so familiar but acted so strange, made me feel more confident in my own choices. Okay, they made feel smug about them. Because I came to them through Judith's still-birth, they represented my greatest fear: that a choice I made could bring about my baby's death. Their strangeness contained this fear, kept it at a comfortable distance. As long as they were whispering in my ears, I could suppress my unease at the medicalization of my own pregnancy.

When the episodes ended, my anxiety returned. Simone the cat lady nailed me: the woman with no birthing instinct, her mind and body out of sync. I could not imagine how a baby was going to come out of me or how I would care for it when it did. My hospital's birth classes were canceled during the pandemic, so I took one over Zoom, but it failed to clarify the issue. I thought of Nikki Giovanni's memoir, *Gemini*, where she reports to the hospital nine months pregnant and reacts with disbelief when a doctor tells her she is going to have a baby. "I was an intellectual," she writes. "I thought things through. I didn't know shit about action. . . . Damn damn damn. Why me?" I asked the internet how you push a baby out. I asked the internet how much it hurts.

The natural childbirth movement has always been a storytelling movement. It tells a story about pain. The phrase itself was popularized by a midcentury British obstetrician named Grantly Dick-Read in a 1933 book for doctors, *Natural Childbirth*. In 1942, Dick-Read published another book, pitched at mothers-to-be, which became a bestseller. Eighty years later, I bought a used copy of the fourth edition online, released under its refreshed title: *Childbirth Without Fear*. The discomfort of birth, Dick-Read wrote, was instigated by the fear of birth itself. Fear caused tension, which caused pain, which caused more fear and tension and pain.

Dick-Read was writing at a time of great change in the management of birth. In 1900, only 5 percent of US births took place in hospitals. By 1935, half of them did. (By 2020, the figure was 98.3 percent.) That shift required pregnant women to buy into the advancing technologies offered in the hospital setting, even as their obstetricians squabbled over how much they ought to be used. In 1914, women's magazines published reports of a faddish European protocol called twilight sleep, in which German doctors injected women with morphine and scopolamine to induce amnesia during highly managed labors. American feminists demanded that their doctors give them the same drugs. Affluent women began to see the hospital as a respectable option and a desirable consumer choice. Twilight sleep lost its sparkle when one of its advocates, Charlotte Carmody, died in childbirth in New York City. But the trend toward doctors administering powerful anesthetics in hospital settings was permanent.

In the foreword to *Natural Childbirth*, Dick-Read warned that obstetric technologies, and the publicity they drew, had not improved birth outcomes. He told doctors and nurses to stop interfering so much. Instead they ought to observe and instruct. In most cases, he advised them to withhold pain medication to laboring women, which he called "the mistaken application of human sympathy." Dick-Read instructed domineering male doctors to trust women's bodies, but he also told women to doubt their own minds. The source of fear and pain, he said, was information. Many young women, he wrote, "have enquiring minds." They are drawn to birth stories "as if by sirens." They "satiate their greed for knowledge by listening to voices that entrance but utterly distort or destroy the truth."

Women told women that childbirth hurts. Dick-Read offered an alternative story, one that he claimed to have gleaned from "historical writings" and from reports of "groups who have not yet come into contact with European civilization." He wrote approvingly of "women whose mental development has not attained a state of civilization," of "jungle women" who birthed in places "where white men seldom go and never stay." These women experienced "very little discomfort," he said. Their children were "born easily, small and firm fleshed." Though he traveled through Africa searching for it, he never witnessed this mode of birth himself. He claimed that the mythical pain-free natural birth now occurred so far off the beaten path that it could not be accessed by white travelers. Still, he assured his readers that the only "true pains" of a natural childbirth were six to eight contractions near the end, a number handily managed by a woman freed of her culture and ego.

Dick-Read was not the first to suggest that labor pains were a side effect of white middle-class women's education, or that the secrets of authentic womanhood could be extracted from a racialized other. "We know that among Indians the squaws do not suffer in childbirth," the suffragist Elizabeth Cady Stanton once told a crowd, leveraging natural-birth rhetoric to promote outdoorsmanship among white women and girls. In 1871, the American physician Martin Luther Holbrook published *Parturition Without Pain: A Code of Directions for Escaping from the Primal Curse*, in which he advised the "luxurious daughters of artificial life" to mimic the nutritional intake of "savage women"; a diet of fruit and rice would produce babies who were "pliable at birth." Even proponents of twilight sleep described it as relieving the "modern American woman" of "her conscious mind and will." When Marie Stopes prepared to give birth to her first child under twilight sleep, in 1919, she warned her doctors, "I am the nearest thing to a physically savage woman that you have ever had the luck to meet in your life."

Twilight sleep was mythologized for its easy recoveries, but Dick-Read pitched his own method as permanently transformative. Birth was not just the "delivery of her child" but "the making of a mother," he wrote. "Childbirth is the perfection of womanhood, and the beautifying of the maternal conscience is one of its most acceptable rewards." In place of anesthesia, laboring women would receive an apex life experience: a "physical, spiritual and emotional achievement" that promised to be "vivid and interesting" as long as the woman capably executed her role. Dick-Read coached her in natural birth's new performance style. He invited white women of the middle and upper classes to put on a fantasy of primitive painlessness, to wear it like a laboring gown. Natural birth was a kind of safari, and when it was over, its participants could return home to idealized and compliant family lives.

Dick-Read pitched painless birth as a feminine ideal in pursuit of a societal ideal: the enthusiastic production of more white babies. In an address to the Eugenics Society in 1945, Dick-Read complained that, if the English birth rate did not rise, the country would soon "cease to be a power or even an influence among the nations of the world." He rose to prominence just as the United States was legislating midwives out of existence. Black midwives were targeted with racist campaigns that slandered them as "witches," "savage," and "unclean" and worked to reform them into a medical model of birth. Midwives were supplanted by white male physicians in hospitals, many of whom had no obstetrical training. In the decades that followed, hospital birth in America came to resemble an assembly line of medical interventions, and Dick-Read's influence over women only grew.

Patricia Cloyd Carter, like any good 1950s Florida housewife, delivered her first three babies in a hospital. "I screamed and writhed and chewed my fingers bloody," she told *Look* magazine in 1956. Then Carter discovered Dick-Read's works. "He's a great man," she said. "He unlocked the door of psychic tranquility at birth." But she soon decided that Dick-Read, and doctors like him, were themselves unnecessary. She birthed the rest of her nine babies at home without assistance, which is how she earned her spread in *Look*. In a photograph, she posed in a sundress on her Titusville, Florida, porch with her many children, the latest of whom had been born just four days earlier. (A newly postpartum Janet Leigh graced the issue's cover, and said of her hospital birth: "I was groggy and I don't remember much.") Carter told the magazine with amusement that an obstetric expert had deemed her "more primitive than the majority of modern women."

Carter was America's first freebirth influencer, and she established the movement's stark cultural contradictions. Even as she resisted the patriarchal control of obstetrics, she embodied the idealized housewife. She was hailed as the " 'do-it-yourself' mother" who sprang up to dust the piano as soon as she put her newborn down for a nap. In one newspaper story, she's photographed reclining on a couch in a tropical-print halter dress a few minutes before birth, a tumbler in her right hand. Carter counseled women to diet and smoke throughout their pregnancies and to mix several whisky highballs to down during labor. "It's easy if you don't let yourself gain too much weight, and the whisky helps you relax," she said. Many of her tips were bent at keeping babies small enough to slip right out. The itsy-bitsy housewife who smoked her way to freebirth was very much of her time, which makes her claims to the "natural" essence of her experiences all the more absurd.

I learned about Carter through the work of Dr. Rixa Freeze, a scholar whose 2008 thesis "Born Free: Unassisted Childbirth in North America" traced the origins of the movement up through the dawn of social media. In 2024, I called Freeze over Zoom, and was pleased to see that she appeared precisely the same as she did in the photograph on her website, with a single blond braid tossed over one shoulder. Freeze told me that she became fascinated by unassisted birth as she started planning to have a family of her own; as a part of her research, she worked as a doula and an assistant to unlicensed midwives, and she spent a lot of time on internet message boards where women planned and executed solo births. She taught herself how to measure her own fundal height and how to resuscitate a newborn. In 2006, she birthed her first child, Zari, without assistance. Her husband joked that their daughter was the "practicum of her dissertation."

In "Born Free," Freeze detailed freebirth's disparate cultural inputs: crunchy mamas, women with birth trauma, religious fundamentalists. When she surveyed more than sixty North American women who had birthed unassisted, and interviewed seventeen more, she found that they were much like Patricia Carter, in that they were overwhelmingly white women who identified as stay-at-home moms. The difference was that now they could all hang out online. Converging in those birth forums, "it's so easy to feel like what you're doing is normal or popular," Freeze said. "But there's an emptiness to online communities, too—a lack of accountability."

Back in 2006, when Freeze delivered Zari, birth forums could feel like organic communities of relative peers. By the time I started looking into unassisted births, I found that that version of the internet had been razed, pumped with capital, and rebuilt as a platform for monetizing influence. Dick-Read's vision of natural birth as a mothering performance has achieved its final form. If natural childbirth tells a story, freebirth is an epic. It is woman vs. nature, woman vs. society, woman vs. herself. It aligns with the imperatives of social media platforms to push content to its furthest extremes. It is a feat of physical and mental but also commercial control. It is birth story as the launch of a personal brand.

In 2023, I revisited the Free Birth Society podcasts that I had listened to during my pregnancy, and I heard an ad I had not noticed before. There were urgent piano plinks, swelling strings. "The time is now," Saldaya said. "We need you to join us in this birth revolution." I navigated to the Free Birth Society's website and was surprised by its professionalism, how action shots of birthing women and clouds of affirmational text floated slickly in and out of view as I scrolled. I signed up for its email list and my inbox grew with subject lines like *How to heal a fever naturally!* And *Are your thoughts your own?*

The podcast's birth stories, I realized, were just the free tier of a vast digital marketing project. Now my inbox was filled with pitches for the society's many programs, which it called *containers* and *offer-*

ings: in addition to joining a *vetted* private membership community ($499/year), I was invited to download an online course called the Complete Guide to Freebirth ($399); attend an intensive retreat called the Midwife Within ($3,000); recruit my partner for a live, interactive couples' module called MatriBirth Family™ ($999); pre-register for the Matriarch Rising Festival, a sleepover retreat in the Blue Ridge Mountains ($900+); school myself in *what's wrong and abusive about the current birth model* with a primer called "The Compass" ($299); purchase a private consultation with Saldaya for processing my birth trauma ($300) or achieving self-mastery (another $300); and enroll in the Radical Birth Keeper School, where I could learn to become not a midwife or a doula but a sort of antimedical attendant of other women's births ($6,000). In 2024, the Radical Birth Keeper School was upgraded to a new offering, called the MatriBirth Midwifery Institute. *Think independent midwifery meets leading-edge business school meets life-changing self mastery tools,* but of course, still with no actual midwifery certification (and now $12,000).

The politics of natural birth had taken many shapes, and now it had fused with a hyperindividualistic entrepreneurial drive. The Free Birth Society once issued palatable progressive statements in its courses, emphasizing that they were inclusive of *everyone who gives birth,* including trans and nonbinary people, and acknowledging that freebirth was a *privilege* that was not always available to Black women due to *systemic racism.* But after I started following the society, in 2020, the language of inclusivity seemed muted in favor of antivaccine conspiracy theorizing, critique of *internet woke culture,* and protest against *transgender ideology.* In the 1950s, Patricia Cloyd Carter had founded a local Democratic Party club at her kitchen table, but now freebirth's political allegiances had completely realigned. In 2024, the Free Birth Society posted a meme to its Instagram account celebrating Donald Trump's tapping of

RFK Jr. to lead his Department of Health and Human Services, with the note: *Sorry not sorry.*

I could understand how, as healthcare became a commodity, some women would find the product so poor that they would eventually refuse to keep buying it. And yet there was something glib about the conversion of freebirth into a content strategy, in how it styled itself as a premium experience even as it aestheticized risk. In its fully commodified form, freebirth was pitched as the origin story for the ultimate self-made woman, the one who could deliver her own baby and start a business, too, staked on the imagery of her own bonkers birth. In 2022, a white German woman went viral after she birthed her fourth baby into the sea like some kind of divine offspring. She posted the video evidence to Instagram, where she documented her Nicaraguan #vanlife under the handle @ragga punzel, earning tabloid recognition and an episode of *The Free Birth Society Podcast.* Soon she was offering one-on-one coaching sessions and access to a guided ayahuasca retreat.

One day I bought the Complete Guide to Freebirth and waded in. There were one hundred lessons. Each featured a video of either Saldaya or her collaborator, fellow birth thought leader Yolande Norris-Clark. They took turns delivering extended scripted monologues on subjects like the evolutionary-psychological roots of fear ("As subsistence hunter-gatherers, living on the land in small groups . . ."), OB-GYNs ("industrial obstetrics is rape culture"), and the prenatal ultrasound ("a scam"). My hand drifted to the seventh lesson—"Birth and Death"—and pressed play.

Saldaya appeared in the corner of a blank room, wearing a loose-knit cardigan over a snug tank top that said "FREEBIRTH" in a faux-typewriter script. A shimmering pendant snaked down her chest, and the cord of a microphone snaked up it. Her lecture corner seemed hastily appointed with elements of nature: a spiny potted plant was plunked behind her head, and a sheepskin rug lay over the curved lip of a leather couch. "Birth is always a life-or-death situation," she began. "Life is a life-or-death situation."

While "obstetric culture" revolves around a latent desire "to thwart death," Saldaya explained, she had come to understand that "death is the shadow side of birth." Choosing to birth at home without assistance, she said, required her to embrace her own mortality, and that of her baby, too. "Sometimes birth is a meeting with death. This happens during home birth, and it happens in the hospital," she said. "I came to the conclusion that I would actively choose to be in my own intimate space even if the outcome was death," she continued. "It is more important to me to receive my baby into my own hands, unmediated by machines and strangers and bright lights."

Sometimes babies died at home: the ultimate unmediated experience.

After my doctor extracted amniotic fluid from my uterus, it traveled by mail at room temperature to a Mayo Clinic Laboratories facility in Rochester, Minnesota. The sample arrived at the clinic's processing center, where a machine scanned its barcode, sorted it, and shuttled it to a lab. The baby's cells were isolated from the fluid, mixed in a chemical broth, and grown in an incubator calibrated to mimic the temperature and humidity of the human body. Then they were harvested, washed, spun in a centrifuge, and split open. Strands of my baby's DNA were mixed with fluorescent probes of synthetic DNA designed to hunt for changes in a region of the eleventh chromosome that contained some of the genes that control cell growth. My baby's DNA combined with the probes, his organic molecules twisting around the artificial ones. When a machine measured the bands of fluorescent light emanating from his sample, its analysis revealed that a maternal copy of one of these genes was switched off that was supposed to be switched on. Like I had forgotten to leave the light on for him when I fell asleep.

When I was thirty-three weeks pregnant, my obstetrician called with the results. The cells had tested positive for Beckwith-Wiedemann syndrome. The call ended quickly, leaving Marc and me in silence on the couch. The diagnostic odyssey was over. The cells in the laboratory had been disposed of, but I sensed that they had been returned to me. Marc found a doctor in Philadelphia who had dedicated her career to studying BWS. A few minutes after he emailed her, she called us on the phone. She assured us that one of the scariest statistics on the internet was outdated, that she had crafted a detailed protocol for treating BWS babies from birth to ensure the best possible outcomes. My son was not yet born, but it felt like she had spent years preparing to meet him.

I knew that other people spent the weeks before a child's birth finalizing the birth plans, preparing their spaces. Marc and I focused on making sure the hospital's pediatric staff understood all potential BWS complications and that they had a high-level neonatal intensive care unit, or NICU, where he could be treated. If the baby's tongue restricted his airway, they needed to be ready to help him eat and breathe. If he was born with an omphalocele, where parts of his intestine developed outside of his belly, they needed to be ready to surgically repair it. If a cancerous tumor was already developing inside of him, a prick of his blood would be necessary to tip them off. One of the symptoms of BWS was persistent neonatal hypoglycemia. The condition was easily managed, but if it was not diagnosed and treated with the correct protocol, it could cause brain damage or, in rare cases, death.

The ultrasound showing a brain abnormality had been a fluke. But now it felt like a premonition. If I had had a wild pregnancy, dismissed prenatal care as a scam, I never would have received that terrifying ultrasound. But I also would have denied myself the information that I needed to protect my child after he was born. I appreciated that the doctors and nurses caring for my son were strangers—professionals. I welcomed their lights and their machines. As Marc and I mapped the NICU treatment plan, I finally felt like I had seized authority over my own pregnancy. It was my job to keep my baby safe, and I knew exactly what to do.

In her death sermon, Saldaya said that protecting babies was a matter of providing "adequate nourishment" to their mothers and "preserving the physiological and biological design of birth," ensuring that it was "beautifully and perfectly executed according to nature." If her own pregnancy presented "clear signs of a medical emergency," she would seek expert care "by all means," she said. But she warned that doctors were so steeped in the myths of pathological pregnancies, they could not differentiate between a true emergency and a hiccup. "But you will be able to," she promised, "by the end of the course."

Natural birth was a storytelling project, and pregnancies like mine did not fit into the narrative. How was I supposed to intuit that my baby had a rare genetic condition that required intervention from birth? Was I supposed to diagnose him psychically? Or else embrace his death, comforted that I had selected the lighting scheme for the experience? The lighting in the freebirth course was unflattering, I realized. The plant behind Saldaya's head was ugly and frail. I watched more and more of the course, waiting for the module where they would reveal how I would single-handedly save my son, and it never came.

Finally, in the eighty-fifth chapter of the course, I reached the unit on "developmental differences." Yolande Norris-Clark sat in front of a shelf of glazed ceramic vessels and spoke about these differences for seventeen minutes. Having no personal experience with the topic, she told a story about a baby born with gastroschisis, a condition where the baby's intestines form outside of the body. I had heard about gastroschisis because it was a sister condition to omphalocele; both were abdominal wall defects that required emergency surgery, though babies with omphalocele tended to have more complications and a higher mortality rate.

In her videos, Norris-Clark spoke with breathy assurance, like she was performing a kind of prenatal ASMR. Her voice made extreme choices feel slick and easy. But here she stumbled. "Gastro—*gastro-isk-us* I think is the right pronunciation," she said. She plowed into a speech about how babies with gastroschisis die in the hospital too, how the attempt to control for such outcomes was a technocratic illusion, but she could barely get through the prepared text. "I know of one family whose baby was born at home with . . . *gastro . . . skis-skis*"—Norris-Clark winced, sucked air between her teeth, and grinned—"and whose birth attendant wrapped their baby's organs and body in Saran Wrap, and immediately transferred to the hospital, and the baby was saved and survived. Umm, so, we just don't know!"

Norris-Clark wanted to give newborn babies "the most intimate and authentic experience of life," she said, from the very beginning. But all she had to offer my baby was a laugh and a sheet of plastic. That was the image she thought he deserved: his little body wrapped up like a day-old deli sandwich.

Chapter 6

Birth

Whenever I called the hospital, the receptionist asked me to hold, and I listened to a crackling recording of a woman's voice. She spoke of the facility's many wonderful doctors and nurses. *See them in action in the critically acclaimed docuseries* Lenox Hill, *now available on Netflix,* she said. I was already a patient of the hospital, but the hospital was still advertising itself to me, nudging me to view its live-action brochure. If I had been pregnant in previous years, I would have reported in person to a childbirth class and a tour of the maternity floor. But I gave birth in 2020, so I was dissuaded from entering the premises before I went into active labor. I lay on my couch and watched the hospital show instead.

The tagline of *Lenox Hill* was *Some heroes wear white coats,* and the series followed a team of neurosurgeons, an emergency room doctor, and an obstetrician, Dr. Amanda Little-Richardson. Little-Richardson was the only Black doctor featured in the show, and many of her patients were women of color, too. As she made her rounds, she spoke to me in a voiceover. "I wanted to work with populations who maybe medicine traditionally has neglected, and women fall under that, frankly," she said. "African-American women die at a much greater rate in labor," she added. She saw it as part of her job to make Black laboring women feel safe and cared for, while watching vigilantly for the "institutional problems that are contributing to these higher rates." Amanda Little-Richardson was Lenox Hill's chief resident OB-GYN, but she was also a patient—seven weeks pregnant when the series began. A pregnant Amanda, just like me.

In the second episode, when she was thirteen weeks pregnant, she lay back in a narrow ultrasound room, the top of her scrubs pulled to her chin. Her husband, Kevin, sat at her side. I saw the technician's back, Little-Richardson's gelled stomach, a skeletal fetus on a black screen. The technician asked if the couple met in California, and Kevin said, "We actually met at the club." Little-Richardson rolled her eyes and laughed. She watched the screen and cooed. The twin hemispheres of a little brain surfaced in the black. "Oh, look at that. That looks good," she said. Then the technician said, "Can you stop the video for a second? Or no. I was just gonna say something. But—"

The scene stopped and restarted. Little-Richardson was again on the chair, belly up, but now a doctor sat in the technician's place. A sad violin played. She appeared chilled over, her eyes steeled. When the doctor spoke, I realized that he was the same doctor who performed my abnormal ultrasound. Once again, he had found something he did not like.

Lenox Hill was filmed months before I became pregnant. But I felt like I was watching a reenactment of my own life. The Netflix algorithm had finally spat out a piece of content specifically for me. I showed the scene to Marc, and he pointed at Kevin's face as he received the news. "That look," Marc said. Kevin's mouth drifted open. His eyes circulated on a track, from wife to technician to monitor. Since Marc was barred from my appointments, he had never sat in Kevin's chair. He learned of the abnormal ultrasound on his phone, alone in the rain. Now his virtual experience had a face, a lost expression.

In Little-Richardson, I found something even stranger and more intoxicating. The Netflix version of my life had replaced me with a double, one who could absolve me of my self-blame. Even as genetic counselors assured me that my baby's condition was random, my shame was adaptive. First, I felt bad that I might have done something to damage my baby. Then I felt bad for ever feeling that my baby was somehow damaged. Now I watched the same scenario unfold in the body of another Amanda. A heroic Amanda— one who had dedicated her life to shepherding her patients safely through childbirth.

I binged the rest of the episodes, skipping past surgeries and accidents to get to the Amanda parts. I stared at the wall behind my TV during the neurosurgery scenes, denying the existence of cancer. I raced toward the conclusion of her story as if it would resolve mine, too. The show served me images of childbirth in montage, faces of pain and surprise flashing from fluorescent rooms. I saw one baby shoot from between a woman's legs and another pulled from a woman's split-open abdomen. The first mother cried gratefully into her baby's hair and the second lay baffled on the operating table with an infection, her baby spirited off to the NICU for tests. Occasionally one of my own doctors flew across the screen, gripping a slippery newborn. The show became a flipbook of birth and death, images of gray lumps shuffled in with tiny bodies. And then Little-Richardson, who seemed to speak directly to me.

There she was again on an exam chair, her pregnancy uploaded to the monitor in black and white. The results of her prenatal tests had returned, and they indicated a rare disorder called Noonan syndrome. When I googled it, it seemed like a mirror image of my baby's own diagnosis: *a genetic condition that stops typical develop-ment in various parts of the body.* "I don't think I'm a crier, so much," Little-Richardson said in a voiceover as an ultrasound wand roved across her skin. "The day I got that news, Kevin said he's never heard me cry that hard. When you hear that something might be wrong with your child, it's, like, devastating," she said. And then she got back to work. Uncertainty, grief, and acceptance, bent into a three-episode arc, ready for me to stream before my due date.

Little-Richardson made me feel better about my pregnancy, and about the hospital, too. I followed her on Instagram and peered into her family life. Her account was set to public, but it still felt like I was standing on my tiptoes, pressing my nose against her open window. I watched a second-birthday montage of her little girl, lying sleeping in a bassinet, wearing a winter hat, peeking out from behind a tree. She looked just like Kevin, this anxious but kind and goofy dad I had to remind myself I did not know.

As my due date approached, I went through the motions of YouTube prenatal exercise videos, pretending to deep-breathe and bear down. But I didn't think much about how my son would arrive or what kind of physiological process would produce him. I felt like I needed to produce him through a psychological process. Or I needed to produce myself, to figure out how to resolve my guilt so I could open the door to his life and make it seem like I had been waiting there all along, his plausible mother welcoming him home. Some days Netflix, and the online searches it inspired, was the only light illuminating my lonely path to birth.

In the show's season finale, Little-Richardson went into labor preterm, thirty-six weeks into her pregnancy. She was back on the labor-and-delivery floor, this time not in scrubs but in a cute custom hospital gown, an oatmeal-colored minidress with a halter top for easy feeding and cutouts at the tummy and the back for fetal monitoring. The screen flashed back to two births she had facilitated—the speedy vaginal birth and the emergency cesarean section. It drew those births as if from a tarot deck, illustrating Little-Richardson's possible fates. I watched her breathe and hobble down the hall, leaning on Kevin's shoulders. She closed her eyes and bounced on a ball. She had resolved to have an unmedicated birth, but as the contractions crashed through her, she wondered why this had been so important to her. She pressed a button and called for an epidural. I saw her rest on a hospital bed, then begin to push. Kevin pulled out his phone to take a picture of the baby crowning and she warned him to put it away. "I was gonna do a selfie," he said. "My bad." She pushed until a silvery baby flopped onto her chest. Then she cried.

When it was over, her mother said, "A vaginal birth." And Little-Richardson said, "I know. Thank you, Jesus."

Lenox Hill was produced and distributed by Netflix, but it had the gritty uplift of high-end sponsored content. Northwell Health, the nonprofit hospital network that owns Lenox Hill, issued a press release praising the show's *unflinching eye* on *the heart and soul of medicine*. *The New York Times* later reported that the show (and others like it) had been effective advertising, making viewers more likely to recommend Northwell properties to others. It debuted at a critical moment, just as New York hospitals were drawing scrutiny about how they managed the labors and childbirths of Black women in their care.

In New York City, Black women are nine times more likely than white women to die of pregnancy-related causes. In the summer of 2020, protests for Black lives made their way to hospital doors. When two twenty-six-year-old women died following emergency

C-sections that year—Amber Rose Isaac at Montefiore Medical Center in the Bronx and Sha-Asia Washington at Woodhull Hospital in Brooklyn—it made national news. As *Lenox Hill* turned its doctors into Netflix characters, Little-Richardson was made to represent both the medical system's risk to Black mothers and its remedy. She was cast as the lone provider who could resolve the inequities of maternity care through her own close attention. A Facebook ad for the series put it this way: *This is Dr. Little-Richardson—she knows there's a problem with how black people are treated by the medical community. And she's not going to stop talking about it until it's fixed.*

When Little-Richardson entered the hospital in a white coat, she was styled as a hero. But when she returned in a laboring gown, her status wavered. She was a doctor of medicine, the daughter of a labor-and-delivery nurse, but this did not confer protection from the institution that raised her. In an article in *Glamour*, Little-Richardson sketched in the details of her destabilizing birth experience. *Lenox Hill* valorized the hardworking doctors who overcame the nebulous challenges of their profession to heal the sick, but when Little-Richardson went into labor early, she questioned whether her punishing medical residency had affected her pregnancy outcome. "I can't help but think that my rigorous schedule contributed to my preterm delivery," she said. "I also wonder if there is something to my being a Black woman that contributed to this as well—an extra burden haunting Black women during and after delivery." When she paced down the hospital's halls in labor, she walked the rhetorical border between protection and risk. Life and death.

The birth stories I absorbed on Instagram and in podcasts were styled to represent the height of individualistic achievement, the climax of a woman's life and the origin of her child's. But Little-Richardson's birth was embedded in the story of a system, one that denied her full subjectivity. In *Glamour*, she described the medical neglect of Black women as both a "crisis" and a "legacy," at once an emergency and a status quo. Even as *Lenox Hill* broadcast her pregnancy as a redemptive drama, the medical system compressed her birth story into a statistic.

When I finally arrived at Lenox Hill one afternoon in September 2020—forty-one weeks into my first pregnancy, a few hours after my water broke—it felt like walking onto the set of a film. Or an immersive brand offering—Netflix's *Lenox Hill:* The birth experience. As I ascended to the labor-and-delivery floor for the first time, I recognized the bank of desks where Little-Richardson typed her notes, the framed photographs of diapered cherubs that watched over her work. But everything felt slowed down, like the production was half-struck.

Watching *Lenox Hill* on my couch, I had identified with the doctors and their propulsive plots. *See them in action,* the telephone recording had said. Now I was one of the show's many nameless patients. My moves were determined by the institution and its processing of the data my body produced. I submitted to its hidden protocols. Immediately Marc was separated from me, diverted to an undisclosed location. I sat in a chair in a narrow room, leaking like a punctured waterbed. Every few minutes a contraction grew in my abdomen and clawed its way out. I was in labor—"I am in labor," I told the nurses and administrators who circulated the area—but I was not to be admitted as a patient until my labor was medically confirmed and coded in the system.

I sat with my hands outstretched, presenting my insurance card. One nurse instructed me to shimmy an elastic band over my midsection and then lodged two gray plastic nodes inside, hooked to long cords. They pulsed signals to a contraption that converted my body into information. A line graph bloomed from a printer, resembling a polygraph test. Another nurse instructed me to peel off my bloated menstrual pad and hand it over for testing. I assured her that it was soaked in amniotic fluid, but she thought I may have just peed myself. "Your water is broken!" she announced when she returned, shaking her head.

I graduated from chair to intake bed to a delivery room, where I sat alone, photographing my surroundings. As if I could seize control of my birth by obtaining documentary evidence of the medical environment. In my phone there is a picture of a pain scale poster, a succession of cartoon faces with mouths that droop methodically alongside caveman-voice descriptors—*No Hurt. Hurts Little Bit. Hurts Little More.* Another photograph shows a plexiglass bassinet sitting under what looks like a salon dryer, a receiving blanket optimistically draped across it. The doctors of *Lenox Hill* were always striding around and conferring in their special language, making judgment calls informed by their compelling personal backgrounds. But when I stepped inside the room, my personal story seemed no longer to exist. My birth plan, a list of preferences I had typed up and printed on a piece of paper, had floated off with Marc, lodged between pillows in a blue IKEA shopping bag.

I am trying to tell the story of my son's birth, to situate myself as its main character, but already my plot has holes. I should tell you that a few months earlier I had hired a doula, Megan Davidson, who became my wise counsel as I faced my pregnancy's gauntlet of medical decisions. After my due date came and went, Davidson and I discussed my options, and—a few hours before I entered the hospital—I asked my obstetrician to perform a membrane sweep, a term I had recently acquired. The doctor stuck a gloved finger into my vagina and swirled it around, loosening the membrane of the amniotic sac from my cervix. As Marc drove me away from the appointment, fluid gushed through my leggings and pooled into the seat.

I requested the membrane sweep because I was told it could subtly prompt my body to go into labor—how, I was not sure. I wanted to go into labor so that I could avoid a hospital induction, which would involve—I did not really know, something about an inflatable balloon. My doctors had wanted to induce me if I passed the forty-first week of pregnancy without going into spontaneous labor, because—I did not know. When my water broke, I went home to labor until my contractions were long and quick, because—I did not know. Those nodes they strapped to my body showed—I did not know. But they were important because—I did not know. When Marc and Megan were allowed to join me in the room, the birth's course only grew more obscure. I offloaded my awareness to them. Only when I sat to write this chapter did I realize how little I understood about how my child was born.

To better understand it, I needed to speak to experts on obstetric practices, consult an archivist at a medical library, and obtain a thousand-page medical record from Lenox Hill. A few days after I requested the document, a PDF arrived in my inbox. A few days after that, an envelope appeared at my address, containing a secret PIN for unlocking the PDF. Inside were reams of pages of data compiled about the birth, along with notes from my provider and medical releases I did not recall signing. I scrolled until I reached my big hospital entrance. I scanned the pages anxiously, wondering how I appeared under the medical gaze. The nurses and doctors who milled about had updated the record every few minutes with the help of their electric probes. I became a demographic sketch, a confluence of electronic signals. I read about my birth in the third person, like it was an entry on FactsBuddy.com.

According to the medical record, Amanda Hess reported to the hospital at 7:24 p.m. that night with the complaint of pregnancy. The patient was married, white, and thirty-five years old. Her membranes had been ruptured and her amniotic fluid was clear. She was experiencing abdominal cramping. Her cervix was three centimeters dilated. Her pain level was a six. Her extremities had a normal range of motion, and her skin was the color consistent with her ethnicity. She was cooperative and alert. She had private medical insurance.

At 9:52 p.m., she was experiencing irregular contractions. She requested an epidural. At 10:12, she sat for the epidural. At 10:25, it was completed. The urine that drained from her catheter was clear. At 11:19, the patient's contractions were still irregular. The patient was okay with starting Pitocin. At 11:52, Pitocin was administered. The patient had contractions every four minutes. Then every two minutes. At 1:03 a.m. the next morning, the Pitocin dosage was increased. At 5:04 a.m., the dosage was increased again. At 7:32 a.m., the epidural was redosed with additional pain medication.

At 7:45 a.m., the patient's cervix was fully dilated and effaced. The dosage of Pitocin was increased. The epidural pump was shut off. The patient was instructed to labor down for thirty to forty minutes. She was instructed on pushing. At 8:22 a.m., the patient pushed with contractions. Her contractions were regular and strong. She pushed in a side-lying position. Her partner was at her bedside. She had no pain. She was offered reassurance and praise. *What is happening* was explained to her. *What to expect* was explained.

At 9:05 that morning, the patient's position was changed. She was placed in a semi-Fowler position. She was given a peanut-shaped ball. The patient was reassured. All of her questions were answered. She felt no pain. The patient's contractions were regular and strong.

The fetal heart rate showed moderate variability. Heart-rate accelerations were present. Early decelerations were noted. The fetal heart rate tracing was a category 2, of indeterminate significance.

At 10:35, a vaginal delivery was anticipated. At 10:37, multiple pushing techniques were attempted. At 10:44, the Pitocin dosage was increased. At 10:49, the patient was pushing with sufficient effort. She was squatting with assistance. Her pain level was a three.

At 11:47 a.m., doctors discussed the option of cesarean section among themselves.

Despite adequate effort, the patient pushed for 3.5 hours with no change in fetal station. The patient experienced an arrest of descent. There was a change in maternal status. The patient desired a cesarean section. A consent was signed. The Pitocin was discontinued. The patient was shaved with clippers. At 12:23 p.m., she entered the operating room for a nonurgent, nonscheduled cesarean section. At 12:40, the doctor cut into her skin. At 12:47, the doctor cut into her uterus. At 12:58, a male infant was delivered, liveborn. The baby was taken to the NICU. There was no skin-to-skin contact. The patient's uterus was closed in one layer with figure-of-eight sutures.

Myth of the week: C-section births are always easier, Flo said. *While "popping them out the sunroof" might sound breezy, a cesarean section is a big surgery and can also be a challenge. So, however your baby arrives, kudos to you, legend.*

I started to write the birth story in my mind when I was still in the operating room. I had not anticipated needing a C-section, but now it seemed inevitable. Thirty-five years earlier, I had been born by cesarean section, just like my older brother had been. It was part of our sibling lore that we were gargantuan newborns; I weighed in at nine pounds. We knew that the doctors first tried to pry my brother out with forceps and suck him out with a vacuum and that when he was finally extricated, his skull appeared stretched into a point, like a member of the Conehead family on *Saturday Night Live*. After my own surgery, my son came out with a pointy head, too, from the pressure of being forced into a canal he would not exit. My obstetrician later explained that I appeared to have a very narrow pelvis. And of course, I had a baby with an overgrowth disorder.

All of this made sense to me until, many months later, I learned what Lenox Hill's C-section rate was in 2020: 31 percent.

Oh.

The Leapfrog Hospital Survey, which evaluates hospitals on a range of metrics, recommends that the C-section rate (defined as the percentage of "first-time mothers giving birth to a single baby, at full-term, in the head-down position") be below 23.6 percent. The statistical gap opened a crack in my story. I trusted my doctors, but I began to doubt my own body. Visions of freebirthers labored in my mind. Maybe I just hadn't pushed hard enough.

All the medical interventions in my birth—like Pitocin, the synthetic oxytocin which had supercharged my contractions—had been deployed to fend off potential emergencies. At thirty-five years old, my chances of stillbirth were ticking up. At forty-one weeks old, my placenta was aging too, growing less capable of providing oxygen to the baby. Inside the hospital, weak contractions prolonged labor, increasing my risk of an infection. But these interventions could also invite infection or hemorrhage or fetal distress, causing their own emergencies. And while a C-section could help resolve those complications, it carried its own risks, especially in future pregnancies. The medical historian Jacqueline Wolf writes that before modern medicine, before antibiotics and anesthesia made successful surgeries possible, a blocked labor might be resolved by a doctor or midwife crushing the baby's skull, dismantling its corpse, and pulling it out with a crochet hook. But also that some babies' heads wrenched free at some point, and they arrived screaming and alive.

When I asked Lenox Hill Hospital about its C-section rate, in 2024, I was connected with Dr. Michael Nimaroff, the hospital's acting Chairman of Obstetrics and Gynecology, who acknowledged the rise in surgical births as a national problem. "Clearly, our rate is too high in the U.S.," he said. While some surgeries could not be avoided—an aging patient population, for instance, tended to have more comorbidities—Nimaroff said the hospital had been working to lower its C-section rate without negatively affecting patient outcomes. One strategy was to leverage the concerning data itself: make each obstetrician aware of their own rate, drill into the reasoning behind each surgery, and celebrate doctors whose rate fell under 30 percent. By 2023, Lenox Hill's C-section rate had dipped to 28.9.

The details of my "birth story" posed no obvious significance to me. My son's birth was not a scene lit by fairy lights. It was not the final exam of my mothering prep course or a premonition of our life to come. Now I realized that it was not even a story. It was a statistical analysis. The outcome was shaped by my demographic position, my risk factors, current obstetric practice guidelines, and the relationship between the diameter of my baby's head and the shape of my pelvis. If a "natural" birth story was about the triumph of the individual, the C-section story represented her disappearance into the system. In *Lenox Hill,* when Little-Richardson facilitates a vaginal delivery, the mother tries to thank her, and she replies: "You did everything! I did nothing." But when Little-Richardson delivers a baby via C-section, the mother is wheeled off-screen, and she tells the woman's family: "I don't want her to feel bad, it wasn't anything she did."

In the endlessly reenacted psychodrama of birth, the C-section presented as the dark mirror of the vaginal delivery. It was the reversal of all of its fortunes. It was styled as a luxury consumer choice, the "easy way out" for the woman who was "too posh to push." But it was also interpreted as a theft, the medical system's violation of a woman's autonomous and authentic birth. It was at once a life-saving procedure and an unnecessary complication. If a vaginal birth was a natural, visceral, selfless, joyful achievement, the C-section was an artificial, numbed, vain, and tragic defeat. These ideas did not add up—the easy tragedy, the luxurious failure. The surgery was made to stand in for all of the promises and contradictions of the American medical system. It was tasked with making sense of the unimaginably wealthy country with the highest maternal mortality rate in the developed world. Which was why the "C-section story" was often totally incoherent.

The term *natural birth* is redundant: *nature* comes from a root meaning "born." It's a birth birth. If a vaginal birth created a child born by birth, what did a surgical birth produce? A child who was never born? This was the riddle at the heart of *Macbeth*, that "none of woman born" could harm him—only Macduff, who "was from his mother's womb untimely ripped." It's not clear from the text whether Macduff's mother was alive or dead when her son was cut from her body, and from the perspective of the plot, it did not matter. Either way, she was not involved. When I started reading women's accounts of their C-sections online, I was surprised by how many were not just angry or depressed over the circumstances of the birth but plagued by the idea that they had not given birth at all. "I wasn't really *there*," Denise Schipani wrote of her C-section on the parenting blog *Babble* in 2010. "I didn't give birth, it was taken from me." In *Self* magazine, Candace Bond-Theriault wrote: "I still grapple with whether or not I can claim to have brought my own baby into the world or if I gave all of that power away to my physician." A vaginal birth made a mother, and a C-section sliced her to pieces.

Modern medicine made C-sections survivable, even protective against other forms of maternal and infant deaths. But they could also introduce their own dangers—bleeding, infection, blood clots. A 2022 study found that healthy Black women were 21 percent more likely to deliver their first child by C-section than white women, that Hispanic women were 26 percent more likely than white women, and that these racial disparities increased their risk of death. In her memoir *We Live for the We: The Political Power of Black Motherhood*, Dani McClain writes about the unsettling experience of becoming a "statistic" when a white doctor diagnosed her with fibroids early in her pregnancy and recommended a surgical delivery. "Was I being steered by a provider with unconscious bias toward becoming another statistic?" she wondered. She sought a second opinion from a Black obstetrician, who agreed that a C-section was warranted. "I felt more confident that she'd be able to see me as a human being, just like her," McClain writes. In the discourse of Black maternal health, the statistics are so dire, unchanging, and tirelessly repeated, they pave another path to erasure. Writing in *The Washington Post* in 2019, Helena Andrews-Dyer called for "a way to digest the numbers without letting them eat us alive."

The public narrative of the C-section threatened to erase the mother, but there were some people who actually did not want her to become a mother at all. "There are those among us who believe that if the baby can't survive a home labor, it is OK for it to pass peacefully," the actress Mayim Bialik, then the "celebrity spokesmama" for the Holistic Moms Network, said in 2010. "I do not subscribe to this," she said, but she nevertheless spoke for members of her community who believed it: "If a baby cannot make it through birth, it is not favored evolutionarily." In *The Business of Being Born*, a 2008 documentary in which the actress Ricki Lake investigated the medicalization of birth, she staked her own claim to the maternal obliteration of surgical birth: "If monkeys give birth by cesarean section, the mother is not interested in her baby," the film claimed. "It's simple."

I did not think my baby should be peacefully dead. I was interested in him after he was born. Very interested! So was his father, who did not undergo the transformative spiritual experience of natural childbirth. Still, after I watched the documentary, I reflexively searched *monkey C-section* and found a YouTube video called *Mama Chimp is reunited with Baby after C-section.* Close enough. I watched a fuzzy newborn rest on a soft bed in the center of a concrete enclosure. A door slid open. The mother, a chimp named Mahale, lumbered in. She crouched against a wall. She stared vacantly for several seconds. My fingers tightened around the phone. Mahale shifted her posture. She glanced into the bed. The baby lifted a pink hand. The mother sprang up and cooed and drew the child to her chest. *Mahale is an exceptional mother and it's clear how much she loves her baby,* the caption said.

In 2023, I took the train through the city, past Lenox Hill Hospital, and up to 103rd Street, to a Romanesque-revival building that houses the library of the New York Academy of Medicine. Across from the library, at the lip of Central Park, a bronze statue of the nineteenth-century physician J. Marion Sims once stood. Dubbed the "father of American gynecology," Sims pioneered a surgical technique to repair obstetric fistulas, a serious complication of obstructed labors—one he developed through barbarous experimentation on enslaved women. In 2018, protesters successfully compelled the city to remove the statue. Now his pedestal was obscured with wooden planks.

Inside the academy I met Arlene Shaner, the librarian who tends to its rare book collection. She had long, muscular fingers, the better to page dexterously through big old books. When I first emailed her, asking about any records on the beginnings of Lenox Hill, she told me that she had rescued a stash of them in 2010, when Lenox was acquired by the hospital network that is now called Northwell Health. A hospital employee had found a closet of historical materials and, when the company suggested they be tossed, called Shaner. Now she wheeled her rescued collection to me on a library cart.

Lenox Hill was founded in 1857 as the German Dispensary, by the German-Jewish physician Abraham Jacobi. He was a friend of Karl Marx and the husband of Mary Putnam Jacobi, the socialist doctor who had published "The Question of Rest for Women During Menstruation," the medical article that marshaled menstrual data to argue for women's equality. In the 1800s and early 1900s, the dispensary provided free medical care to poor and working-class German immigrants under a model of community charity. One report, from 1903, said that its patients that year included 111 bakers, 52 carpenters, 48 butchers, 29 brewers, 16 farmers, and 2 journalists.

At the time, the hospital was located in lower Manhattan, in a district called Shantytown, just north of a swamp that Jacobi described as a "sea of dirty water." In the coming decades, the hospital's community of patients moved uptown, and eventually the hospital building did, too. Park Avenue grew stylish. Tenements flipped into luxury apartments. Skyscrapers rose above the railyards. Middle-class patients started coming to the hospital, then wealthy ones. Wards were replaced by rows of private and semiprivate rooms.

As I sat at a broad desk in the hushed library, an oil painting of Jacobi hanging just out of view, Shaner delivered me a 1955 pamphlet produced by the hospital called "AND NOW, PLEASE RELAX!" Like the phone recording touting *Lenox Hill* on Netflix, it advertised the hospital to people who were already there, overwriting their experience with sleek midcentury illustrations. "Why are you in this hospital? It does not have to mean that you are very ill—and if you are a maternity case you have an extremely healthy ailment," it said. "It's simply because only a hospital has the equipment and the specialists your family doctor feels are necessary for someone in your condition." The pamphlet emphasized the complexity of the machines, their heft and size. It described the hospital's gift shop and television sets and compared its food to that of a resort hotel. "We do not know whether *hospital* is derived from *hospitality* or *hospitality* from *hospital*. This much is certain, Lenox Hill Hospital means hospitality," it said.

As she guided me through her Lenox Hill materials, Shaner suggested that I read *Cesarean Section: An American History of Risk, Technology, and Consequence* by Jacqueline Wolf, the medical historian. The 2018 book investigates the procedure's dramatic rise to become the most frequently performed major surgery in the United States. Wolf describes the C-section rate rising as it became safer, but also as the American medical system fused with consumer imperatives. Insurance companies billed C-sections at higher rates than vaginal births, which raised the question of whether providers were incentivized to call for more surgeries and rack up greater returns. A 2024 study of births in New Jersey hospitals found that doctors were most likely to recommend healthy Black women for C-sections when hospital operating rooms sat empty, suggesting that some medical decisions were in fact opportunistic. And another financial incentive could be at play: bereaved family members, mourning the loss of a mother or child, had sometimes accused providers of withholding necessary surgeries—failing to call for a C-section, or calling for one too late.

C-sections were once performed only in the direst of circumstances, and then in true emergencies, but increasingly they were performed to eliminate risk, or the perception of risk. Wolf writes of the surgery's frequency rising alongside the popularization of the electronic fetal monitor—the device that I had strapped to me in the hospital, leading to monitors and the polygraph-style readout. These electronic readings, Wolf writes, were no better at diagnosing fetal distress than a stethoscope intermittently applied to the belly. But they produced more incidents of potential fetal distress, indeterminate readings that could point in multiple directions. The increase in C-sections helped to mitigate the risk that these readings were emergencies, but it also mitigated the risk of future lawsuits.

The strategy for suing OBs was architected by the future Democratic senator and presidential candidate John Edwards, who, as a trial lawyer representing parents in the 1980s and '90s, argued that stillbirths and birth injuries could be prevented if doctors called for C-sections at the right time. In court, he ventriloquized the voice of the unborn child and presented evidence of fetal heart tracings that purported to show its distress. One midwife complained to Wolf that obstetric residents had stopped attending to patients and started to attend to the data instead. "They sit outside at the desk and watch the monitors," she said. The woman's experience was subordinated to the fetus's data outputs—the virtual depiction of its life on a screen.

Doctors and nurses watched patients through their screens, and now patients were invited to watch them back. By 2020, when I gave birth at Lenox Hill, Northwell Health had spun off a for-profit arm, Northwell Holdings, which leveraged the company's "enterprise data assets" and licensed its intellectual property with an eye on "private equity and venture class returns." *Lenox Hill* was the first docuseries featuring the network's facilities and staff, but it would not be the last. In 2024, Northwell launched Northwell Studios, its own production house that would help develop documentary and scripted stories to *break down the walls of our hospitals, amplify the voices of our frontline heroes, and shed light on critical health and societal issues,* a press release said. When healthcare transformed into a commodity, patients became consumers. Now healthcare was content, and even patients who had baffling or disorienting medical experiences could turn on the television and stream a more compelling story.

When I navigated to the App Store to download pregnancy apps to compare against Flo—Clue, Glow, Expectful—I also found Irth, an app developed by the journalist and entrepreneur Kimberly Seals Allers. Irth presented as a kind of Yelp for birth, a place where women of color were invited to rate their hospital experiences on a range of metrics, like: *Lack of eye contact. Dismissiveness of pain levels. Rude comments. Forced to accept unwanted treatment. Treatment withheld.* It struck me how explicit Irth was about operating in a marketplace, how clear-eyed it was in challenging the healthcare system in its commodified form.

In 2024, I called Allers and asked about the origins of the app. She had her first child in 2000, in New York City, when she was pursuing a joint graduate degree in journalism and business at Columbia University. During her pregnancy, she joined a message board for Manhattan moms, where parents shared resources and discussed their experiences at different hospitals. She decided to deliver at one where women had described their births in glowing terms. "I learned this later, of course, but a lot of those parenting spaces were dominated by white women," she said. When Allers arrived at the hospital in labor, her experience was "confusing and disrespectful and traumatizing." She felt that she had to fight to receive the minimum standard of care. She was not supported during labor, and when her cervix did not immediately dilate, her doctor rushed her into a C-section she is not convinced was necessary. "I had no medical emergency except I was taking too long," she said. "Birth simply takes time. And hospitals are built for turning beds over. Because time is money."

Entering a hospital in labor, she expected that her "education and accomplishments would be protective," she said. "But the data consistently shows that for Black women, that is not the case." Once Allers changed into her anonymizing hospital gown, she felt that the system reduced her to a demographic idea, an unmarried Black woman using student insurance. Discussing the months following the birth, she said, "My first reaction was to blame myself." But as she spoke with other Black mothers, she found that their experiences mirrored her own. A few years later, she had a second child, and when he was a preteen, he learned how to code. Together they developed Irth. "I gave birth to my coder," Allers said.

As a nonprofit, Irth functions as a challenge to both the hospital system and the commercial pregnancy app. The typical app, the one that features the headless white pregnant woman, guides users through what it assumes to be a normal pregnancy experience, administering glib outbursts along the way: *however your baby arrives, kudos to you, legend*. Irth leverages its user data not to discipline its users' bodies but to hold systems accountable. "Hospitals hate us," Allers said. "They hate us and I love it."

. . .

Patient desired a cesarean section, my hospital report said. That line first struck me as a euphemism generated by the medical record, but now I understand that it was true. In 2023, I called my doula, Megan Davidson, and asked her what she thought would have happened if I had tried for one of those undisturbed physiological home births. When we spoke, Davidson had just attended her eight hundredth birth. She played many roles in my pregnancy, but one of her most crucial responsibilities was as a close observer of my labor, one who held the churning medical staff accountable to the shifting signals of my body. She made sure that the system registered me as a person. In answer to my question, she told me, "I still don't think your baby would've come out. I think you probably would have labored for a long time, you probably would have fully dilated, and you probably would not have felt a huge urge to push." Then would have come the infection, the fever, the spike in the baby's heart rate, the rush to the hospital. "Ideally, you would have done that early enough that it was not catastrophic for you or the baby," she said.

As nurses wheeled me from the delivery room to the operating theater, I cried. The surgery was not an emergency and it was not a preference. When the paralyzing anesthesia entered my bloodstream, I vomited into a kidney-shaped dish. Doctors converged on my stiff body and rolled it onto an operating table. Marc appeared in a funny paper outfit and held my hand.

A blue curtain fell between my mind and my body, and it felt appropriate. Like after years of practice I had finally achieved total disassociation. I shivered on the table and stared into a white light. There was time for a nurse to ask if I wanted to play any music during the birth, and for me to request the Taylor Swift album *Folklore*. When the nurse instead selected a chaotic Spotify mix that began with the duet that Swift had recorded with the former One Direction member Zayn Malik for the soundtrack to *Fifty Shades Darker,* the 2017 sequel to *Fifty Shades of Grey,* there was time for me to ask her to please turn it off.

It was a pain-free supernatural childbirth for as long as the morphine was dripping into my veins. I felt the pressure of hands rooting and yanking inside me. An alien suction. Then my own hollow center, emptied of its wriggling form. Marc shot from his seat, sat back down, and said, "I think I saw something I'm not supposed to see." He vanished and reemerged on the border of my vision, staring into a bundle. "He's so cute," he said. "He's so cute!" Marc lowered the baby for me to kiss, but my mouth could not quite meet his cheek. Then he disappeared and I stayed stuck to the table. A nurse, preparing for his transfer to the NICU, paged back through my medical records. She turned to me—the paralyzed, split-open, twenty-second-old mother—and said: "When did you stop taking the Ativan in pregnancy?"

"Alma"

According to FactsBuddy.com, we named the baby Alma, so that is what I'll call him here. I repeat Facts Buddy's error for two reasons. One, because I don't want to publish my son's real name. Two, because the baby character who appears on these pages is not exactly my son. I have tried and failed to pin him down with my words. I have observed him more closely than I have any other person and still he twists and jumps from my grasp. The "Alma" of this book is a representation of a child—mediated by technology, distorted by the internet, and filtered through my own limited perspective. I will call his little brother Brayden because I would not give that name to a real baby.

Chapter 7

Work

An hour after the birth, Marc sent me a video shot through the window of an incubator. I was deadened with anesthesia in a recovery room, and Alma was beginning his life as a patient, too. Skinny tubes snaked from his body to a beeping monitor. He wiggled in his blanket, peeped at his surroundings, and stuck out his tongue. When unrolled to its full length, it reached past his little chin. I wondered whose was bigger, his or mine. I absorbed his beauty, searched his eyes for clues to his personality. An hour before, he had lived inside me, and now he was wearing a newborn beanie.

Once the anesthesia drained from my body, my injuries screamed for my attention. My stomach, my crotch, my shoulder, my back. Nurses offered me Tylenol and Motrin, stuff I could score at the drugstore. On a whiteboard hung in my hospital room, in a box labeled "MOST IMPORTANT THING," a nurse had written three things:

Breastfeed every 2–3 hours

Pain management

Fluids & rest

When I had arrived at the hospital in labor, I told the nurses that I planned to breastfeed. But now Alma and I were trapped on opposite ends of the hospital floor, a city block apart. A nurse wheeled a pallid yellow device in on a trolley and parked it next to my bed. A network of tubes sprung from its humming core. For the first week of Alma's life, I would not feed him. I would feed this thing instead. The nurse tore two holes into a belly band and showed me how to pull it over my head and thread my nipples through it. I hitched each teat to the milking machine and sat rigidly in bed as it yanked at my breasts for thirty minutes. Nothing came out. Three hours later, I did it again.

When the board said *every 2–3 hours*, it meant *every 2–3 hours*, not *every 2–3 business hours* or *every 2–3 waking hours*. Each interval was counted from the beginning of the session, not the end, so by the time I had pumped, drawn any moisture into a syringe, and washed the pump bottles and parts, my next pumping session was already barreling toward me.

Everything in the hospital seemed to occur on a three-hour schedule, but these events were not synced, so a scheduled horror confronted me approximately every fifteen minutes. My door was always swinging open, throttling me from sleep. Every three hours, a nurse entered the room—"Hey, mama"—offering me pain medication. Every three hours, an alarm purred on my phone, prompting me to pump. Every three hours, the nurses in the NICU fed Alma, and so every three hours I attempted to intercept them so that I could try to latch him to my breast instead. Every three hours I called a nurse, waited for her arrival, hobbled into a wheelchair, rolled across the floor to the NICU, and arrived to find Alma already fed, a few minutes earlier than scheduled. "Sorry, mama," they said as sweet formula leaked from the side of his mouth. When I did manage to lift his mouth to my nipple, he stuck out his pink tongue, covering his lower lip and preventing a seal. I could not do MOST IMPORTANT THING. Also, my flailing attempt to do MOST IMPORTANT THING prevented me from doing anything else.

Marc spent much of his time with Alma in the NICU—until I showed up, when the one-parent Covid-safety rule forced him out. We both downloaded an app called Baby Connect and linked our accounts, simulating a shared parenting experience through its data-logging system. Marc recorded the baby's formula feeds, and I marked my pumping sessions. For the first four days my log looked like this:

0 ml expressed. 0 ml expressed.

"You should be producing milk by now, mama," a nurse in the NICU said, rolling past me and Alma on a desk chair. "If you had a natural birth."

"I didn't," I said.

"I'm just trying to help you," she said.

0 ml expressed. 0 ml expressed. 0 ml expressed. 0 ml expressed. 0 ml expressed. 0 ml expressed. 0 ml expressed. 0 ml expressed.

Then, at 2:38 a.m. on the fifth day: *1 ml expressed.*

I was familiar with the concept of tracking feeds. My time using the Lose It! app had coached me in recording my calories, then modifying my diet and activity in an attempt to pull my body weight downward. Baby Connect's logging prompts flipped a switch in my brain. Now I would juice my pumping stats, focus myself on lifting those numbers up. *2 ml expressed. 3.6 ml expressed. 4 ml expressed.*

5 ml expressed. 10 ml expressed. The milk I made disappeared easily, into a belly or down a drain. But a lasting record of my productivity was forever inscribed in the Baby Connect app.

When Alma was cleared to go home, I spent weeks trying to get him to fasten himself onto my actual boob, and then, eventually, to a silicone super-nipple that I applied atop my own. In desperation, I turned to a lactation consultant, who appeared with pixelated edges atop a fantasy Zoom background, like she was beaming to us from the Holodeck. She helped me to reposition Alma and led me in stretches to ease my back, but she was cruelly optimistic about his ability to nurse, and she made me feel as if failure were not an option. She advised me to log more stats: I was supposed to plop my baby in a bowl on a medical scale before and after every attempted feed, to track precisely what he had swallowed.

At the same time, she counseled me to access the wisdom of my ancestors, who did not have breast pumps or scales or formula to feed their young. "Babies with large tongues existed back then, too," she said knowingly, "and they survived." But I had read the ancestral medical reports of the babies who could only nurse if the *nipple was large and elongated,* babies who had to be fed by *introducing liquid aliment very far into the mouth to be enabled to drink it.* And I knew that some of them did not, in fact, survive. I stopped consulting the consultant and started pumping exclusively. Every three hours, I sat at a miniature version of the hospital's yellow breast pump and filled Alma's bottles.

Before Alma was born, I couldn't imagine spending so much time interrogating and negotiating the way a baby ate. I had assumed families did whatever was most convenient for them. Now I awoke to a strong preference for feeding my child in a highly inconvenient manner. I would say that I wanted Alma to have my breast milk because he was born amid a pandemic with a cancer-predisposition syndrome, because breast milk was said to pass on Covid antibodies, because it could reduce my own risk of cancer—and that was all true. But my appeals to science also hid an irrational drive. I wanted to breastfeed because I believed it would redeem my body from all the ways I worried it had failed my child. Like I could drown my weakness in a five-ounce bag of expressed breast milk.

On my Instagram feed, I saw women blissed out on endorphins with their young hooked greedily to their chests. My breast pump and my tracking app unlocked access to an alternate parenting style, one couched in data and expertise. The figures I logged in Baby Connect told me when my supply was dipping, and a website called ExclusivePumping.com taught me how to up my game. I ate special cookies and drank gross teas. I pumped until my nipples cracked and my milk flowed pink with wisps of blood. First I was happy to fill Alma's next bottle, but soon I desired bigger yields. *250 ml expressed. 280 ml expressed. 290 ml expressed.* Sometimes I awoke and strapped into the pump for a morning "power hour," pumping four times in quick succession to simulate a baby cluster-feeding. I banked a stash of breast milk bags in the freezer, thick bands of yellow fat congealing at the top.

Pumping provided the satisfaction of productive activity. The pump made food for my baby, but it also kept me away from him, literally at arm's length. As the machine pulled at my chest, I couldn't do much else. Marc often fed Alma with the bottle while I pumped. In time, he would start to seek comfort not at my breast but at Marc's shoulder. And so my mothering technology was also a sneaky exit from the expectations of mothering. I spent many hours a day pumping Alma's milk—which meant that I spent hours reading, listening to podcasts, and writing on my computer. Birth had reduced me to a primordial ooze, but in those hours I staggered out of the goo, reconstituting myself. Eventually I became so myself again that I wondered what this meant—that I could only feel like a person now when I was being milked.

When I opened Flo again, I logged the birth. I flicked its psychic fetus into the trash can of my phone. Boink. *We are happy to hear about the arrival of this new blessing in your life*, Flo said, dropping confetti from the top of the screen. A pink butterfly flew from a bassinet. Flo quizzed me about the circumstances of the birth. Then she said: *Are you planning to lose the weight you have gained during pregnancy?* And: *When are you getting back to work?*

What was I really doing when I produced milk for my baby? The pediatrician and psychoanalyst Donald Winnicott described breast-feeding as an "experience" I shared with my child, a form of communication by which I established the foundations of his "strength of character and richness of personality." La Leche League said that I was practicing "the womanly art of breastfeeding." Simone de Beauvoir said that I was engaged in "exhausting servitude." Of course, I wasn't breastfeeding, I was pumping breast milk, and this clarified the transactional nature of my operation. The patent for my Medela pump described its technology as *the extraction of body fluid by suction*—roughly the same process that yanked the milk from the udders of industrial dairy cows. On its website, Medela referred to pumping as a *journey* and called my breast milk *liquid gold*, as if I were a prospector mining a natural resource from my own chest. My body and my baby were translated into economic forces; my milk became a *supply* that I could increase to meet his *demand*.

And who was I working for? The lactation consultant had called Alma "the boss," like she was training me up to work in his service. In her 1940 essay "What Socialism Will Mean to the Women Who Toil at Home," the Marxist feminist Antoinette Konikow advised a housewife that when she performed unpaid work for her kids, she was actually laboring for the benefit of her husband's employer. "The wife thinks she slaves day and night for her husband and children—in reality she works for the same boss who exploits the husband," she writes. Inside the nuclear family, a husband became a kind of middle manager, passing some of his wages to his wife. I was not working for my husband's employer, however—I was working for my own. For the first few months of Alma's life, my salary was paid by New York State's paid family leave program and by the mass media company that employed me. When my parental leave was over, Marc and I paid parts of our salaries to a childcare center in our neighborhood, where Alma spent the workday. After his little brother, Brayden, was born, two years later, the center provided his care, too.

My employer supplemented my parental leave because this was a benefit demanded and negotiated by my union. But also because it helped to ensure that I would not disappear from the workforce into the home forever, that I would eventually return to the office and resume producing media—even if I was still producing milk.

Once I went back to work, I pumped breast milk under the same conditions that many working women do when they are physically separated from their babies. "This is the 'fix' of choice in a country with a high rate of female labour-force participation, no mandated paid maternity or parental leave, and a love-affair with technology," the feminist theorist Nancy Fraser writes of pumping's rise in the US. "No longer a matter of suckling a child at one's breast, one 'breastfeeds' now by expressing one's milk mechanically and sorting it for feeding by bottle later by one's nanny." The most desirable breast pumps for this purpose, she writes, are hands-free ones that "permit one to express milk from both breasts at once while driving to work on the freeway." Or while sitting at a desk, a mere block away from the center where Alma drank my breast milk from a chilled bottle. I had become the baby manager, supplying the materials and pay for other women to feed my child. As a consumer in the childcare economy, I flexed the height of my privilege. Federal law guaranteed no paid leave, the childcare was bruisingly expensive even as childcare workers' wages were unacceptably low, and the broad inaccessibility of care revealed a total system failure. But *even with* these benefits, and even as Marc and I split our childcare responsibilities down the middle, the work of cooking, feeding, bathing, clothing, and cleaning for a family in addition to full-time work overwhelmed us, especially after Brayden was born. Our equitable arrangement failed to alleviate the stresses of the second shift. I was not totally naïve about the institution of heterosexual marriage; I knew where such arrangements could lead. And yet I was annoyed to find myself there, bone-tired in our private apartment, reenacting the claustrophobic dramas of family life.

It wasn't the work itself that I found difficult to manage. I didn't mind getting on my knees and wiping scraps and saliva off the floor. It was the isolation of the work that made it so inefficient, depressing, and dull. It would be almost as easy to fill a dozen water bottles, to spread a dozen peanut butter sandwiches, to mop the floor after a dozen toddlers, as it was to do this for just the two of them. Especially if the dozen other parents were folding clothes and filling baths as we worked the kitchen. Then our kids could play together and we could, like, talk. Whenever our friends piled their kids onto the subway and brought them by for an afternoon, I wished they did not have to leave. They closed the door behind them and left me to fold laundry while Marc washed dishes, our life shaved down to its bare family unit once again.

When I opened my phone, however, I found my isolation transformed. My social feeds were stacked with videos that eroticized the secluded mother. Robed in a prairie dress, she stood in a kitchen as white as a near-death experience, whispering ASMR incantations into my ears.

My pregnant fascination with freebirthers bloomed into a postpartum online ecosystem of homemakers, homesteaders, free-schoolers, and intuitive mothers. They role-played domestic scenarios in which time appeared to stand still. In one video, a faceless toddler requested French toast for breakfast and his pregnant mother delivered it seemingly seconds later in an unsoiled lace slip. I watched her mix, knead, bake, slice, and fry her own bread, then mash her own fruit topping and hand-whip her own cream. The video compressed her work into a mirage of a child's desire instantly met. In another scene, another woman wore a cloud-white nightgown as she made her kid cinnamon-toast cereal from scratch, her neck permanently outstretched, her smile an unnerving mask. The video was expertly spliced to make it seem as if ingredients simply floated into her grasp, while her bare feet stayed stuck, mannequin-like, to the same spot on the kitchen floor.

Though these women presented as a category of influencer known as "tradwives," they were performers and video producers, crafting images that flirted with fetish content. In their homemaker fantasies, the kitchen expanded to fill the whole frame, to constitute a woman's entire life. Characters beyond the central mother rarely appeared in the shot, save for a husband swooping in for a forehead kiss or a bundled baby briefly pressed to her artfully obscured boob. Any hired domestic workers were scrubbed from the scene. The peeps of hungry children were smothered under the mother's narcotic voiceover, in which she breathily narrated a routine that rarely strayed beyond *morning vitamins* and *wild-berry compote*.

Trending alongside the homemaker was her outdoorsy cousin, the homesteader, who escaped the kitchen and ran as far as the chicken coop before being incapacitated by her own domestic bliss. If the homemaker spun a fantasy of unlimited time, the homesteader promoted a vision of endless space. She took a wrecking ball to my dark apartment, filming her children frolicking in grass as she hand-fed a cow or foraged for medicinal herbs. Still, no figures from outside her heterosexual nuclear family appeared. Presumably she had neighbors, surely she had some help, but the content elbowed them out of the frame to zoom in on her virtuosic solo performance.

This vision of "tradlife" was, as Zoe Hu put it in *Dissent,* an "agoraphobic fantasy," though one filtered through a modern lens. "The twist that makes tradlife a phenomenon of our times is that it also includes earnest criticisms of life under capitalism," she writes. "Only tradition can salvage love from modern indignities and the early-morning commute." In *Dazed,* Niloufar Haidari described how the tradwife fantasy poked at the "scam" of working life, where women were dispatched to work in drab offices only to return home to a "second shift of domestic labour." The tradwife could at least seem to be performing her first and second shifts simultaneously, as she mined her very housework for profits. I started following one trad account, @nataliealaska_rewild, on Instagram after listening to her Free Birth Society podcast episode, where she discussed birthing unassisted while traveling Australia in her van. Now she was wearing a floral kerchief and promoting her practice of *intuitive motherhood* with her *three wild boys.* Over a video where she twirled in a gingham dress and bent down to present a live chicken to her sons, she wrote: *I wasn't created from a billion years of stardust to "reply to emails."*

Of course, stardust did not generate an income, especially one large enough to sustain a vast homestead or fund a kitchen renovation with a $15,000 oven. Even as tradlife content spun a gauzy critique of laboring under capitalism, it delighted in uncomplicated celebrations of wealth. Angela Davis, writing of the emergence of the housewife ideal in the 1800s, wrote that while she presented as the sacred guardian of "a devalued domestic life," she "was really a symbol of the economic prosperity enjoyed by the emerging middle classes," a vision of domestic excess built on exploiting other women's labor. The housewife could afford to stay home because her husband had so much money, and she and her home looked fresh and appealing because servants or enslaved women often performed her more menial domestic work. Davis writes that even as more and more American women worked outside the home, the ideology of the era "established the housewife and the mother as universal models of womanhood." The value system that exalted her diminished the worth of women who worked outside the home—which also meant that when the housewife hired them to perform work in her own house, their wages were artificially suppressed.

The homemakers of Instagram and TikTok represented the mother who telegraphed so much surplus wealth that her image became remunerative in and of itself. She slipped ads for acupressure mats and organic bars into her videos or else instructed her followers to buy her farm's beef fat and slather it on their faces as a sunscreen alternative. As I followed more and more homesteaders, women who projected a kind of immersive farm experience, I was first amazed that there were so many homesteaders on Instagram, and then I wondered if there were any homesteaders who were *not* on Instagram. It seemed like a lifestyle that could persist only through the promotion of the idea that some people lived that way.

One day, I noticed that @nataliealaska_rewild and a cluster of her fellow mom accounts were sprinkling in mentions of an exciting new business opportunity. I too could raise my boys slowly and reverently by creating my *own stream of online income* based on the sales of a *high ticket product*. I would only need to take twenty minutes to watch a video on the curative properties of the Kangen Water Ionizer, a product produced by a Japanese *innovator in alkaline water ionization technologies* called Enagic. I could become an Enagic distributor, advance through all six ranks of its eight-point compensation structure, rise from 6A to 1A, all after an initial investment of course, an investment that began with my purchase of my very own Kangen device—only $4,980 for the K8 machine, plus annual upkeep, but that's not counting all the money I would save by replacing all of my facial cleansers, laundry detergents, and bug sprays with my new supply of innovative water.

The tradwife worked to obscure that she worked. Seeming to live a life of leisure so desirable that she could recruit other women to the cause—that was, in fact, her job. *I am currently receiving multiple applications per day from driven mamas and individuals who are READY and eager to take action on creating the freedom that they desire and the life of their dreams,* Natalie wrote. At the bottom of everything, all the foraged tinctures and sourdough starters, online motherhood was a multilevel marketing opportunity.

One night Marc texted me the link to an article published on Slate.com. I could feel his smile spreading across the room as the page loaded onto my phone. The title was "The New Opt-Out Revolution: Not Having Kids." I had no memory of the story, though I had written it myself seven years earlier. It was framed as a response to a *New York Times* article on high-earning corporate women who had decided to "opt out" of the workforce to stay at home to care for their children. I opened the piece by sneering at the moms, whom I described as "women who quit work in order to fashion wreaths."

Then I veered drastically into personal testimony. I had, I said, joined an "opt-out revolution" of my own: I was opting out of having kids. (Oh, God.) I was "choosing to forgo diaper-changing in order to pursue a risky, impractical, and modestly-paying career that I love," I continued. (Oh, no.) Also, "In order to enjoy some luxuries, I've opted not to share my life and paycheck with a family." I couldn't finish reading it. Just looking at the website's signature typeface made me sick.

When I wrote those words, I was a freelancer paid by the article to pass judgment on cultural trends involving women. This "opt-out revolution" article was one of hundreds I had written at the behest of various online news outlets, in the service of various social algorithms, often with the assistance of several cigarettes. My job required me to produce opinions more frequently than they naturally formed in the human brain. When Mitt Romney said "binders full of women," I posted. When Miley Cyrus rubbed her butt against Robin Thicke at the Video Music Awards, I posted. When *The New York Times* ran a think piece about women, certainly, I posted. Every morning I generated a new skin, sloughed off my previous form, and slithered away. But the internet ensured that all my passing impressions were preserved, waiting to be rediscovered by my future spouse. I met Marc a few months after the article was published.

I wasn't sure which part of the story was more ridiculous: that I had chosen to be alone (I had not), that I loved my career (I did not), or that I was basking in luxury as a result (was I talking about . . . the cigarettes?). Then there was my reference to fashioning wreaths, as if this were a central childcare responsibility. When I searched back through the *New York Times* article, it didn't even say anything about wreaths. Obviously, I had not been breezily dismissive about having kids. I had been in denial and posting through it on the internet. My job so consumed my identity and my time that I couldn't imagine taking care of another person. Instead, I rhapsodized about buying stuff.

Years before I had Alma, before I got inducted into the motherhood internet, I had already absorbed the idea that caring for them was little more than a craft project, an opportunity for a dull woman to express herself. I had picked a side in the mommy wars, and I wasn't even a mom. Now I understood how difficult it was to take care of children all of the time, or even some of the time, like I did. When I dropped Alma off at daycare, the damage and hypocrisy of my little article revealed itself. The only reason that I could pay other women to care for him while I worked was because my work was valued more than theirs. My salary was higher than the cost of the care, even as it was obvious to me that the true value of the caregiver's work exceeded my own. If I had to choose which was more important, publishing an article or feeding children, I would choose the children every time. Especially if the article was of the quality of "The New Opt-Out Revolution: Not Having Kids."

In her essay on housework, Konikow sketched out a program where the work of parents—mothers, in her letter—would be integrated with the means of production, with nurseries installed on factory floors and cooperative lunchrooms organized to relieve the mother of her "kitchen drudgery" and draw families into shared meals. bell hooks envisioned collectivized childcare that recruited people of all genders and parental statuses to raise the community's kids, and Davis imagined "radically transforming the nature of housework," where it "need no longer be considered necessarily and unalterably private in character," and where instead teams of well-paid and well-trained workers efficiently managed each other's homes.

These were my real domestic fantasies, visions that exploded the boundaries of the lonely Instagram square. In my early years of parenthood, flashes of them appeared instead in WhatsApp threads and Slack channels, where neighbors organized mutual aid with residents of a nearby migrant shelter and claimed shifts stocking the community fridge that hummed outside a corner bodega. As I prepared breakfast for Alma and Brayden, I dreamed of making fifty breakfasts. I never wanted to watch a lady spend five hours making cereal for her toddler ever again.

The tradwives taught me that there was a form of work I disliked more than isolated mothering: the virtual staging of isolated mothering for social media. Replicating oneself in front of an online audience was now a job requirement for a range of professions, one that I struggled to perform. I had always lacked proficiency in playing myself. Many times, I had paged through slideshows that promised to reveal top influencer secrets about how to pose for flattering selfies. I knew that you were supposed to sink into a wide squat and lean an elbow onto a knee, like you were casually shitting on the ground. But whenever a camera appeared, my mind emptied of this special knowledge. My muscles fired at random.

Now, motherhood threatened to render me totally invisible. The ad networks that pitched my pregnancy as a sexy romp pivoted to postpartum body horror. A bra brand said: *When you're done, your boobs die, they turn into flat little pancakes.* The vitamin company that offered me prenatals early in pregnancy circled back around, recommending a pill for crow's-feet wrinkles. My friend Reyhan, who was in her forties with two small children, shared an ad for drop-shipped stretchy pants that confronted her on Instagram. *Every woman in her 60s loves these pants,* it said. *Your granddaughters will be calling you the cool grandma when you wear these.* When we gave birth we reached consumer capitalism's peak feminine form, and now the brands were patting us on the hand, leading us reverently to the grave.

And yet there was something seductive about the prospect of becoming irrelevant. One day I was listening to the podcast *Las Culturistas*, when the cohost Bowen Yang said, not in a mean way, "Moms are the terminus for anything cultural." The context fell away but I carried the line with me. It was uncomfortable at first, but then it was interesting. I could exit at the terminus of culture and leave all claims to relevance behind. I would never have to learn who Tate McRae was. After a lifetime of posting, I could stop trying so hard to build an identity online. "I found motherhood to be an experience of self-abnegation," my friend Sasha told me soon after Alma's birth, and that prompted her to consider who she actually was. Who was the person that motherhood had swept away? I wasn't sure how to answer that myself, but I felt a tinge of relief about her sudden departure.

My old blogger self would have found this pathetic, but I liked the person I saw reflected in my son's eyes, his competent and joyful caretaker. I felt relieved of my cynicism, gifted with new observational powers. The city opened a vein to me. As I ventured out with Alma strapped to my chest, I gazed upon strangers, impressed that every one of them had been created by the same process, more or less. Someone had gestated and birthed and fed and burped and changed and soothed them all. The work that went into every one of them. Now they waved and clapped at Alma, hid their faces behind their fingers and smiled as they pulled them away. Two young men at the coffee shop made me a latte and I thought, *They are my sons.* I watched *My Dinner with Andre* and thought, *Wallace Shawn is my baby.* Impossible, damning, how I never noticed the stunning beauty of Wallace Shawn.

Without quite realizing it, I started strapping Alma in front of me in my online persona, too. Before he arrived, I asked Marc what we should do about Instagram. I wondered if we would be like the couple that never posted photos of their baby, or the couple that obscured their baby's face with an angel emoji, or the couple that sealed its baby in a special locked profile only friends and family could see. Marc wasn't sure how he felt about it, either. But once he arrived, we didn't discuss it. It was clear what had to be done. I held out for eleven days, then posted a picture to Instagram of the baby swaddled and sleeping, a human chrysalis. It felt absurd, the idea of not posting baby. All I wanted to post was baby.

The Instagram posts represented a slim fraction of the thousands of photographs I took of Alma. Google automatically recognized his features, accumulating his portraits in a special album. It seemed urgent to view him through the field of my phone. I tapped and tapped, discovering every angle of his little face—the strawberry birthmark between his eyes, the pad of fat beneath his chin, the slim thigh poking out of his bouncer, the blond hair that grew in like a funny buzz cut.

I did not take the photos to look back on later—I created more than I could ever possibly review. The act of photographing him was a compulsive expression of my wonder at his existence. It's him: *tap*. He is here: *tap*. He remains: *tap*. But he was never quite as charming and vibrant through the lens as he was through my own eyes. And when I broadcast his image to an audience of a few hundred people, none of them admired him quite as much as I did. I posted his pictures to my Instagram story and then played them back over and over again, observing him in this public space he did not know he occupied. As he rolled about on his mat, I stalked him with my phone's sensor, turned him into an electrical signal and exchanged him for the currency of the web.

Once my Instagram grid had been stacked with selfies, pictures of bodega cats, and screenshots of articles I had written. Now it felt like I was Alma's social media manager, maintaining his page. I hid gratefully behind his celebrity image. I felt like the picture of Dorian Gray—he the youthful beauty scampering across Instagram, me the portrait decaying in the attic. On December 31, I posted a picture of him smiling on the play mat in a kitten-pocket onesie, with the caption *new year, new me.*

When Marc and I enrolled Alma in daycare, the center prompted us to download an app through which we could communicate with his caretakers and receive updates on him during the day. I opened it to find a stream of photographs of Alma. I scrolled down and reviewed his private life. I watched him nap in a crib, socialize with a friend, upend a bottle of my breast milk into his own mouth. It was tender but also a little odd, how Alma appeared to be toddling about the center independently. His caretakers were always obscured behind the camera, as if the photos were deliberately staged so I could imagine that I was watching (and photographing) him all day by myself. This was, I realized, part of the service I was now paying for. The work of childcare professionals had expanded to meet a new demand. As they cared for my child, they reproduced him for my parental gaze.

Chapter 8

Gear

"The tongue is prominent," a doctor said when she saw the video Marc shot of Alma after he was born. But she also said: "I've seen bigger." Alma had a big tongue, but it wasn't clear what challenges this posed. Already he was defying categorization. He could swallow and breathe. Oxygen circulated normally through his blood. But a specialist insisted he undergo a nightlong observation to see if the tongue blocked his airway while he slept. At the end of his NICU stay, a couple of burly baby-EMTs strapped Alma into a special stretcher and drove him in an ambulance to a children's hospital with the tiny equipment necessary to run the test on a newborn. Marc and I followed behind in the car, me milking myself in the passenger seat, the pump plugged into the cigarette lighter.

At the new hospital, Marc left to find me some Advil, and I found Alma napping in a clear bassinet. I pumped again in the room, my back complaining from the blows of the pregnancy, the surgery, the pump that required my body's compliance. I rubbed my neck with one hand and steadied a television remote in the other, wheeling through the children's entertainment available in the flat-screen looming above us. Then I saw it. I pressed eagerly on the icon for the 2017 animated film *The Boss Baby*.

For three years, I had wondered intermittently what the movie was about, my curiosity never rising to the level of investigation. What was the nature of this "boss baby," the smug, sunglasses-wearing tot voiced by Alec Baldwin? Finally I would know. The opening credits revealed a heavenly skyscape fitted with a vast Rube Goldberg–like contraption. A line of CGI babies bopped down the fluffy white conveyor belt that primed them for birth. Robotic limbs and knobs assigned the babies sexes, tickled their tummies, and stuffed their mouths with binkies. Then the babies slid down a chute toward delivery—all except for one, who stared unfeelingly when a tickle feather tried to make him laugh. This baby was selected, instead, for a management role at Baby Corp., the very company that had manufactured him.

As the boss baby sharpened his crayon inside his Baby Corp. cubicle, Alma's monitors bleated in alarm, and I tore the pump from my chest and ran topless into a crowd of nurses. One walked airily into the room and assured me there was nothing to worry about. The pulse oximeter had just shifted out of place when Alma kicked in his sleep.

Two days later, tests complete, Marc brought Alma home with a diagnosis of obstructive sleep apnea—meaning that Alma's tongue fell back in his throat as he slept, sometimes blocking his airway. A technician trudged up the stairs to our apartment and dropped off a metal box the size of a rolling suitcase: the Philips Respironics EverFlo oxygen concentrator. The machine had an analog glass gauge, a panel of indicator lights, and a long translucent tube that split into a circle and pumped oxygen into the prongs of an itsy-bitsy cannula. We were instructed to insert this into Alma's nostrils as he slept, ensuring a steady stream of oxygen made its way to his lungs. We wheeled the device into our bedroom and parked it next to his bassinet.

A few hours earlier, Alma's vital signs had been monitored continuously by a team of pediatric nurses. Now it was just us and the machine. Its hulking body challenged us from the corner of the room. We had just had a baby, and now we were expected to competently deploy a medical device to stop his own tongue from inhibiting his brain and heart functioning. Alma's doctors recommended against using a pulse oximeter to monitor the efficacy of our work. As in the hospital, the probes were easily dislodged. We'd just have to . . . assume it was working. When we flipped its switch, the machine screeched alive. It clanked and wheezed at five-second intervals, a push-button monster breathing from beneath our baby's bed.

Alma did not like having prongs stuck up his nose—he wailed and yanked at the tube whenever we tried to fit it in—so we spent our nights and days workshopping a routine to get him to actually sleep while hooked up to his sleep-protection machine. Every night we dressed and swaddled him, traced the tube up the back of his onesie, read him books, and rocked and sang him to bed. When he finally fell asleep, we lay in wait outside the door, then crept back in to slip the cannula over his head, rest the prongs in his nostrils, and press a square of medical tape firmly to each cheek. As Alma grew stronger and more willful, he fought the cannula harder, and the routine's degree of difficulty leveled up. Many nights, when I peered into his crib to check on him, I'd find the tape unstuck, the prongs dropped from his nose, and the cannula encircling his neck. We put Alma to bed with the machine to keep him safe and woke to find it transformed into a threat.

Every few months, Alma spent the night at a hospital for another sleep test, where he was fitted with streams of wires and wrapped in gauze that made him resemble a synthetic jellyfish. He lay in a prisonlike crib as Marc sat on a slick couch next to him, trying to soothe him through the bars. Then one day, when Alma was seven months old, Marc surprised me by walking into the bedroom and silently packing the cannulas and tapes, unplugging the device, and wheeling it away. Alma's latest sleep test had revealed no more apnea. It was a victory for the three of us: Alma was freed of his uncomfortable tubes, and we were freed of our parental-anxiety machine. But that was not the only new device in Alma's life.

Before Alma arrived, Marc and I had no idea what we were supposed to buy for him, and I had never been so vulnerable to a pitch. I found myself selecting lotions for skin that I had never touched, diapers to clothe a butt of unknown size. When we visited our friends David and Amanda in the suburbs, we picked confusedly at their offerings and came home with a kind of baby slot machine that called itself a "learning farm" and a rubber . . . placemat? With . . . a trough? Around the same time, Marc's friend Martha sent us a full baby-gear primer, including a 114-line spreadsheet she had inherited from another friend with slightly older kids. The brand names resembled incoherent babble: Keekaroo, Woombie, Ubbi. Soon all the plugs in our bedroom were filled. We got a video baby monitor that looked like a big black eyeball, a conical sound machine that rustled and hissed, and something called a *smart sleeper bassinet:* a crib that rocked a baby to sleep on its own.

We bought a Snoo (which is a very expensive robot bassinet) and now I feel so dumb about it, Martha had written to us, but all I digested from her message was *very expensive robot bassinet.* I navigated to its website and found that new models sold for over $1,000. Did *we* need a very expensive robot bassinet? Happiest Baby, the company that manufactured the Snoo, assured me that we did. *Babies who sleep in SNOO clock 1 to 2 more hours of sleep a night than babies who sleep elsewhere*, it said. The claim was a picklock, accessing our deepest anxiety about becoming parents. I needed a lot of sleep, and famously, babies disrupt this. Marc was wired the opposite way—he had trouble falling asleep, and he could never nap—and that was bad, too. Covid's unrelenting spread meant that we could not invite a rotating cast of family and friends into our home to assist us with the baby. Would it be so bad if we surrendered him to a Wi-Fi–enabled bosom instead?

Marc scoured a local parent message board for secondhand Snoos, and a few weeks later, we snagged one off a doctor who had used it with her own child. It had a midcentury-modern design—hairpin legs, curvy walnut base—and I was irritated at how pleasing it was to my eye, how exactly it had been tuned to my blunt millennial taste. I shimmied my pregnant body onto the floor beneath it and worked to decode its impenetrable instructions. Then I inspected the special swaddle that came with it: a white baby straitjacket that clipped into the sides of the device to steady the child as it rocked. I installed it and left it there to await its guest.

This was all before we knew that Alma would be coming home from the hospital with a different, necessary sleep machine. By the time we finally clipped him into the Snoo, the charm of the mechanical helper had dissipated. But I had already cast my lot with the robocrib, and the pulmonologist said it was safe to use. We watched the machine sputter to life, swaying Alma's body back and forth and emanating whooshes and squawks near his head. When we left the room, we monitored Alma's Snoo experience via its paired app, where the Snoo converted his sleep habits into a shifting mood board. The Happiest Baby logo, a smiling cartoon tot with half-moon eyes and a single curl popping from his scalp, hovered in the center of the screen. If Alma slept motionlessly, the app flooded blue and said: *Alma is calm.* If he fussed or cried, the app turned red and said: *Snoo is soothing Alma.* And if it soothed him harder and faster and he cried still, the Snoo powered down and my phone jolted with a notification: *Alma needs your care.*

Quickly the device's lexicon slipped into my conversations with Marc. "He's being a calm guy," I would tell Marc as Alma slept in the Snoo or loafed happily outside it. But Alma was not, as a rule, a calm guy. We were somehow getting even less sleep than we had feared. His condition cranked up the difficulty level of every component of his caretaking. Marc and I agreed that I would take the late-night feeds so he could have a window of protected sleep, and I could nap while he took the lead during the day. I spent my nights wading through the inky sludge of our bedroom, blinking gadgets lighting my way.

Every few hours, Alma awoke crying. I released him from the Snoo and let him suckle ineffectually on my breasts for forty minutes; placed his wriggling body on a digital medical scale, which indicated that he had ingested as little as one half ounce of milk; fed him expressed breast milk from a bottle, which he drank frustratingly slowly; changed his diaper and often his onesie, swaddle, and sheet as pee leaked easily from the holes around his skinny thighs; tried to place a pacifier in his mouth, which he sucked gratefully until his tongue pushed it out of place; rocked him until he fell asleep again; lowered his body into the Snoo and wriggled my hands out from beneath him like I was Indiana Jones swapping a precious artifact on a booby-trapped pedestal; frantically clipped his swaddle into the sides of the machine and pressed its on button, hoping he would not notice that he had been transferred from his mother's arms and into a robot's; replaced the cannula in his nose as in a game of Operation; hovered above the crib when he instantly roused, sticking my upturned pinkie finger into his mouth to take the place of the pacifier that had already tumbled out; repeated,

repeated, repeated; and finally crept away to hook myself to a pump that yanked at my boobs for twenty minutes, producing milk for the next bottle, while I looked at my phone. Soon Alma would awake shrieking, and the cycle would begin again. Sometimes as I rocked him, my smartwatch blinked at me, asking if I wanted to record an elliptical workout.

As we cried and sweated and sucked through the night, the Snoo app produced a horseshoe-shaped graph tracking Alma's sleep patterns. I awoke in the morning with my memory wiped clean and reviewed the graph to piece together what had transpired the night before. The Snoo was our uncompromising governess, delivering her report card on our soothing progress. If Alma slept calmly, the graph showed long stretches of blue, but if he did not, it was sliced through with streaks of red and gray, an angry wound. When Alma awoke screaming, I felt a tender respect for his need. But when I saw the moment reddened on the grid, I seethed at my defeat. Sometimes I screenshotted the page and sent it to Marc, proof of the harrowing experience I had endured. In this theater of sleep deprivation, the Snoo assumed a totemic importance. I projected longings and recriminations onto its vacillating form. The more I doubted its efficacy, the more I invested in its promise, searching for the trick to unlocking the elusive *1 to 2 more hours of sleep* it had promised.

In my late-night reading, I learned that the Snoo had been invented by a California pediatrician named Dr. Harvey Karp, and I ordered his book *The Happiest Baby on the Block*, which sold his personal baby-soothing methodology. Karp urged me to soothe harder. With his permission, I shushed Alma louder and jiggled him more vigorously than I would have on my own. I complied with his instructions even as my doubts deepened with every page. The book opened with an extended acknowledgments section that thanked the actress Michelle Pfeiffer and the Fleetwood Mac rocker Lindsey Buckingham, and it went on to suggest that Karp had discovered a previously uncharted response in babies—an innate "soothing reflex" that could be engaged only by a caregiver who followed his advice exactly. By priming the baby with his "5 S's"—*swaddling* him, *shushing* him, soothing him on his *side or stomach, swinging* him, and giving him something to *suck*—a parent could flip the baby's "off-switch" for fussing and engage his "on-switch" for sleep.

On-switch, off-switch: it was not clear where Alma ended and the device began. The Happiest Baby website referred to its charges as *SNOO-babies*, a kind of corporate cybernetic hybrid. This blurring between baby and crib made it impossible to confidently assess whether the machine was working as advertised. Maybe Alma was not a great sleeper, and the Snoo could not do much about it. Or maybe he would be a great sleeper, if only we released him from the Snoo. Or maybe—and this was the fear that ensured my compliance—he was a truly awful sleeper, and the Snoo was already helping him to sleep more than he otherwise would. Even as the Snoo heralded the insights I could glean through its app, it blocked me from understanding the real baby I held in my hands.

Happiest Baby was ostentatiously confident in its tech. An article on the typical four-month sleep regression in babies said, *SNOO is so effective, it's very rare that a "SNOO-baby" goes through a sleep regression.* But it encouraged parents of uncooperative babies to call its helpline and troubleshoot their kids. Our secondhand Snoo was not covered by a warranty, so I set out for Snoo-inspired internet communities instead, where Snoo owners past and present convened to hack and tweak the device to compel their babies to sleep inside it. They advised me to pre-warm the mattress with a heating pad, lift the bassinet legs with cans of tuna, and rest a one-pound bag of rice on the baby's chest before I zipped him up. I should also probably wrap his arms in a dish towel as I swaddled him, or else release one of his arms entirely, or else release both arms. I should double-swaddle him, preferably in the Ollie swaddle or the Merlin swaddle or the Kyte. I should limit the motion of the Snoo to a feeble wave or dial it up until the baby was practically vibrating. I had watched just a few minutes of *The Boss Baby* while Alma slept, but now its nightmarish vision of assembly-line babies had come true. I didn't weight Alma with dried goods or lift him with tinned fish. The more I tried to control his sleep environment, the more I gained a grudging appreciation for his resistance to it. He was a Snoo objector. He wanted to be held by a person, not a machine, and he refused to go down quietly.

There was another reason I did not abandon the Snoo: it all but promised that our baby would not die in it. *Here's a shocking truth: Each year, around 3,500 healthy American babies go to bed at night . . . never to wake up again,* the Happiest Baby website said. *Unfortunately, some babies die for totally mysterious reasons that nothing can prevent. However, the good news is that SNOO keeps babies safely on the back—all naps and all night.* Happiest Baby was nodding at a phenomenon called sudden unexplained infant death (SUID), a category that includes babies who die of accidental asphyxiation or strangulation, undiagnosed disorders, infection, and sudden infant death syndrome (SIDS)—deaths that could not be attributed to any known cause, even after investigation.

Marc and I piously followed recommendations for safe sleep— Alma slept on his back, on a stiff mattress with a tightly fitted sheet, alone in his crib with nothing else inside—but his nooselike cannula worried me. I felt reassured that the Snoo's swaddle clips would, at least, prevent him from rolling into the tightening grip of the breathing tube. My nighttime fear was specific, contained within the cannula's transparent loop, but in other parents I saw sleep anxiety stretch in all directions. One online "mamas" chat group I joined pealed with anxious updates, with mothers sharing the thoughts that loomed like shadow puppets over their children's cribs. They worried that their babies would bonk their heads on the bars, or get their feet stuck within them, or go to sleep peacefully and never wake up. I understood this pervasive fear of death, its irrational pull. The mamas shared recommendations for therapists, self-help books, SSRIs. And lots of products.

The Snoo's technique—physical restraint—was crude compared to the other gadgets that some parents used on their kids. Like the Owlet Dream Sock, a pastel bootie that wrapped around a baby's foot as she slept and beamed her pulse rate and oxygen saturation level to her minder's phone. (In 2024, it was priced at $299.) Or the Nanit, a smart video monitor that, paired with a patterned band wrapped around the baby's midsection, could detect her chest movements and sound an alarm if she stopped breathing for twenty seconds. (Camera systems started at $249.) One mother said that she affixed both the Owlet sock and the Nanit band to her baby at night. *Because I'm crazy,* she explained.

I scrolled back through Owlet's Instagram account and watched rose-tinted montages of loving smart-sock applications. The company's influencer partners eerily parroted the same lines. The Owlet was *the best peace of mind you can get* . . . It gave *parents peace of mind and comfort* . . . because *peace of mind is everything when it comes to being a parent* . . . and *you can't put a price on peace of mind.* Glow, one of the pregnancy apps I signed up for with a fake due date, sent me a targeted email when it thought I was thirty-eight weeks pregnant, with a push to *pre-pack peace of mind* by buying an Owlet for my hospital go-bag. I saw on Instagram that when the box arrived, it opened to say: *Rest assured.*

The Owlet Dream Sock was marketed not to treat any medical condition but rather to affirm to the parents that their babies were not experiencing a medical condition at all. In fact, it treated a parental condition: anxiety. But of course it could cause that, too. The company telegraphed its charitable partnerships with a number of foundations, lighting a constellation of traumas—miscarriage, infant loss, premature birth, NICU stays. On its website, users could pay $10 to donate a tree seedling to the parents of babies who had died. It hosted an Owlet *rainbow baby day giveaway*, raffling free socks to parents who had experienced pregnancy loss. And it described its *mission to end SIDS* by donating some proceeds to scientists researching the phenomenon. Owlet did not outright state that its biometric tracking would prevent deaths, but the mysterious nature of SIDS opened the possibility in a parent's mind.

In 2021, the FDA issued a warning letter to Owlet, dinging it for marketing a medical device without its blessing. But two years later, the agency granted the company de novo approval—the right to market the sock as a "novel medical device," an over-the-counter infant pulse oximeter for home use on healthy babies. (The FDA also approved a hospital-grade Owlet sock called BabySat, available by prescription to children with certain medical conditions). In the announcement, the agency was clear that the Owlet was not approved to detect or prevent sudden deaths. In 2023, the FDA also extended de novo approval to the Snoo as an "over-the-counter infant sleep system," though it again cautioned that the data could not determine whether the device could protect against death. A bulletin from the American Academy of Pediatrics warned parents: "Do not use home cardiorespiratory monitors as a strategy to reduce the risk of SIDS."

In late 2023, after the Owlet's FDA clearance was announced, I dialed into the Owlet earnings call and listened to Kurt Workman, the Owlet cofounder and CEO, tell investors of his plan to finally dissolve the distinction between a sick baby and a healthy one. "The gap between consumer and medical technologies and channels continues to shrink," he said. "Our vision is to drive that tipping point." Workman and Karp both expressed hope that FDA approval would clear a path to health insurance coverage of their products. Karp envisioned a Snoo in every new parent's home and predicted that the practice of putting babies to sleep in cribs "totally unsecured" would one day be a relic of ignorant parenting. If these companies had their way, every baby would be strapped into a robotic bassinet and fitted with a surveillance sock from birth.

And that was just the beginning. On TikTok, I watched a coterie of pregnant influencers hawk an Owlet Beta product: a mint-green *pregnancy band*, which, the Owlet website explained, cast a *net of sensors* over the belly in order to *track an unborn baby's wellness*. (Owlet paused its development of the product in 2022). The band could detect the baby's heartbeat, lead the mother in a kick count, and track her contractions. An IVF influencer named Baylie Janis filmed herself beaming and strapping it on. *Owlet just released this insane new product for pregnant women to bring you added reassurance and insights to your pregnancy,* she said. *I literally am so obsessed.* A white button stamped with the Owlet logo stared unblinkingly from the top of her stomach.

It was, I agreed, insane. I had been so excited for Alma to be discharged from the NICU, then released from his infernal oxygen tank. Now the baby-monitor industry was recruiting peppy moms to sell a vision of the perma-hospital, restyled as comfy and chic. The fact that many of these devices did not come recommended by actual medical professionals seemed only to enhance their appeal. They emphasized the parent's superior authority over a child's health, confirmed her expert status. With these new tools, I could play the doctor, my body the clinic, my baby kept forever under my care.

As I scrolled through the Owlet's Instagram account, I found a video republished from one of its ambassadors, an influencer named Lizzie Appel, who posted under the handle @thats.darling.mama. In the Owlet video, her camera floated toward a crib to find a new-born wriggling in a knit blue pinafore. *As a mama I crave peace of mind. If you know my story you know why this is so important to me,* Lizzie wrote in the caption. *This past month I've been trying the Owlet Dream Duo with my surviving twin James and I can't tell you how much relief it's brought me.* Her grateful pitch for the Owlet fused with the dread of that phrase: *surviving twin.*

I tapped on Lizzie's account and waded into a stream of gauzy images of her children, who wore natural fabrics as they romped happily inside her boho home. Threaded between them were emotional dispatches from Lizzie's experience of vanishing twin syndrome, processed through montages with crackling filters. Early in her pregnancy with James, a doctor had detected a second embryo on an ultrasound, without a heartbeat. The lost embryo did not affect the health of the surviving baby, but the discovery of its existence—and nonexistence—affected Lizzie. *It's been hard watching Twin A slowly vanish away appointment after appointment,* she wrote during the pregnancy. *Now there is no sign of her at all, like I never carried her.* After James's birth, a vacant bassinet became a tableau for her loss, staged with Twin A's unworn ruffled onesie and her unclaimed stuffed rabbit. On Instagram, a grief Lizzie experienced through the ultrasound screen gained shape and took its place in her home. When James was born, she posed him swaddled next to a slack, empty blanket.

I was startled by the flash of myself I saw in Lizzie's stories. Our online personas were not similar—she had an earnest aesthetic with a romantic color scheme, and I made my baby wear custom merch inspired by *Phantom Thread*—but we shared this strange modern form of technology-assisted grief, as well as an impulse to try to make sense of it for an audience. I felt a little guilty for my initial discomfort at encountering stories like hers under the imprimatur of the Owlet brand. I reached out to Lizzie over email, and she told me how much she appreciated the company's recognition of her situation, which had once felt confusing and obscure. "This was a partnership I was desperately praying for," she said. "The loss has definitely left me with some sort of trauma, and this device helps me know that my son is all right." I wondered if, had I known about the Owlet before Alma's birth, I would have bought one, too.

The Owlet made grief its brand, and this made some parents feel less alone. It recognized their traumas, and then it amplified them until they were big enough for every expectant parent to see. On the Owlet website, I took a quiz to match my baby to his optimal Owlet product. One question—*How do you feel about keeping an eye on your baby's health?*—prompted three choices. I could code myself as A) *on high alert due to specific health concerns;* B) *generally concerned, like any parent;* or C) *not too worried, but a little peace of mind goes a long way.* Each assumed a baseline need for the sock.

Over Instagram, I posted a request to interview Owlet users, and I connected with a woman named Lorna and called her over Zoom. She sat in her darkened bedroom in Canada, laptop screen angled up at her face, and told me about her twenty-two-month-old son. He was born with a heart condition, and Lorna identified on Instagram as a *heart mom*, though she did not advertise her use of the device on her feed. Her son lived in a hospital NICU for the first six months of his life. When he came home, Lorna was spooked by the sudden revocation of the constant monitors that had assured her of his safety. She had seen the Owlet on the feed of a pregnancy-loss influencer she followed when she experienced her own miscarriage, and she thought, *Maybe we need a baby monitor like this.* Her son had abnormal oxygen saturation levels in his blood, and the Owlet could tell her if they were dropping even more perilously, requiring a call to a doctor. "As a parent, you're just kind of left to your own devices," Lorna told me. Quite literally: "The Owlet is one of the tools that parents with children with special needs can use to take care of themselves, in a way."

The next day, I went for coffee with my friend Rachel, who I learned had bought the Owlet a few days before she went into labor with her own child, though her pregnancy had been normal. "I know myself," she told me. "I have a lot of anxiety." The pandemic only heightened advertisers' leverage over new parents—they were more worried, more isolated, more online. Buying the sock made Rachel feel "in control of the many unknowns," she said, her way to get ahead of her own anxieties about having a baby. Her mother had told her stories about bending over her crib when Rachel was a newborn, watching her chest rise and fall. She figured that the sock could, at least, spare her an aching back.

But when the baby came, she had an unexpected complication: colic. "She just cried for six months straight," Rachel said, and the Owlet did not help. "It probably made our lives worse." When her baby finally stopped wailing and went to sleep, Rachel found herself watching the Owlet app, which "gamified the baby." Its real-time readings made Rachel doubt whether her sleeping child was even really sleeping, and if so, whether her sleep was light or deep. Sometimes, after she rocked the baby into a blissful slumber, the device sounded an angry alarm for no apparent reason. Still, "I would endorse it," she said. "It's more for peace of mind than anything else."

I asked Lorna how she felt about parents of healthy kids using the Owlet, and she said, "I try not to judge. I understand everyone has their anxieties." Still, as her son grew, she unfollowed the pregnancy-loss influencer who had introduced her to the product. The influencer was sharing her anxiety about her healthy baby's sleep, while Lorna's anxiety was rooted in her child's complex medical needs. "I just couldn't relate anymore," she said. I had often seen parenthood pitched as a universal experience, but it was riven with imperceptible fissures. Every aspect of raising a child presented an opportunity to divide us into our own isolated experiences. But there was one thing that united Lorna, Rachel, and Lizzie: they all wrapped an Owlet around their baby's foot.

Long after Alma grew out of his bassinet, I lingered in the internet's constellation of Snoo groups, watching as the conversation stretched beyond tips. Strangers in far-flung cities convened in a recognizable consumer landscape, united by the folkways of the Snoo and the ease of a shared class position. Its users felt comfortable whining and preening in front of one another. On Reddit, a dad posted a triumphant screenshot of his four-month-old's sleep graph, showing off its oceanic expanse of blue and tagging it *#SNOOporn*. On Facebook, a mother shared a photo of a hotel porter hoisting her thirty-eight-pound Snoo over his head and carrying it across a dock of a tropical resort, where she had brought it along on vacation. Another woman signed in to a Snoo group from the hospital. She was in active labor and wanted to know when she ought to place the epidural.

A Facebook group featuring Snoo talk, Bougie Baby Banter, made it explicit: consumption was the new community. *It truly takes a village to raise a child and let's be honest, it also takes a lot of bougie (and non-bougie) products,* its description said. *In this digital day and age, not all of us have literal villages to lean on, so we look online for advice, a sense of community, and product recommendations.* Karp also evoked the proverb "It takes a village to raise a child" as he pitched the Snoo. "The real stressor in modern families is that they don't have extended families," he told *The New Yorker* in 2023. "We are re-creating the village, a quasi-village, if you will, to support parents." He advised his customers not to worry about the robotic nature of the help. "That word, 'robot'—it's kind of a problematic word," he said. "No one wants to put their baby in the care of a robot. 'Robot' comes from a Slavic word, *rab*, meaning 'slave.'"

Once he said it, I never saw the Snoo the same way again. The phrase "a village" conjured an idealized past, one where childcare was communal, aid was mutual, and non-parent helpers were close at hand. This utopia was positioned so safely in the past, so unrecognizable to our present, that we were not bothered with wondering whether it had ever truly existed and what conditions had made it possible. Karp's explication of *robot* was a reminder that the history of childcare in the United States was also marked by forced and coerced labor. In the early twentieth century, domestic servants were what the historian Faye Dudden called "a vital element of middle class domesticity." Most middle-class American families employed at least one servant, and that figure fell in the coming decades not because the desire for servitude diminished but because workers demanded better jobs with higher wages. Enter vacuum cleaners, dishwashers, and prepackaged foods, the new helpers that middle-class parents employed to shape their domestic worlds.

It seemed to me that the Snoo's customers did, on some level, desire robo-slaves. After all, the Snoo functioned more like a minion than a surrogate aunt. It was much more affordable than a human night nurse, especially if bought secondhand or rented by the month, but its sleek machinery also obscured the other laborers who made it—the Chinese factory workers who built its body and the call center employees who kept it humming.

In his *New Yorker* interview, Karp argued that the village model wasn't all it was cracked up to be. It required "everyone knowing your business and everyone giving you their opinions and whatnot, and you have to deal with surly family members." Even as these online consumer-communities yearned for the village and lamented its irretrievable loss, they positioned the tech as an upgrade. Leah Plunkett, a Harvard Law School professor who studies the digital privacy of children, told me that these technologies sell themselves as "removing the discomfort of interpersonal relationships," eliminating the frictions that arise from close human contact. The smart baby device pitched itself as a solution for a lost communal life, but really it represented the pure commodification of care.

"Our best machines are made of sunshine," Donna Haraway writes in *A Cyborg Manifesto*. They are light and clean and "a matter of immense human pain in Detroit and Singapore." When I interrogated my own relationship with the Snoo, I realized that its subhuman status was part of its appeal. I was frustrated that my baby would not stop screaming in the middle of the night. I was insecure about my own capability to soothe him. I hurled all those feelings at the Snoo's unfeeling frame. "Goddamn you," I told it on multiple occasions. "Goddamn you, you fucking piece of shit!"

Two years after Alma was born, in October 2022, I gave birth to his little brother. By the time Brayden came around, I felt inoculated against the anxious pitches of many of these devices. I was too busy and worn down to worry about anything that wasn't directly smacking Brayden in the face, which Alma sometimes was. Most of the time, though, Alma was reaching over to pat Brayden gently on the head and say, "Awww, look at the little guy."

We used the Snoo again, because it was there, and though Brayden slept easily in it, I was eager to banish it from my life as soon as possible. When I offered it to a friend who was expecting a baby of his own, I did not exactly endorse it. I felt like an ill-fated figure in a folktale, forced to remove a cursed object from her home without telling an outright lie. We used our video monitor to check in on Alma and Brayden as they slept together in the room they now shared, but when the camera finally died, I happily threw it away. In its place, we plugged in a $15 audio monitor. It did only what we needed it to do: tell us if Brayden was crying.

Our new baby monitor was not much different from the oldest one: the Zenith Radio Nurse, a two-sided radio marketed as the first baby monitor in 1938. It was developed by Zenith Radio Corporation president Eugene McDonald Jr., whose first child was born the previous year. The radio was designed by the sculptor Isamu Noguchi to resemble a human head with a grilled face, and the marketing suggested that its mechanical perception was superior to that of a human caretaker: ads called it "the guardian that never sleeps." A review in *Parents* magazine praised its industriousness. "The radio nurse goes on duty at once without any fuss or tinkering and remains faithfully on the job as long as you need it," it said. "It saves worry and steps, for it will transmit to you every sound, even a whisper." In its ads, the Radio Nurse promised "greater safety for your baby, greater peace of mind for yourself." But the manual warned of complications: "serious distortion," "speaker rattle," the hum of interference.

The Radio Nurse was released in the wake of the kidnapping of Charles Lindbergh's baby in 1932, a nightmare saga that resurfaced regularly in the news even after the boy's accused killer was executed in 1936. The kidnapping was like an urban legend turned real, and because it targeted the child of the most famous person in the world, it suggested that no baby was safe. It also fanned wealthy families' mistrust of their domestic employees; some had suspected the Lindbergh boy's nanny of aiding the kidnapping, or else allowing it to happen. The Radio Nurse promised to override the nanny, instantly alerting a parent to a child's cries, and to the steps of an intruder breaching his nursery.

By the time my children were born, baby monitors were probing a new fear: they would tell you if your baby could not cry, because he had stopped breathing. A simple audio feed, even a video feed, could not detect this silent threat. So the Owlet slipped over a baby's foot, the Snuza Hero clipped to his belly, the Angelcare cased his mattress with a sensor pad, and the Nanit wrapped a band around his chest and used machine-learning algorithms to determine that it was rising and falling at proper intervals.

After I learned about Nanit through the mom group, I reached out to the company, and it sent me a camera to try. When I opened the box, it said, "Welcome to Nanit! Your baby is about to *sleep like a baby.*" In a few minutes, I had followed its simple instructions to erect a freestanding camera that peered directly down into Brayden's crib, its neck bent over him like an aluminum bird. I opened the Nanit app and the image beamed to my phone dazzled me with its clarity. Immediately I understood how an expensive camera could have improved my postpartum life. When Alma was still sleeping on oxygen, I could never manage to find a vantage point high enough for our video monitor to reliably report back on the placement of Alma's cannula. I was always hunching down, creeping to his crib like a storybook crone. I imagined owning a Nanit instead, lying on the couch and casually thumbing from Reddit to Instagram to my Make Sure the Baby Is Not Strangling on His Home Medical Device feed.

By this point, however, I had grown accustomed to my radio monitor, and now the Nanit overwhelmed me. The breathing-tracking function, which I could engage by swaddling Brayden in a special band (though I did not), was only one feature of many. I would open the app in the morning and find dozens of notifications of various movements Brayden had made over the course of the evening. I could set up the app to send me a push notification every time the camera detected a noise near his crib. If I wanted, I could turn off the audio feed from his room, replacing his screams with the neutral plink of a phone alert. Or I could flip on a speaker above his crib and speak to him from a remote location, like I was his God. Every week, the Nanit sent me Brayden's report card, grading his nighttime performance on a range of metrics.

A few weeks after I installed the camera, I reported to Nanit's offices inside a sleek shared space in lower Manhattan. There I met its director of research, Dr. Natalie Barnett, and its vice president of brand marketing, Quynh Dang. Near the end of my visit, I told Dang that I had been relieved, scrolling through Nanit's Instagram feed, that it did not brand itself by suggesting my baby would die if I didn't use it. That impression was "very intentional," Dang said. "You brought up SIDS earlier—it's not something we ever talk about. We're not a medical device. That's not our role." When Nanit partners with influencers, she said, it makes clear that it is not interested in fear-based content. "The spirit of the brand is to support and to build confidence and to alleviate stress. Not to add to it," Dang said.

If the Owlet branding struck at parents' hearts, the Nanit appealed to their minds. It was created by a computer scientist who, working on a PhD in computer vision while caring for his unsleeping newborn, realized that he could apply his research lessons to his own child. As a scientist, "he was using computer vision to look for defects in computer chips, tracking dust and things," Barnett said. Now he would leverage machine-learning algorithms to identify flaws in his own baby's sleep patterns.

Pediatric sleep researchers had long used a method called actigraphy to study sleeping babies, and this required attaching a Fitbit-like monitor to their wrist or ankle, which—like Alma with his cannula—children disliked. But now the Nanit could watch a baby with its mechanical eye, its algorithms calculating the child's sleep patterns without having to touch his body at all. And it could recruit research subjects on a large scale, through thousands of Nanits trained on thousands of babies at once. Barnett told me that the Nanit sought user permission to pull their babies' data, and that many of its users were eager to comply, happy to aid in the mission. Even sleep labs were starting to integrate Nanit cameras into their research.

The Nanit cofounder who built the camera to help his sleepless baby went on to have two more kids. They both struggled with sleep as babies, too. I asked Barnett what the point of the camera was if it didn't help babies sleep better. "There's so many reasons people use the product," she replied. As I toured its functions, I felt my relationship with my baby supplanted by a relationship with his information. If I used the company's "smart sheets" in Brayden's crib, the Nanit could automatically chart his growth and tick off his developmental milestones. Brayden's Nanit report card came in the form of a *weekly sleep dashboard*, which charted his *sleep efficiency, sleep onset,* and *total nighttime sleep* against what it called the *optimal range.* If an algorithm determined that Brayden was out of range, it triggered a *sleep coaching tip* that I was encouraged to implement to bring him back in line. I was not going to let an algorithm decide how I sang my son to sleep, so I ignored these prompts. But I remembered how I had felt in the bleary first weeks of Alma's life, when the Snoo stopped and said: *Alma needs your care.* I felt shamed by the machine and motivated to improve. Smart devices could make new parents feel inadequate, but they also offered a simple solution: tweak the baby-parent relationship to juice your standings on the dashboard.

As these machines promised to help babies rest, they inducted them into a winking culture of meritocratic achievement. Nanit told me that Brayden was sleeping more efficiently than 96 percent of babies, a solid A. On Instagram, I watched Snoo users style their kids as pupils, posting when their #snoobaby, a citizen of #snoonation, outgrew the device and became a #snoograd. Several times I saw a picture of a baby smiling in the bassinet, a tiny tasseled mortarboard perched atop the head. This all sounds like a joke, and parental participation could feel disarmingly silly. "I get a sick pleasure out of my daughter's 'report cards,'" a friend joked of the Nanit's weekly emails. But it was a short distance between fake baby rankings produced by consumer surveillance gadgets and real baby rankings run by the state.

When I installed the Nanit for its trial run in my home, my family was mired in a months-long process to convince the public school system to provide Alma with speech therapy. This required that he be observed by a psychologist, a trained educational evaluator, and a speech pathologist in a range of settings. When a PDF of the final report arrived in my inbox, I raged through its findings. I glared at the educational system as it described my son's relationships, his personality, and his abilities, all ranked against various markers of normalcy. The report assigned him an IQ score calculated using the Stanford-Binet Intelligence Scales and assessed his social skills based on the Vineland-3 Adaptive Behavior Scales. He was two years old. It was not cute.

Alma's speech was *very difficult to understand*, the report said. *He tried his best to share experiences.* Marc and I never had trouble understanding him. We knew how conversant he could be, how brilliantly he adapted his communication for people who were willing to listen. The state's perception of Alma was a betrayal of our intimate view. But in order to secure the accommodations he deserved, we were required to endorse it, to sign our names at the end. There was one line in the report that I held on to, a kind aside included by an evaluator: *Alma presented as an adorable little boy.*

The Nanit did something that my old video monitor never could. It let me play back the video from the night before, and it automatically curated select moments of interest. The Nanit's Instagram and TikTok accounts, which leaned more playful than anxious, often featured adorable clips culled from users' feeds, like triplets standing up in their side-by-side-by-side cribs to hug one another through the bars.

It was strange, how quickly I got used to seeing Brayden through the Nanit's cyclopean eye. He appeared in grayscale night vision, as if I were his guard observing him through a CCTV monitor. Seeing him from above, he appeared comically Pooh-like, his belly spilling from his pajamas as he rolled about, stretched with his butt in the air, and sucked on his thumb. When he opened his eyes, they were alien and white, though this too came to seem normal. First I had learned to track my periods, then my pregnancy, and now I was tracking my kids from a surveillance camera perched above their beds.

As I scrolled back through the Nanit's saved footage, I realized that it did not just capture Brayden. It filmed me, too. I watched myself stride into the boys' room, bend over the lip of the crib, and sweep Brayden into my arms. I had been a mother for several years then, and still it was odd to see myself outside of myself, capably executing a classic mom move. I rewound the footage, captivated by my own performance. The next day, I found a different clip waiting for me, a record of the minutes before the boys fell asleep the night before. The video, which the app automatically sped up to compress its time, showed me walk into the room, put the boys down, and leave. When Alma sat up in bed and screamed, "Mama! Mama! Mama!" I did not turn around. I walked right out the door and closed it behind me. Marc and I had learned that these swift exits helped our kids fall asleep, but now I questioned whether I should try a different approach. Something that played better on-screen.

I didn't think much about how my own children experienced the Nanit, until one night I saw it for myself. I lay down with Alma in the dark, ran my hands through his hair, and rubbed his back. Then a sinister presence appeared in the corner of the room. From the vantage point of his low toddler bed, positioned a few feet away from Brayden's crib, I could finally see the camera from a child's perspective. Four glowing red dots stared back at me. The next morning, I packed the Nanit back in its box and plugged the $15 audio monitor back in.

Martha had used the Nanit camera, too, and she told me that eventually her daughter insisted that she remove it from the room.

"She started referring to it as 'the eye' and saying that she didn't want to sleep with 'the eye' over her bed," Martha told me. "It felt very Foucault." Checking the Nanit app on my phone made me feel like I was reaching out to care for my children, even at a distance. But it only brought them closer to the machine.

Chapter 9

Growth

I remembered one thing about *Dumbo:* the elephant flew. One morning, when Alma was two years old, I played the movie on our television and cleaned the kitchen while he watched from the couch a few feet away. (Long ago, Marc and I had culled our own streaming subscriptions, sacrificing them to the altar of Disney+.) I listened as storks cruised down from the sky, delivering baby animals to the various enclosures of a traveling circus. One bird dropped a baby elephant in front of a new mother, and she named him Jumbo Jr.

I glanced up and saw a line of lady elephants staring at the baby with stunned amusement. Released from the stork's beak sack, Jumbo Jr.'s ears flopped out, revealing their extra-large size. *Just look at those, those E-A-R-S,* one lady said. *Oh, these! Aren't they funny?* said another, grabbing at the baby with her trunk. Jumbo's mother whipped her own trunk around and slapped her in the face. The lady elephants gasped, then resumed their nasty conversation.

What did I do? Tell me, did I say anything?

A perfectly harmless remark.

I said they're funny looking, they are funny!

They certainly are.

After all, who cares about her precious little Jumbo?

Jumbo? You mean "Dumbo."

The elephants laughed. Alma gazed neutrally at the screen. My hand reached for the remote. I threatened the television with my finger on the button. Then, something interesting happened: Jumbo's mother scooped up her baby with her trunk and wrapped him in the fabric of his own ears. They smiled together as she rocked him to sleep. I sat on the couch next to Alma and searched *Dumbo disability studies* on my phone.

Once the cruelty of the elephants would have struck me as old-fashioned or melodramatic, but now I recognized the realism of the scene. Alma's tongue usually rested outside of his mouth, and strangers sometimes interpreted it as a provocation. As I guided him down the sidewalk in a carrier or a stroller, people stuck their tongues out at him, then laughed in confusion when he didn't pull his back in. They yelled after us as we walked away, hooting about the tongue's size. They neared Alma in the park or drugstore and said, "Whoa!" or "Is he sick?" When I slipped Alma's passport application under a slot at the post office, a worker gruffly pushed it back, saying that his photograph looked illegal. I was always caught off guard by how difficult it seemed for people to say nothing. The comments just spilled from their mouths. Not knowing what to do, I usually kept mine shut. Now I wondered if I should have slapped somebody with my trunk.

On my phone, I read about how *Dumbo* recycled damaging tropes about disabled people, casting the big-eared elephant as a *victim*, then a *freak*, then a *supercrip*. It infantilized disability, removing it from its complex human context and planting it in a cute baby animal instead. But the movie also had an alternate reading, one expressed in an essay by Victoria Lucas, a woman born with a rare genetic condition called cherubism that produces an enlarged lower face. When she watched *Dumbo* at age nine, she saw a hero with an "extremely enlarged facial feature," she wrote. "For the first time, I'd found someone I could relate to. I didn't realize it then, but I had reclaimed him as a disabled role model."

As Alma watched *Dumbo,* I watched the character's mother. I followed her story closely, tracing the boundaries of her role. After she named her baby, she did not speak another line. Her child's bullies multiplied. She raged against them until she was subdued and imprisoned in a cage. Only when Jumbo discovered that he could use his big ears to fly was he able to charm the circus, earn the world's respect, and free his mother. *Dumbo* taught me that a good mother wielded righteous anger on her child's behalf. But also that this anger was dangerous, and it could cause problems for my son. I could become one more burden he was expected to resolve.

When Alma was a few months old, he and I were sitting on a blanket in the park when a friend walked by. My friend's partner was pregnant, and he expressed relief that she had aced her prenatal tests. The tests also told them that the baby was a girl, though this did not matter to them. "We're just happy that she's healthy," he said.

As long as the baby is healthy—this was a standard line. It was meant to emphasize the expectant parent's total acceptance of their future child. They had no superficial preferences, but their protective concern was without limit. Now, whenever I heard this, my mind receded into a back room and rehearsed possible responses. I wanted to say, *No test can tell you if you will have a "healthy" baby,* and *It feels like you're saying you don't want your baby to be like mine,* and also, *My baby is not* not *healthy.* A few weeks later, after the encounter paced around my head several more times, I realized how I truly felt about his comment. When parents say that they want their baby to be healthy, they mean that they want their baby to be normal. I had been one of them, and now I was sickened by my own ableism. I didn't say any of that, though. I just smiled at my friend and said: "Such great news."

During my pregnancy, I was wrecked by the loneliness of my "abnormal" experience. Now I moved from pregnancy world to parent world and closed the door behind me. I didn't expect parents-to-be to carry the baggage of my own pregnancy's events. They walked away and left me to drag it around myself. There was no reason why the average expectant parent would have ever heard of BWS, much less tested for it. But their easy announcement of prenatal results assumed a rooting interest against all conditions, and fetuses that have them, and people. Just a few months earlier, I had been the pregnant woman fetishizing the normal test result. Now that I was the mother of a child with a rare condition, I found an enemy in my past self.

My friend Dave also has a child with a rare genetic condition, and when I ran into him at a friend's birthday party, he told me the question everyone had been asking him: *Did you know before she was born?* It was another way of saying: *Did you choose this?* The real tragedy, these interactions seemed to say, was having a baby with traits that you did not personally select. The obsession with choice, Dave said, was a symptom of a class of professional strivers who needed to control and optimize every aspect of life. Babies don't work like that, and that's part of what makes parenting meaningful: you do not get to choose. But that did not stop people from trying.

During my pregnancy, my blood, urine, and amniotic fluid was screened and tested for countless conditions, some of which did not yet have names. Additional tests could have searched for many more. By 2020, prenatal testing had become a standard medical offering and a billion-dollar industry, and options were made available earlier and earlier in pregnancy. Take the NIPT—the *noninvasive prenatal test*, which could analyze fragments of fetal DNA in the mother's blood and screen them for a band of chromosomal abnormalities. I took one when I was thirteen weeks pregnant, yielding unmemorable results. That was in the spring, when the American College of Obstetricians and Gynecologists recommended the test for women with certain risk factors. By the summer, it had revised its recommendation, advising doctors to offer a NIPT to every pregnant patient.

My NIPT test was created by the biomedical company Natera, and the product was called Panorama, like the photographic gimmick that could take a 360-degree view and flatten it into an image. *Pregnancy can be exciting for families, and also bring concerns about medical decisions or the challenges of parenting,* the Natera website said. It promised that its test delivered *unique insights* into this problem by screening babies for conditions like Down syndrome and Turner syndrome. The website was laced with pictures of able-bodied pregnant women smiling down at their bumps from above. Also, a photograph of curly-haired twin babies with delicious fat rolls and gurgling smiles, like a doubled stock image for *healthy baby.* There were no pictures of babies or adults who appeared to have any condition screened by the test—only brief written sketches of the narrowed lives you could expect for children who did. Panorama was supposed to tell you if your baby was likely to have a genetic condition, but all its iconography pointed toward a negative result—a normal baby.

"Panoramic" insight promised an all-seeing mechanical eye into the womb, one sold as an improvement on human powers of observation. *Every pregnancy deserves Panorama,* the website said. Natera did not elaborate on the implications of this knowledge. The test could help expectant parents pursue care and treatment for their future children, or it could prompt them to abort their pregnancies. I had wanted as much information as possible about my future child, but I hadn't thought about what I might do with it. The eerie pictures on the website suggested that in Natera's biotech fantasy world, no affected pregnancy was carried to term. *NIPT* could be pronounced "nipped," like, "in the bud." The test's panoramic view could not see children or adults with disabilities, much less envision communities in which they thrived. The branding suggested that abortion was a parent's personal decision, so personal that the word could not even be published. And it implied that caring for a child with disabilities was the parent's responsibility alone.

It was not very common to receive a prenatal diagnosis of Beckwith-Wiedemann syndrome, but I knew from my research that some parents who received it chose to terminate their pregnancies. Others said that a prenatal diagnosis helped them to decide against termination. I supported a parent's right to choose an abortion—my right to have chosen—for any reason. I also knew that the imagined BWS baby that confronted expectant parents was a fiction. Alma looked nothing like the jarring medical photos that appeared online. And the list of his potential complications, out of the context of a life, felt like a smear. I imagined my own life, at thirty-five years old, compressed into a similar kind of list: surgery for an unexplained neck lump at age one; later, two abdominal surgeries; mole removals; Celiac disease; HPV; social anxiety; depression; bunions; intermittent nicotine addiction; sometime binge drinking; chronic sleepiness. Then I imagined all those factors tossed in with complications that I might have had but did not. People said they wanted information, but it often seemed like what they really wanted was a blank slate.

As the prenatal testing industry dangled its buffet of choices in front of expectant parents, reproductive justice was yanked further from our grasp. Abortion laws around the United States grew more restrictive and punitive, exaggerating inequities and conscripting some women into unwanted, doomed, or lethal pregnancies. Even during a pandemic, the country was loath to provide sufficient support for raising children, much less children who required additional resources. In this context, the Natera website came to resemble an advertisement for a luxury good. The unspoken possibility of a TFMR—a termination for medical reasons—was available only to expectant parents with the considerable resources required to get themselves to an abortion clinic in a permissive US state before the legal deadline.

Every year this reproductive technology gap widened. In 2023, a startup called Orchid Health started advertising whole-genome sequencing of five-cell embryos for $2,500 a pop. Its founder, Noor Siddiqui, had captured Silicon Valley's imagination by publicly promising to engineer "healthy" children for her elite clients. She waved away accusations of eugenics by claiming that she was granting parents more choices on how to reproduce, not fewer. Siddiqui encouraged her customers to avoid natural conceptions and opt into IVF because "sex is for fun, and embryo screening is for babies." *The Information* reported that Siddiqui advised one of her investors to hire a gestational surrogate to carry her first child, not because it was medically indicated but because, as the investor recalled her saying, "it's not that expensive." The project to eradicate disability would be built on a reproductive underclass.

I wondered what might happen if prenatal testing for BWS grew more sophisticated, if it became quick and widespread. I asked Dr. Linda Hasadsri, a clinical molecular geneticist at Mayo Clinic, whether it would someday be possible to develop a NIPT-style blood test that screened for BWS and related conditions early in pregnancy, and she said the technology was already here. I told her I wasn't sure that I wanted it to exist. I thought about the expectant parents who might jump, scared, at an early chance to prevent kids like my son. All their private, data-informed decisions, adding up to the total elimination of his genetic code.

The results of NIPT tests were not always straightforward. Genetic testing companies once offered early screening for chromosomal conditions that were relatively easy to detect, like Down syndrome, which is caused by a tripled twenty-first chromosome. But in recent years, the offerings expanded to include rarer conditions that were harder to accurately pinpoint in maternal blood. These screening tests ended up snagging plenty of normal pregnancies in their nets. Many pregnancies flagged as potentially high-risk were actually not. The sudden ubiquity of the NIPT created a new pregnancy experience: the false positive.

One day Instagram served me a reel of an influencer kissing her newborn on the forehead. She rubbed her lips back and forth against the sleeping baby's skin, and I watched it on a loop, reliving its familiar plush sensation. Over the video, the woman unspooled a diagnostic saga. *When I was twelve weeks pregnant, I got a call from my OBGYN*, she wrote. *His words were: "Your NIPT came back positive for Turner Syndrome."* The mother pointed viewers to continue the story in the caption below. I scrolled and started reading: *Right at that second my world stopped! I couldn't sleep anymore . . . I couldn't eat or work . . . I couldn't function! . . . How would I take care of a special needs child? How would my life change? . . . Would I ever be able to work again? And of course the biggest of my concerns: all the health issues that would come with Turner. How could I be able to see my child possibly suffering so much?*

The story paused there. The mother said she had continued it in the comments, but they had not threaded properly, so I could not see them. Instead I saw comment after comment from kind strangers:

I'm 41 years old a nurse practitioner and have Turners Syndrome and am more than happy to talk with you.

I'm Turner's if you ever want to chat!

I have Mosaic Turner's Syndrome, and I am 50 years old and very healthy, one said. She added: *You love your baby girl. There is nothing broken or wrong with her.*

When I found the rest of the mother's story, scattered throughout the vast comment section, it became clear that her daughter did not have Turner syndrome. Rather, her DNA had been flagged by the NIPT screen, but a more accurate diagnostic test returned negative. The mother rejoiced in her good luck. *I look at her and I can't believe she is here,* she wrote. *She is here and she is completely healthy!* Women with Turner syndrome flocked to her story, eager to build a community around her and her daughter. Then she revealed that her daughter was not like them. They were images in her rearview mirror, reminders of her averted tragedy.

This was happening all around me, I realized. Expectant parents were experiencing the threat of a diagnosis and reeling from its phantom traumas. In 2022, a group of American women sued Natera, alleging that they had been "subjected to unnecessary stress and anxiety, and additional medical costs," due to "false positive indications of rare disorders." (Natera has denied their claims; as its NIPT is a screening test, not a diagnostic one, the company refutes the idea that a high-risk result constitutes a "false positive." The case was ongoing as of January 2025.) The suit described each woman's experience with the Panorama test, but they all told similar tales. Typically the woman "suffered substantial distress," "considered terminating," "worried she might miscarry," and "felt fear throughout the entire pregnancy." She spent money on further tests and specialist doctors. Many of the stories ended with a line describing the whiplash of the result: "Her son was born healthy," it said. Or, "Her daughter was born healthy."

I was just like them—I had lost my mind over a scary ultrasound that turned out to be nothing. But I was also unlike them, because I then had a baby with what turned out to be something. To stake a legal claim against a biomedical company, a spurned consumer had to publicly detail a nightmare—the nightmare of having to consider that a child might have a medical condition. I kept returning to the lawsuit's repeating line about how, at pregnancy's end, the child was "born healthy." A mother's emotional distress only had currency because she ultimately produced a normal kid. My distress was, I guess, warranted. I had no damages to claim. These women's nightmares ended when their kids were born with no genetic issues. My nightmare had also ended when I met my son. But now our projects felt opposed. Their pregnant imagination squared off against my reality.

Late at night, I found myself thumbing over to Reddit and searching for pregnant strangers. Through them, I staged deeper simulations of all my unspoken conversations—with friends, influencers, litigants. I started lurking on r/NIPT, where people sometimes came to Reddit to post their atypical test results and float their anxieties into the crowd. *ONLY ABNORMAL RESULTS CAN POST!!!!*—that was the sub's number one rule. *This NIPT/NIPS sub is for FALSE POSITIVE, FALSE NEGATIVE, TRUE POSITIVE & those stuck in limbo,* it said. I had once been stuck, and now I was unstuck, but I was still there, watching.

As I slipped through the sub, I was struck by the pregnant posters' confident deployment of prenatal testing jargon. They used terms like *fetal fraction* and *SCA panel* and *soft markers* without elaboration. They spoke like scientists studying their own pregnancies. But they were also devastated and anxious, parents getting comfortable with their potential grief. An ambiguous finding abruptly forked the path of their pregnancies, splitting their loyalties. They wanted nothing more than to have their baby, or to avoid having their baby, depending on the result.

One day, I watched a woman break the first rule of the sub—she posted about a NIPT test with normal results. She worried that the results were wrong and wondered if she ought to repeat the test. *All came back with low probability but I'm still worried about a false negative result, since we would terminate if there is any genetic issues,* she wrote. I read the post again. She would terminate if there were *any* genetic issues? I had never posted a comment before, but now I thumbed in a response late at night. I told her that even a second test could never rule out *any genetic issues,* but that this was not as worrisome as it seemed. *You can't control for everything in pregnancy, and I'm ultimately grateful for that, because my son is amazing!,* I wrote.

It felt like I had a time machine, like I could travel back to my pregnant self and give her the gift of knowledge. But when I read my comment again, it looked canned and aggressive. My enthusiasm was a thin disguise for my irritation at the words she had used. I knew that past-me would dismiss the perspective of present-me, suspect that she was desperate and lying to herself. Past-me saw a prenatal diagnosis as a tragedy; present-me knew that no tragedy had occurred. Present-me believed that if past-me had gotten an abortion based on that diagnosis, *that* would have represented a kind of tragedy. But if past-me had gotten the abortion, present-me would not be present-me, and there would be no child to reveal my mistake.

As I typed out the comment, I felt omniscient. When I saw my words on the screen, my powers dissipated. No one acknowledged them or replied. Alma's birth slammed the door between my parent-self and my pregnant-self, and now I was knocking, asking her to let me back in.

The first picture of Alma ever posted to the internet showed him resting on a lounger, arms above his head, tongue sitting on his bottom lip. Marc tweeted it when Alma was one week old, announcing the birth. In the stream of congratulation, strangers waded in with advice. His image prompted theories, demanded explanations. It looked like he could have a tongue tie, they said. We should investigate getting it snipped. Marc messaged these people, informed them Alma had BWS, and assured them we were on top of all tongue-related matters. One of them deleted her tweet.

Alma's image was vulnerable, but it was powerful, too. I had seen many clinical photos of kids with BWS, their eyes covered with anonymizing black bars. Online fundraisers featured photographs that emphasized the child's dire medical situation. They were snapped in hospital settings, cased with sensors, their tongues stretched out as if to prove the extent of their need. On the internet it could seem that our children were defined by the medical system. But inside the camera app on my phone, I could reverse these images shot by shot. I thought of bell hooks's insight in *Art on My Mind: Visual Politics*, where she writes about how "the camera became in black life a political instrument, a way to resist misrepresentation as well as a means by which alternative images could be produced." Also, as she put it, "Taking pictures was fun!"

As I photographed Alma, I reveled in his beauty and verve. I documented his ingenuity as he learned to drink and eat and comfort himself with his own tongue, placing it against Marc's shoulder and sucking on his shirt until his eyelids dropped and his breath slowed.

I admired how the tongue emerged from his mouth, a pink half-moon, as he concentrated on a task, and how it pulsed softly as he slept. In *Beasts of Burden: Animal and Disability Liberation,* Sunaura Taylor writes about "the sensuality, the unruliness, the beautiful potential of living alternative ways of moving through space and of being in time." I didn't like that Jumbo Jr. had to take flight for the circus to accept him, but I loved the scene with his mother, when his ears transformed into the soft material of his own baby blanket.

As I scrolled back through my Instagram feed later, I noticed something. First Alma's tongue was inside his mouth, then outside it. Inside, then out. In many of the pictures I shot, his tongue was long and thick, protruding to his chin, but these never made it to the grid. In the ones I shared, his tongue usually rested between his lips, not quite in and not quite out. Schrodinger's syndrome.

With my vacillating posts, I seemed to be saying: *He is normal, but he is different, but mostly normal—only a little different.* Every new photograph seemed like an opportunity to signal his difference or to obscure it. In "On Photography," Susan Sontag describes photography as a tool of family storytelling, but also a defense against anxiety. Photographs "help people to take possession of space in which they are insecure," she writes. I realized that I was trying to use my phone in both ways at once, to build our family story while putting myself at ease. I wanted everyone to delight in Alma as easily as I did, but I also did not want to have to justify him to anyone. And so, on Instagram, I hid a part of him from the world.

There was one place where I felt I could share more freely. A pediatrician Marc contacted suggested that we consider joining a parent support group but advised us to find one moderated by a legitimate advocacy organization. There are *a lot of nutty groups online,* she wrote. *Alien DNA etc etc.* Instantly, I searched for BWS groups on Facebook and requested access. I wasn't sure who was

moderating them, and I didn't care. Just the size of the groups—
they had thousands of members—steadied me. When they unlocked
their doors, I slipped inside gratefully.

Parents shared stories, concerns, and photos of their children,
in sickness and in health. Often they attached an image of a smiling
child to their posts, in the hopes that the Facebook algorithm would
not bury their contribution in its algorithmic feed. A typical post
ended with the phrase: *Photo so this doesn't get lost.* The groups were
not straightforwardly reassuring. Often they coursed with uncertainty and pain. But the groups were comforting in a deeper way,
in the shared framework they presented for our children's lives.
Through reading the posts, I familiarized myself with the contradictions of my role. I started to work out how to embrace Alma's
BWS while preparing ourselves for the distress that it could cause,
in operating rooms and on playgrounds.

The parents in the BWS groups told stories about how their kids
were perceived. Every ignorant comment could be inscribed into
our secret book: the pediatrician at an appointment who said, *She
might not go to Harvard;* the grandmother at the aquarium who said,
That baby looks retarded. Every word felt torpedoed straight at my
son. I had encountered the word *retarded* only infrequently since
junior high school, but now it seemed to follow me around. Most
kids with BWS did not have intellectual disabilities, but some other
children with large tongues, like kids with Down syndrome, did.
The grandmother at the aquarium had said, *Oh, sorry you heard me,
your Down syndrome baby is cute, you know that.* That slur, *retarded*,
was a blunt reminder of the punishment exacted at any suspicion of
difference. As I read about these encounters, I prickled with guilt
over the relief I experienced after Alma's brain scan. Even before he
was born, he had been slotted into a hierarchy of disability; doctors
had spoken of potential syndromes as if the medical system main-

tained a hidden internal ranking of them all. The barely contained subtext was that physical disabilities were preferable to intellectual ones. Which would also mean that a child's pain was an acceptable cost for a typical brain.

The parents I encountered online differed in their approach to disclosing their children's diagnoses, especially on the open internet. Some of them wanted to guard their kids' medical privacy; others wanted to present their whole selves proudly to the world. My mind marched restlessly between their camps. If I revealed nothing, I worried that it meant I was ashamed of my son's condition. But if I emphasized it, it meant that I felt he needed an affirmative defense. I resented the idea that he needed to be explained, but I also wanted to smooth his entry into the world. To find the combination of words and images that would secure his easy acceptance.

Though BWS was rare, the world of social influence was vast enough that I found a handful of accounts where parents posted about having kids with the syndrome. I followed them and watched them perform our life in the form of a burlesque. I looked closely at the creators who did not theme their whole online projects around the kids but who nevertheless integrated them into their personas. There was a nonbinary apocalypse-themed baker who danced while gesticulating to their daughter's symptoms in floating text bubbles, and the father of an extreme-couponing family who bought items on clearance and resold them on eBay and Amazon. His fourth child's BWS diagnosis, he said in a video titled "Never Give Up!!," set them on the path to couponing. Their son's extended hospital stay did not stop them. *We bought more stuff,* he said. *We couponed harder.* Images of a baby fitted with sensors and tubes cut to a panning shot of a vast storeroom. Inside were stacks of detergent bottles and cereal boxes. The video ended with a nod to the family's many doubters and haters. *You weren't there at our lowest. You don't need to be here during our best,* it said. Also, *Shout out to the doctor that told us to terminate the pregnancy.*

During my own pregnancy, I resented the doctor who suspected my baby had a syndrome, but now I realized how many parents suffered from the reverse position. They suspected a diagnosis that their doctors denied. Alma's diagnosis was a ticket that guaranteed automatic entry to a protective protocol for newborn care, early intervention services, specialists who dedicated their careers to him. Many BWS posts I encountered on Instagram and TikTok were crafted under a framework of *raising awareness.* I had always been confused as to why it was important to make others aware—it seemed superficial and insufficient as a cure for anything—but now I understood the appeal. If a parent did not realize that their child had BWS, or their doctors dismissed the suspicion, then the kid could not get a genetic test, or a diagnosis, or early cancer screenings, and he could face potentially life-threatening complications as a result.

I followed a Pennsylvania mother named Theresa Thomas, who posted on TikTok under the name @largerthanbws, and I watched a video she posted under the trending prompt *Show your baby as a newborn vs. now.* It opened with a shot of a big-cheeked newborn, sleeping in a lap, sucking on his own big tongue as if it were a natural pacifier, just like Alma did. Then—*pop!*—he became a mop-haired little boy with a toothy smile. In this TikTok trend, the videos with the most dramatic transformations traveled further on the app, and this one had been viewed more than four million times. I picked through the comments that stuck to it like old chewing gum. There were heart emojis, laugh emojis, skull emojis. Some expressed confusion: *Why TF is this on my fyp.* Others just said *Nauseating* or *Terrible* or: *i'd send it back.*

When I called Thomas, in 2024, she told me that she started posting about her son's BWS in the hopes of finding someone who understood her experience. "I felt very alone," she said. Through a blog and then social media accounts, she started connecting with other families affected by BWS, and soon her posts were attracting the attention of other lost parents seeking guidance. She lived close to the Children's Hospital of Philadelphia (CHOP), an institution with a leading BWS clinic, and she embraced the opportunity to publicize its resources. She helped parents pursue diagnoses; she scheduled playdates for their kids. But she also heard from strangers with no connection to BWS who insulted her son and judged her parenting choices. "I would have people saying horrible things about him, and then I would have people saying that I'm exploiting him, and I could never wrap my brain around that," she said. "Just because other people are ignorant about it doesn't mean that I have to keep him hidden."

For an isolated parent, TikTok could be a site of connection, a seed for growing an intimate community. But when a video went viral, the audience transformed. A mother could submit her child's image to the internet's awareness-raising machine only to watch an audience tear greedily through the pictures, performing repulsion and accusing the parents of seeking clout. As I scrolled through the @largerthanbws page, I noticed how Thomas's presentation of her son seemed pulled and shaped by the crowd. Like many babies with BWS, he grew big and fast. Over the years, he underwent two tongue-reduction surgeries, and the size of his tongue in relationship to his body fluctuated over time. Some strangers would alight on her feed and leave shocked at the size of her son's tongue, or his body. But others would act confused, even suspicious, suggesting that he was perfectly healthy. In one video, Thomas might reply to a stranger who accused her of failing to manage her son's weight; in another, to a stranger who suggested he required no care at all. Even as she worked to normalize his existence, she was compelled to publish receipts of vulnerable moments, to prove his identity as medically complex and her own competence as his caretaker.

As her son got older, Thomas started asking him for permission to post stories from his life to her feeds, and she refocused her storytelling on herself. She documented her long recovery from spinal surgery and her progress in the gym. She launched a podcast with a friend about mental health. "In the first year of his life, I lost who I was," Thomas told me. "I almost took on his BWS. Not as, like, a 'persona,' but it is all-consuming. And I didn't want our life to be that way."

The accounts of BWS parents gifted me with public representations of children like Alma. But social media algorithms misread my interest as a broader enthusiasm for child medical content. Soon my feeds coursed with unrelenting pediatric dramas. My phone became a virtual hospital ward, staffed with parents proffering updates on their *rare genetic kid* or their *special needs spice*. I had just become a mother, but already I had been assigned a subidentity: the medical mom.

The prototypical medical mom was a mom who executed at the highest levels. Simultaneously a long-suffering caretaker and a fearless combatant, she meticulously managed her child's complex medical needs, documented her family's challenges, and fused her identity with her child's condition. Her central struggle was fighting the medical establishment to get it to accept her unique form of expertise and reward her family with adequate care. Through grief, rage, and financial insecurity, she endured. Instagram and TikTok surfaced scores of women who had appointed themselves representatives of the group, each with their own affective style.

The medical mom posted images of little IV ports and feeding tubes set to repeating choruses from Sia songs. Or she shared imageless earth-toned squares with somber quotations like: *My child's health issues have changed me forever.* You could find her soliloquizing about her child's struggle from the dark edge of a hospital bed, a front-facing smartphone camera illuminating her fatigued expression. Or else weeping in front of a dashcam in a parked SUV, her bewildered child just out of frame. She identified as a *hospital mom,* a *rare mom,* or a *disability mom.* She quilted together a community through hashtags like *#healthanxiety, #disabilitylife, #NICUlife, #specialneedsreallife, #tubefed, #griefwarrior.* The biggest medical moms had steroidal followings—in the hundreds of thousands, in the millions—and their children occasionally became famous, their medical journeys aggregated by *Us Weekly* and E! Online.

I circled this new identity at an alarmed distance. I meticulously managed nothing. Marc was the one who was on top of all the medical stuff. He made the appointments, monitored the online portal, ordered the nasal cannulas, ordered the smaller nasal cannulas when those nasal cannulas were too large, reminded me of the hospital staffers' names, saved their phone numbers, found specialists, found alternate specialists to those specialists. I read an inspirational quote online that said, *Medical moms are the equivalent of Batman, Captain America, and the Incredible Hulk, all rolled into one, with a side of Mary Poppins.* But I was just the equivalent of me, rolled into a hospital waiting room. Sometimes Marc would ask me to raise a sensitive issue with a doctor: "They listen more when it comes from the mom," he would say. It didn't matter who I was or what I did. I was perceived as having supreme authority over the body of my child.

The medical mom crafted an identity for her kids, too. She

described them as *strong, resilient,* and *brave.* As *warriors.* I was struck by the tireless promotion of these clichés. It felt like they were trying to convince a skeptical public who saw our kids as pitiful and unfortunate. And I wondered how the children themselves internalized those words. It was not always clear what the children, those warriors, were fighting against. Unlike the compliant soldier, the warrior is iconoclastic. He wages a lonely battle. I was not eager to cast my baby as a superhero, to build his psyche to those rigid specifications. And I also knew that one of the forces he might come to battle was me.

As Alma grew, a backlash mounted against the practice of sharing images of children online, and some critiques called out medical moms for special censure. In a 2023 article for *The Washington Post,* Fortesa Latifi questioned the costs of growing up with one's intimate medical events streamed for an audience. Every ambulance ride. Every intubation. Adults with disabilities described it as a dual betrayal: a child's autonomy revoked first by the medical system, then by her own parents. The camera's presence in the hospital room converted treatment into a monetizable scene—one that was sometimes leveraged to cover the child's medical bills. As if the quality of care were contingent on the strength of the performance.

I wondered if some of these medical parents posted out of a magical belief in their own attention—that if they witnessed their child's hardships closely enough, they could neutralize them. "I really wanted to protect her by sharing online so that people could understand her story before they met her," one medical mom with seven million TikTok followers told *The Washington Post.* "And then she wouldn't be faced with so many questions." Only when I read her quote back again did I register how bizarre it was—a mother's fantasy that she could clear a path for her child via repeated viral exposure of her body.

Even as the medical mom sought acceptance for her disabled child, her performance glorified the able-bodied mother and her sacrificial drive. The impossible standards of intensive parenting "pose particular dilemmas for disabled mothers," the sociologist Angela Frederick writes. For all the criticism visited upon medical moms and their kids, it was mild compared to the comments I saw under the accounts of parents who were themselves disabled. On Instagram, I watched Alyssa Higgins, a wheelchair user, demonstrate how she bottle-fed her newborn using a special band to position the baby in her lap on the chair, and when I swiped up to read the comment section, I saw that it had been defaced. *Really didn't need to have a child . . .* , one commenter said. Another said, simply: *I'm not ok with this.*

I never posted images of Alma in medical settings, or in distress for any reason. And yet I was familiar with the currency of his pain. When I spoke the words *children's hospital* in conversations with colleagues or friends, sympathy rushed my way. I was privileged that my medical duties were not all-consuming, that I could keep my regular job, that my private insurance funded the majority of Alma's care. And that I could write a book about my feelings instead of projecting them into a TikTok sideshow. The internet medical moms poked at the raw skin of my new identity. They amplified my most anxious and vain impulses. How badly I wanted *my own* experience understood. How selfishly I wanted *my own* sacrifice affirmed. I sliced off little bits of my child's life and turned them into content, too.

Outside of the glow of TikTok, people with disabilities and their parents were subjected to a broader surveillance. Families were sometimes threatened with separation if they failed to meet unarticulated standards of care and attention. When I searched medical journals for Beckwith-Wiedemann syndrome, I also found a handful of lawsuits that mentioned the syndrome in their statements of facts. The lawsuits were custody disputes. In each case, the state had removed a child with BWS from his birth parents and assigned him to an alternate caretaker or made him a ward of the state. These cases began when a doctor or social worker raised a flag about the parent's ability to handle the child's complex medical needs. The cases only filtered into the legal database when parents fought them long and hard enough to spark appeals, and yet I was surprised by the number I found: three.

The cases were anonymized, and I could not investigate them beyond the facts selected for inclusion by the court, but some of the arguments were distressing on their face. In one case, a mother living in poverty argued that, in a court-facilitated visitation of her son with BWS, she had "exhibited some of the parenting skills necessary" to care for him: she "held him throughout the visit, stroked his face, fed him, changed his diaper and took pictures of him on her cellphone." Though this is all normal parenting behavior, the court did not think it was good enough, because it had decided her child was not normal. Only the child's court-appointed "resource parent," the court decided, was "attentive to the special needs occasioned by Beckwith-Wiedemann Syndrome."

This was the voice of the state speaking—it was speaking on our behalf. If a mother who strokes her baby's face and takes pictures of him on her cell phone can't singlehandedly manage his complex medical needs (along with the needs of her three older children), the state will not step in to help her in every way possible; it will take her baby. As I scrolled back through these cases, I noted the years when the children were removed—2016, 2014, 2008. I did the math in my head, calculating the long cold absences of their kids. Every parent who filed an appeal lost.

When I reread my hospital records from Alma's birth, I noticed something I had not seen before: a two-page "psychosocial assessment" of me, written by a social worker. I had not understood why she had visited me, other than that the hospital had sent an endless supply of disturbances to my room during my stay. I wondered if a social worker visited every mother with a child in the NICU, or if a nurse had pointed me out after seeing me crying while holding Alma in the nursery. "I'm just so worried about him," I told her. As I read through the social worker's report, I was struck by what it included. It noted that I was *cooperative and alert*. It noted that Marc and I had learned of the diagnosis in pregnancy, had consulted with a genetic physician, were seeking a sleep study to evaluate Alma for apnea. It noted that we lived together, that we had *all baby provisions,* and that we were both newspaper reporters. It noted that I was *breastfeeding and pumping*. It noted my *criminal justice status* (none), whether I was *known to CPS* (no), and whether I *received cash assistance benefits* (also no). It did not note that I had ingested prescription drugs during my pregnancy.

Later I sent the psychosocial report to my friend Sarah, a social worker who works to defend families whose children have been removed. "Yeah, that's the cops," she said. The social worker visit can lead in different directions depending on whether the mother is white or not, rich or poor, she said. A social worker could be dispatched to help connect a mother to resources for postpartum depression or to alert child protective services. Years after his birth, I was still working out my relationship to Alma's diagnosis, trying to understand what it meant for my own identity. Now I realized that my performance had been watched and rated from the moment he was born. It felt like the eye of the state had scanned me and recommended me for a provisional stamp of approval. But I hadn't really done anything. I had just touched his face and taken his picture with my phone.

When Alma was three months old, Marc and I drove him to Pennsylvania for two days of appointments at the Children's Hospital of Philadelphia. Over the next few years, he would see many experts there. The words *children's hospital* once scared me, but now they brought relief. The facility's vast atrium suggested the scale of competent care that revealed itself to us there. Its exam and waiting rooms were fitted with televisions streaming Disney Junior, so Alma absorbed reruns of a computer-animated program called *Mickey Mouse Clubhouse* while he whimpered through an ultrasound examination of his distended belly, a reenactment in miniature of my own exams during pregnancy. It was a punishing day of appointments, and also January 6, 2021, and as my phone pulsed with news alerts about an attempted coup, I annoyedly swatted them away. I understood why a parent might fashion an identity centered around the hospital, devote herself to investigating its complexities.

On that first visit, I was asked whether I wanted to enroll Alma in a BWS research study and consent to the collection of his information and genetic material in a biorepository. Marc and I agreed that we ought to support the research. But it felt eerie, signing on Alma's behalf, as if his body were mine. The consent form briefed me on the risks of the study. If a participant's medical information were somehow leaked, it could affect his *stigmatization* and *insurability*, it said. It could affect his social value or his monetary value; he could be seen to be worth less. The researchers asked for vials of blood, tissue left over from surgeries, a cheek swab, and photographs that could be used for *research analysis, publication in medical journals,* and *materials to advertise the registry,* including *brochures, broadcasting,* and *print media.* I signed my initials consenting to the blood, the tissue, and the swab, but not the photos. I would let them have his flesh but not his image.

A few years later, the hospital reached out with a new research request: it wanted to study me. It sent me an online survey seeking to understand the psychological effects of acting as a caregiver to a child with BWS, and as I completed it, I was surprised to find its questions surfaced thoughts and reactions that I had experienced as intensely personal. The survey asked me about my *fear, horror, anger, guilt,* and *shame.* But also about my resilience, my shifting priorities, my faith in other human beings. It had been composed by a young researcher at CHOP named Rachel Ottman, as a part of her dissertation on the psychological effects of medical diagnosis in children. Ottman had BWS herself, and I had seen her weigh in occasionally on the BWS Facebook groups, waving invitingly at distressed parents and generously detailing her own experience.

After I took the survey, I called Ottman, and I asked her what had made her interested in the caregiver's experience. She told me that at first, she was not interested in us. She had hoped to study children directly, but the most intense medical interventions related to the syndrome are concentrated in the first years of life. By the time the kids could speak for themselves, they would not remember. So she studied their parents instead, investigating how their psychological responses could come to affect their kids.

I asked Ottman how she felt about parents sharing their kids' medical information online, and she said, "It's tough. I can see both sides of it." Regardless of how they navigate that choice, "it's important for families to co-create a narrative around BWS that is positive and kind of embraces it," she said. When Ottman was a kid, she and her mother experienced "an intertwining" between their identities, she said. "That can happen when a BWS child has a strong medical advocate in their family, which is needed." As she got older, her medical needs lessened dramatically, and that shifted her identity and her relationships, too. "For a caregiver," she said, "I can imagine it can feel hard to let go."

On the internet, it could seem that Alma was me, that I was him. But this was not the case. When Marc and I brought him to the hospital for the sleep test, it was Alma's body fixed with sensors and wrapped in gauze. At his quarterly ultrasound scans, it was his shirt pulled up, his stomach bared, his organs on view. Later, when Alma neared three years old and his surgeon finally recommended a tongue-reduction operation, it would be his body deadened with anesthesia, his tongue cut down, his tissue preserved in the bio-repository. It would be his mind awaking to a pain and confusion that I could not foresee and that medicine could not easily resolve. But lasting memories of these events would persist only with me. Whether or not I posted about them online, I had to decide how to integrate them into his sense of self, and my own.

In 2023, the summer before Alma turned three, I went to a BWS conference at CHOP where all the characters of these narratives converged: parents, doctors, kids, and adults. We made an audience together in front of a giant slideshow screen, then lined up to poke at cocktail meatballs with toothpicks. I scanned the faces in the conference room, trying to match them with thumbnail photos from Facebook. A few days earlier, Marc and I had agreed to the surgery and scheduled it for just after Alma's third birthday. I wove through the conference grounds until I found a group of parents whose children had the procedure at a similar age. Then I sat in on a session on the relationship between BWS and assistive reproductive technologies. The incidence of BWS in the IVF population was many times greater than in the general population, and a researcher was running experiments on mouse embryos to try to understand why. When she finished her presentation, one of the mothers raised her hand.

She had more of a comment than a question. The woman's daughter had been conceived via IVF, and she had been watching the research closely, investigating the potential causes of her condition. She wondered whether IVF companies had unleashed lucrative technologies on babies without concern for the unintended consequences. "Is there a class-action lawsuit in this story? Because I've been waiting," she said. "Any other mouse in the room—come talk to me." After the session, the mother pointed me to a group of clinics that performed preimplantation genetic testing on embryos, assuring parents that the process would produce a healthy child. She wondered whether the hubristic effort to create a genetically perfect child had in fact triggered a genetic change. "It's like *Frankenstein*," she said.

For so long I had wondered about what caused Alma's condition. I worried over what I had done to trigger it, over the dark secret of my body that had determined his suffering. But the more I cared for him, the longer I spent as his mother, the less this seemed to matter. I realized my great luck now: I had no outside entity to blame, no corporation to fight to make us whole again. If this was "like *Frankenstein*," that would make Alma a monster and me a tragic figure. I did not believe this about us or anyone else. We were just made this way. And each day, we remade each other.

Chapter 10

Judgment

When Alma was ten months old, we moved into a new apartment a couple of miles away, with a bedroom for Alma and a washer-dryer stacked next to the fridge. In that place, Alma learned to crawl, then walk, then run and jump and launch himself off the couch. He learned to pick things up, drop them, whack them against each other, and throw them across the room. He learned to open doors and slam them. He learned to sing. He learned to blow bubbles, to spill all the bubble solution, and to pound the floor in desperation. In time he would learn to perform many of these behaviors simultaneously.

The only thing that he did not seem to pick up easily was how to *not* do these things. When he was eighteen months old, new neighbors moved into the apartment beneath us, and a few days later, I found a plate of white-chocolate cookies wrapped in plastic and a note sitting on our doormat.

Fuck.

I knew that the building was loud. The floorboards above us cranked and squeaked. Voices routed mysteriously through the walls. I could hear a man greasing his clients over the phone, a girl practicing show tunes, a woman disciplining her cat. I could only imagine the macabre domestic drama that emanated from our unit. The note contained a phone number. I arranged a call with the downstairs neighbors, who seemed to be a young couple. On the call I was the quietest person on earth; no one had ever been quieter than me. The neighbors described disturbing thuds, racing steps, random screams. I pitched my voice into a gentle lilt. As if screaming were a concept I had learned about only through dedicated academic study. I empathized, I apologized, I promised to guide Alma away from specific rooms at specific hours. I pledged to buy another rug. I also suggested that, Alma being a human child, successfully regulating his body and voice was a project that could take many years.

For the next few months, the neighbors and I texted passively about his noise, as if sliding a virtual plate of cookies back and forth. Occasionally, my phone would ping with a note like: *Hi Amanda. Hope all is well! There seems to be quite a bit of noise coming from the apartment, it sounds like something is being dropped or bounced,* and I would assure them I would confiscate the offending object, though I knew that he would easily find another. I felt like Alma's crisis communications manager, absorbing public disapproval and spinning his critics. When I got pregnant with Brayden, I called the neighbors to warn them of the new development.

When he arrived, just after Alma's second birthday, I got a text from an unfamiliar number. The neighbors also had a new roommate, I learned, and this person had instantly secured my number and assumed control of the noise-complaint process. Their style was blunt and uncompromising, though these were not the words I used to describe them to Marc. As I rocked a whimpering Brayden in the morning, Marc weaved and bobbed through the apartment, trying to catch Alma and escort him out the door to daycare, only for Alma to escape his clutches and race back down the hall. Ping: *i hear someone running around with shoes on and it's really loud,* the roommate texted. My unnerving niceness had no effect on my new correspondent. Their annoyed texts were the new soundtrack to our eight a.m. exodus from the house. Ping: *i'm being repeatedly woken up this morning.* Ping: *Please quiet down above my room. I am being repeatedly woken up in the mornings now.* Ping: *Hey someone is being really loud above my room.*

I bought vaster rugs and thicker pads and sweated through my shirt rolling them under couches and beds. (Ping: *Hey did you put the rug in the bedroom? I was woken up again this morning.*) Each time, before I texted back, I reapplied my ghastly nice-mommy mask. I did not say: *Quiet hours in our building end at seven a.m., after which my baby and toddler will unfortunately be unable to maintain a monk-like silence.* I did not say: *To me it is odd that you sleep past 8 in the morning, good for you though!* I imagined that the remoteness of text messaging made the roommate more aggressive and relentless than they might have been in person, but it had the opposite effect on me. If they had come upstairs and yelled at me, I would have yelled back. But inside my phone I felt compelled to project the persona of the obsequious mom. As the roommate and I texted about my loud children, viral posts about loud children climbed atop my social feeds, dispensing parenting advice like: *If your child can't reliably obey the command "quiet" they don't belong in public spaces where they can bother others,* and: *Parents. Stop bringing your annoying shithead kids to the supermarket.*

The more I tried to contain Alma, the more implausible this pursuit became. Invitations to deep-breathe or scream into a pillow were met with seconds-long periods of compliance. Marc and I took him outside for hours, but we could not do this for, literally, every hour of every day. Toddler experts who proffered tips on Instagram to desperate parents advised us to physically remove an unruly toddler who was disrupting a public space. But our apartment was the private space we were supposed to haul him back to. I felt lousy for trying to stop Alma from letting loose in his own home. I didn't think he was doing anything wrong. But I was also aware that my neighbor thought *I* was doing something wrong. It had happened faster than I had imagined. Somebody thought I was a bad mom.

I never met the roommate, I never spoke to them on the phone, but text messaging provided unlimited access to me. They could make judgment radiate up through the floorboards, issue a performance rating at any time. The texts were significantly more upsetting than the blunt bang of a broom handle on the ceiling (a technique the roommate also employed). Whenever my phone vibrated in my hand in the morning, it felt like being shocked by a novelty buzzer. What impossible situation was I expected to mitigate now? I started to think about the neighbor so frequently, it was as if they had walked upstairs and moved right in. When Alma threw himself on the floor, crying, I thought of the roommate. When he jumped gleefully, singing a song he wrote himself, I thought of the roommate. When I got up to feed Brayden in the middle of the night, I thought of the roommate. When we left the apartment, I thought of the roommate still, as they had expanded in my mind to embody all the judgment that I imagined radiating toward the parents of young children. It was the first time, but not the last, that I would understand that being seen as a "good parent" by strangers was not the same as being a good parent to my kids.

My anxiety over the texts reached its height one afternoon in May 2023. I had been offered a fellowship at an artists' retreat to work on this book, and I guiltily left Marc alone with the kids while I moved into a little cabin and typed for two weeks. It was the first time I had been alone in three years. I told myself that I would "unplug" in this place, and I tuned the alarm clock to a Christian talk-radio station, so that I would awake in the morning not to a child screaming through a monitor but to a megachurch pastor assuring me that *God has a dream for your life far greater than one you could ever dream of on your own*. My body stretched into a life outside of the apartment, my mind wandering past my family's immediate needs. On the tenth day, the roommate buzzed my phone. The complaint found me in my quiet forest cabin, hundreds of miles away. It said: *This is so loud.* It was four p.m. on a Sunday, and I knew that rain had been pummeling Brooklyn for days. I explained that Marc was alone with a toddler and a baby, and that I imagined that the weather had only intensified the difficulty level of the situation. The roommate replied: *we are also stuck inside because of the rain.* I imagined shaking them by the shoulders in the psychic split-level living room we shared. *You are not a baby,* I wanted to say. *You are a childless adult. You can hold an umbrella over your head. You can sit in a chair in a coffee shop and sip a hot drink. You can sit on a bar stool and have a cold one instead. You can walk down the steps to our subway station and ride it wherever you please. You can put noise-canceling headphones over your ears and take a nap. You are free!*

Marc told me to block the number, but I couldn't let it go. There in my cabin, where I was supposed to be writing, I googled the roommate instead. The internet footprint was frustratingly sparse, so I built an imagined personality profile out of scraps of online materials. I stalked through Reddit boards like r/childfree and r/neighborsfromhell, where I read long, unsparing complaints about demonic kids and oblivious parents. Sometimes videos appeared, recording screaming kids through the walls. Commenters recommended calling 911 or child protective services. I imagined the posters delivering their judgments directly to my face. When I had visited the r/NIPT board, I was casting about for women I could fashion into adversaries, but this time, I was looking for strangers who saw a villain in me. As I moved around as a parent in the world, I sometimes got the eerie sense that I was being watched. The internet intensified this phenomenon and clarified it. I wanted the objections to my parenthood to be stated plainly, for the subtext to become text.

Did the internet reveal the judgments that stalked me just outside of my awareness? Or did it conjure judgment where none existed? When I told Marc what I was doing, he said, "*Of course* you followed the subreddits that made you into the bad guy." His impulse was to seek out content that made him feel better. My impulse was to find content that made me feel worse. Strangers brought me their judgments, and I brought them upon myself.

Reddit's r/childfree sub was a community for *those who do not have and do not ever want children (whether biological, adopted, or otherwise)*. Its 1.5 million members convened to compare notes on birth control methods, discuss how they enjoyed their copious free time, and vent about the kids with whom they were occasionally forced to interact. Many of my best friends did not have kids, and I often identified with them more easily than I did the parents in my life. But I was not on Reddit to delight in our similarities; I was there to read posts about how children were disgusting and their parents reprehensible. I wanted to know just how selfish these strangers thought I was.

I clicked eagerly on posts that called kids *trophies* and *accessories*, *crappers* and *turds*, *crotchgoblins* and *spawn*. Similar complaints surged on TikTok and Twitter, where they reached parents directly. I made a mental list of the spaces where children were unwelcome: Restaurants, breweries, libraries, planes, grocery stores, sidewalks. Apartment buildings, of course. Often, the posters boasted of how well-behaved they were as small children (though it was improbable that they could remember much about such a young age) and directed their contempt at the parents who failed to modulate their children's behavior. (I did not say: *Actually, child development experts advise us to underreact.*) Screens, and the millennial parent's overuse of them, were often to blame. Young adults monologued into TikTok about the scourge of *iPad kids,* children who were said to terrorize society whenever they snapped out of their YouTube-induced dissociative fugues.

As I skulked around the childfree internet, Reddit suggested that I follow another sub: r/antinatalism. The antinatalists regarded children with more pity than rage, but they cut deeper into parents like me, mounting a more profound philosophical critique: It didn't matter where we brought them or how they behaved. It was morally indefensible to have children at all. The melting of the polar ice caps, the rise of authoritarianism, the existence of childhood anxiety and depression, the global spread of novel viruses—all of these contributed to the case against procreation, which one user referred to as a process of generating *dying painmeat.* The antinatalists threw the book at me. As one poster put it, *it is inherently immoral to bring a new life into a cruel and unforgiving reality masked by the comforts of modern life.* Another posted a meme in the sub, written from the perspective of a gape-mouthed baby staring optimistically upward. *TRADE OFFER,* it said. *I receive: the burden of human consciousness. You receive: a false sense of purpose in your monotonous existence.*

It was somewhat pleasurable to imagine sparring with the people who wanted kids barred from public life. But faced with the objections of the antinatalists, my mind spun unproductively. Before I got pregnant, I agonized about whether I was ready to become a parent, but I never considered whether my future children would want to exist. Now that they were here, news of unnatural weather patterns and school shootings followed me around like cartoon rain clouds.

I, too, had often viewed the world as a cruel and unforgiving reality masked by the comforts of modern life. And Alma's birth had lent a sense of purpose to my monotonous existence, had it not? One day, I logged on to Reddit and saw that an antinatalist poster had discovered BWS. They reposted a picture of a baby and said: *That simply seems unethical to let it be born with a adult tongue.* When another user accused the post of *nazism*, someone replied: *The point is to bring attention to childrens suffering.*

My children were vulnerable little babies, deserving of humanity's grace. But once the internet flagged them as "my" children—coded as my accessories, my possessions—strangers put their entire lives up for review. They were reduced to mere extensions of my own selfish decision to have children. After I put down my phone, I lugged their critiques along with me, heaved them onto the pile of judgments that had accumulated in my short time as a mom. In Reddit's stark digital scrolls, parenting was inscribed as a lifestyle choice—a poor one. There would be no support extended for those who opted in, only judgment. I was expected to raise my kids in isolation. Ideally in a manner that maximized the comfort of other adults.

When I hopped to Instagram, I found an antidote to this pessimistic view. As I rode around its pastel carousels, I learned that my decision to have children could indeed be justified, as long as I kept making the correct parenting choices again and again. First, I had to follow the right experts, implement the necessary tips. Together we could parent better, parent harder. We could change the world by making the best kids ever.

I was sitting at the playground's edge with my friend Sarah when she asked if I had heard of something called Big Little Feelings.

Sarah's daughter was six months older than Alma, and as they navigated the playground's rubberized structures, we traded notes on the various parenting gurus who were peddling their wares on our feeds. I had not heard of Big Little Feelings, but it felt familiar, probably because its name evoked the ubiquitous online rebranding of childhood where kids were referred to as *littles* and their most extreme behaviors were styled as *big feelings*.

When I typed *Big Little Feelings* into Instagram, I found Deena Margolin and Kristin Gallant, two women who were on a first-name basis with their 3.5 million followers. "Deena and Kristin" presented as white millennial moms from Denver. They styled themselves in stretchy headbands and messy buns, soft pants and minimal makeup. Their posting aesthetic, which featured blobs and rainbows rendered in muted pinks and earthy browns, felt indistinguishable from Flo's house style. *Tame those tantrums*, their bio said, followed by a tornado emoji and a link to an online course called Winning the Toddler Stage, priced at $99. Big Little Feelings' posts stretched back only a few years, to March 2020, when I was three months pregnant. Deena was pregnant for the first time then too, and she gave birth around the same time I did. Already they had become my generation's reigning toddler experts, as if they had been delivered to Instagram directly from Zeus's forehead.

Big Little Feelings, or BLF, fought the toddler wars on two fronts. Deena, a trained family therapist, delivered much of the advice on how to handle kids. Kristin, Deena's childhood best friend and a self-described *mom of two toddlers*, spoke to the parents, talking us through our own emotional outbursts. Every day, BLF issued fresh instructions on how to be *the cool, calm, confident leader of your home* who guides her toddlers to become *emotionally healthy adults*. As I scrolled down its feed, I absorbed an *easy hack to get your kid to stop screaming* and a *life-changing hack to avoid sibling rivalry* and a *really easy tip you can start using week to week to minimize the meltdowns* and then a sponsored ad for a new line of wooden toys from Fisher-Price. Eating paint, resisting baths, ruining the holiday family photo: any permutation of normal childhood behavior could trigger a specialized, expert tip. Often Deena and Kristin provided "scripts" for these scenarios and practiced them in front of the camera, playing both the parent and the toddler roles, ventriloquizing their followers' relationships with their own kids.

BLF, as Deena put it, was forged from the impulse to simplify the lessons of child psychology for busy parents. It was made for those who came to the internet pleading, *I'm so tired, tell me what to do and say!* Even as it instructed its followers precisely how to modulate their behavior to perform acceptably as parents, it sympathized with the impossibility of perfect compliance. In between tips, Kristin appeared in home-based montages, giving us permission to stop apologizing for our messy houses, to put our postpartum bodies into swimsuits, and to serve our kids pasta with butter for dinner because, as she'd come to realize, *pasta was self care.*

Whenever I opened Instagram, I got spun about in the BLF content feedback loop. The tips were inoffensive and often commonsensical, but they also assumed a stock two-year-old who responded to controlled scenarios in a predictable manner. If you tried a *hack* and it failed to *fix* your child, you could at least leave reassured that the experts, too, had been personally decimated by the work of parenting, which was *so hard*. I suspected that much of the content was less effective at "taming" a human being than it was at pacifying parents as they endured the unavoidable features of the toddler years. Even though I told myself that I checked BLF "for research," I occasionally heard lines from its scripts come out of my mouth, *Exorcist*-style, as Alma thrashed on the sidewalk or tossed his dinner plate to the floor. Sarah called the account a "security blanket for parents," an authority that they could reference to assure themselves that they had done everything right, even if the results failed to materialize.

BLF's relatable posts often referred casually to my *trauma*, which I was assumed to have sustained in childhood due to the suboptimal techniques employed by my own parents. The brand called its followers *generational cycle breakers* and suggested that our various personality quirks were the product of childhood neglect. *(Are you a chill, easygoing person or is it trauma?)* In one video offering, BLF seized a popular Instagram audio track and layered it over extended shots of a waterfall surging over a rock cliff. *Excessive overthinking is usually a trauma response from childhood where you were criticized too much and had to analyze everything you do just to feel accepted by your parents,* an unnervingly confident man said. *Because you're disconnected from your intuition, you feel like you're not enough. So you become a stressed-out career chaser trying to prove yourself.* When I searched for the source of the audio, I discovered that it was a monologue filmed by the life coach Ehsun Anwar, who instructed his followers in *freedom from stress, healthy relationships and easy weightloss.*

Was I vulnerable to *excessive overthinking?* See the past two hundred pages: yes. Was this a *trauma response* caused by overly critical parents? I wasn't so sure. BLF assured millennials that we were perhaps the first good parents who had ever existed. But its constant invocation of our trauma also served as a nudging reminder that we could easily fuck up our own kids if we failed to implement the recommended hacks. And it promoted a seductive fantasy: that, with enough research and development, parents could achieve psychological control over their kids. The BLF brand spoke of a toddler who could be *tamed*, with behavior that could be *hacked*, in a life stage that could be *won*. As parents worked to avoid reinscribing their own scarred personalities in their children's minds, they were advised to strategically promote positive experiences, a process the BLF experts called *laying down core memories.* Our kids could be programmed for optimal human life.

Big Little Feelings, Instagram's most popular parenting influencers, were grouped into a broader online movement that came to be known as *gentle parenting* or *conscious parenting.* As I absorbed its tips, I was served flashes of superior results. I watched a dad nuzzle his newborn's nose until his baby fell asleep smiling. I saw a seventeen-month-old toddler sucking on his pacifier as he capably maneuvered a snowboard down a ski hill. I witnessed a two-year-old unloading the family dishwasher, and a three-year-old preparing his own breakfast in his fully functional toddler kitchen (complete with hot plate and cereal dispenser), and a six-year-old steaming milk for his parents' morning espresso. After a while, my Instagram reels began to resemble a nostalgic advertisement for child labor. When I read the comments on these videos, I found that even these feats of parenting were not impressive enough. Of the little chef, they said: *Breakfast cereal is highly processed food. It has zero nutritional value. Give your child real food.*

Still, the parenting influencers posted on, congratulating themselves on their achievements and implying that nobody over forty had ever done it before. *Can we take a second to acknowledge that we are the first parent generation to apologize to our kids?* Deena asked in one reel. She led us through a thought exercise, where we envisioned our parents apologizing for yelling and telling us they loved us. *Imagine how different the world would be, and we are doing it. I'm very proud of us,* she said. On the subreddit r/parenting, users spoke of the highly evolved parenting advice millennials were blessed to receive. In the past, *parents wanted their children to be fed and bathed and if they got annoying they would beat them,* one poster said. Said another, *Yeah, lately I've been getting myself so down over how awful the world is turning: climate change, covid, racism, sexism, etc. But then I think about how far we've come in what we know about mental health and child development.*

After I found Big Little Feelings, I ordered an early edition of Dr. Benjamin Spock's *Common Sense Book of Baby and Child Care* from an online rare-books dealer, and it arrived bound in green linen with cracked gold letters across the spine. "Don't be over-awed by what the experts say," Spock writes in the book. "Don't be afraid to trust your own common sense." But this sentiment was betrayed by the book itself, which featured five hundred pages of expert instruction. First published in 1946, its many editions dominated the parenting advice genre for multiple generations. By the time Spock died, in 1998, it had sold fifty million copies.

My version, from 1948, was published a few years before my own parents were born; its pages were marked up with pinched cursive that recalled my dead grandmother's handwriting. The previous book's owner—a mother, I assumed—had charted the medical histories of her children in its thin pages. I read about Karen, Bruce, Paula, and Peter, and learned about their measles cases, broken bones, and polio vaccinations. In 1958, Peter suffered a serious accident: *tongue cut ¾ across,* the mother noted. As if sending me a message through the decades that our experiences were somehow aligned.

I paged through my copy, looking for evidence of the ignorant parenting instructions that millennials were finally dismantling. Instead, I found that the advice was virtually unchanged. Spock advised parents against scolding children, threatening them, punishing them, giving them time-outs, or shooting them cross looks. He advised them to embody the role of the "friendly leader," the parent who casually redirects their toddler with the full understanding that pushing boundaries is the child's job.

There were a few key differences between Spock and his millennial heirs. One, he counseled parents to consult pediatricians and child psychologists when they encountered trouble, whereas the new wave of experts often coached parents to operate in a therapeutic mode. Two, he referred to his reader as "the tired-out mother," whereas the modern gurus embodied that figure themselves. The paradigmatic millennial parenting guru was a professional white woman who nevertheless, as a friend put it to me, "posts videos where she looks like the Cryptkeeper." Her aesthetic of mess challenged the image of the midcentury housewife who clutched Spock's guide to her chest like it was the Bible. But she represented a different heightening of the mothering ideal. Now, from the moment her first child was born, she could be positioned not just as a student of parenting but as the expert herself.

The American studies professor Jay Mechling observed in 1975 that "childrearing manuals are the consequents not of childrearing values but of childrearing manual-writing values." The rise of Big Little Feelings may not say much about how millennial parents interact with their kids, but it revealed something about how they interact with their experts. I thought again of the BLF waterfall post. It had pegged excessive overthinking and career-chasing as a product of poor parenting, but I suspected that a more ubiquitous force was at play. In *Kids These Days: Human Capital and the Making of Millennials,* Malcolm Harris examines how millennials were raised under "an accelerated and historically unprecedented pace of change as capitalism emerged as the single dominant mode of organizing society. It's a system based on speed, and the speed is always increasing."

Millennials grew up fusing our identities to a neoliberal demand for hypercompetition. One possible response was to anxiously prime our children for achievement by taking on parenting as a kind of second career. In between absorbing parenting advice, reparenting herself, and working her actual job, a parent could find she had space for little else—and that didn't include the hours she spent actually spending time with her kids. Sometimes I wondered whether these Instagram experts were so popular because they made parents feel like they were looking out for their children even if they were just sitting in their workplaces, studying their phones.

Shortly after Alma was born, I read a kind of anti–parenting manual by the child psychologist Alison Gopnik called *The Gardener and the Carpenter*, then immediately forgot everything it said. I picked it up a few years later, when my mind was again capable of absorbing information. The idea of good parenting was a myth, Gopnik suggested in her 2016 book, because "parenting," as a careerist program schooling parents on raising children, was itself bad. The accumulation of expertise was no substitute for what she called "wisdom and competence," multigenerational communities, and traditions of mutual care between neighbors and friends. "In the past 30 years, the concept of parenting and the multibillion-dollar industry surrounding it have transformed child care into obsessive, controlling, and goal-oriented labor intended to create a particular kind of child and therefore a particular kind of adult," she writes. And yet this obsession with parenting had utterly failed to make children's lives better: "The United States, where all those parenting books are sold, also has the highest rates of infant mortality and child poverty in the developed world."

The parenting experts exulted in the decimation of tradition.

Now that American children had been raised through canned parenting advice for several generations, each new wave of parents could look back at the previous generation's product and rightfully announce that it had expired. The Instagram experts spoke of *breaking generational curses* in styling modern parenting advice as a revolution against all that had come before. When another expert, Dr. Becky Kennedy, sold what she described as a *record* number of gift memberships to her private advice platform, at Christmas in 2023, she said on Instagram: *This is cycle-breaking. This is the movement.* It . . . was a gift card. But she was not alone in promoting parenting products as political materials. Mary Van Geffen, who pitched herself as a teen-parenting expert versed in raising a flavor of child she called *spicy ones,* herself published a sappy monologue about parental apologies. *Can you imagine what it would be like to get a call from your parents saying: "You know what? I'm sorry. You were a child. I didn't have the tools. I didn't have calm class. I didn't have parent coaches on the internet,"* she said. *It's revolutionary.*

In June 2020, after Derek Chauvin murdered George Floyd, BLF posted a long message to Instagram punctuated by sparkle emojis emphasizing its points. *If we want our kids to lovingly show up and sit alongside someone who is hurting, someone who has been wronged, then we must sit alongside them when they are hurting or having big feelings (yes, even if they're having big feelings because their purple crayon is too "purpley"),* it said. Do this and *short term: your child will be the change we need in this world,* stepping up to stop *racism on the playground.* Long-term, *if we can JUST get this right, we will be building a generation of healthy, emotionally resilient, empathetic, powerful adults who will NO LONGER engage in the horrific acts of our current generation.* Hatch, the maternity brand, chimed in: *Your greatest contribution to the world may not be something you do, but who you raise.*

I was starting to believe that parenthood was inherently political. But the politics it produced were not automatically progressive. As a white, American "medical mom," society had awarded me a bizarre and unearned moral authority, which appeared to be its consolation prize for my withdrawal from public life. This was the Instagram-friendly, corporate-sponsored parenting revolution: sinking more energy into our own families, anxiously attending to our own children, caring for them with such focused intensity that they would grow up to spontaneously fix all the social problems we had gestured to along the way. Big Little Feelings appeared to be sincerely suggesting that racist police violence would not exist had Derek Chauvin's parents bought Winning the Toddler Stage for $99.

In 2022, the Big Little Feelings TikTok account picked up a meme that had been circulating on the platform. *I keep hearing it takes a village to raise a child,* a woman's voice said. *Do they just show up? Or is there a number to call?* The meme had passed from parent to parent, each one lip-syncing along to the track, as if speaking as one generational voice. Deena joined in, holding a toy in one hand and a bottle in the other. I understood the broadly relatable feeling invoked by the meme. The American model of parenting in the 2020s was a punishing and isolated ordeal. Still, it was depressing to watch a succession of influencers demand a community materialize as if it were a product they had added to their Instacarts.

In 2023, the joke of a dial-a-village became real. Deena and Kristin debuted a podcast, *After Bedtime,* a chat show that opened another monetizable peek into their imperfect family lives. *Real talk? Modern parenting is a doozy. Where the f*ck is that village every-*

one talks about? the promotional copy asked. Then it supplied the answer: *Consider* After Bedtime *your village.*

Where was the village that was supposed to raise our children? Traditionally it might have been found in previous generations of parents, the ones who were often disparaged on these parenting accounts. I was always seeing "relatable" parenting memes about how grandparents, in-laws, and other relatives were obnoxiously bent on sabotaging the millennial parent's enlightened approach. In this claustrophobic worldview, where only the expert parent was deemed capable of interacting with the child, a sense of community was safely routed through consumer technologies instead. The whole-genome prenatal test to assess the embryo's optimal health. The robot crib to soothe the baby. The artificially intelligent camera to spit out sleep tips. The parenting podcast to simulate the mom friend. The iPad to silence the toddler, and the downstairs neighbor, too. One of the Nanit's brand touchstones was: *No judgment.*

In "Revolutionary Parenting," bell hooks put it this way: "Child care is a responsibility that can be shared with other childrearers, with people who do not live with children," but not "if parents regard their children as their 'property,' their 'possession.' Many parents do not want their children to develop caring relationships with others, not even relatives." The hoarding of resources and attention also made it impossible for parents to make meaningful contributions outside of their own families. They could not care for other people's kids, or for their adult neighbors, either. It is a model that "isolates children and parents from society," hooks writes. The same forces that styled parenting as self-sacrificial also ensured that it would be entirely self-centered.

The more I versed myself in millennial parenting culture, the more I understood the deep annoyance of the most aggressive child-free posters, the ones who accused me of reproducing my blithe narcissism and loosing it upon society in the form of snot-nosed kids. But the solution to the selfishness of parenting culture was not to drive families further into insulated private lives. It was to rebuild the public world for the collective benefit of all people. And children are people.

There was such a thing as a good parent, I decided. One defined not by how much they invested in their own kids but how much they invested in everyone else's. My anxious fixation on being perceived as bad—this had only narrowed my vision onto my own home. When I lay down with Alma one night, I realized that I had been carrying around rifts and animosities that did not exist in his vision of the world.

"Who loves you?" I asked Alma, as I sometimes did.

"Mommy and Daddy," he replied.

"Who else?"

"Brayden."

"Who else?"

"Grandma and Grandpa."

"Who else?"

"My neighbors," he said.

Chapter 11

Free

When Brayden was born, I reverted again to my primordial mother self, where all I existed to do was feed him and look at my phone. Late at night, my eyes paced back and forth through Instagram's hall of mothers. But now I was wise to its claims of expertise, and I already owned more baby items than I actually wanted. Slowly my online attention led me back toward broader human dramas, like unsolved murders and ill-fated expeditions. One by one I unfollowed the birth workers and homemakers and parenting instructors I had welcomed into my phone as research. Then I scrolled back upon the Free Birth Society account, and I paused on an advertisement for an upcoming offering: the Matriarch Rising Festival, an in-person retreat that would unfold at the sprawling North Carolina homestead of the group's founder, Emilee Saldaya.

A video advertising the retreat showed her land shot from high above, filtered to appear overexposed and crackling, like a filmstrip recovered from a seventies cult. Women and children flowed over a grassy hill, gravitating toward a domed structure. They wore airy dresses and brimmed hats. They coalesced on the lip of a wooden deck, then turned and waved back at me. *Imagine gathering under the Solstice Sun, surrounded by your sisters, barefoot and free, completely immersed in the here and now,* the video said. The festival, another ad explained, was *the opportunity you've been waiting for to go off grid for a few magical days and simply breathe as Mother Nature holds you.* It would feature five days and nights of programming for women, girls, and boys under six. There would be sessions on broom making, breast massage, guided breath work, conscious conception, and something called German New Medicine. It would all culminate in a solstice ritual on the longest day of 2023.

As I picked through the material on the festival, I noticed that the society had refreshed its branding. Now it deployed curvy cream letters, rose and terra-cotta backgrounds, digital stamps of flowers and suns. As its posts passed through my feeds, I often mistook them for Big Little Feelings tips or advertisements for Hatch. Everything had fused into one ubiquitous millennial-mom aesthetic, regardless of the ideologies undergirding the posts. I wandered back to *The Free Birth Society Podcast* and found that its cover image had changed to a picture of a pregnant Saldaya wearing an open white robe. On her head was a headband emanating a spray of golden spikes, recalling a Renaissance painting of a saint. Or an Etsy dupe of the headpiece a pregnant Beyoncé wore at the Grammys in 2017.

The freebirthers had been speaking to me for so long, though of course they did not realize this. They had emerged as a foil in my construction of myself as a mother. They were always talking about the importance of a birth story, and now they would help me to close mine.

I bought a $900 ticket to the festival, booked a flight and a rental car, and immediately regretted it. The closer the Matriarch Rising Festival came, the less interested I was in becoming a matriarch who was also rising. I had a toddler and a baby, whom I was still nursing, and I did not want to leave them for five astronomically significant days and nights. Specifically, I did not want to leave them to go to what Marc had started calling "the freebirth convention." At the same time, I did not want to take them *with* me to the freebirth convention, though the festival WhatsApp group that unlocked with my purchase suggested that many of the other attendees were prepping to take their children along. I couldn't imagine carrying Alma and Brayden on a plane, driving them hours into the woods, sleeping with them on a damp tarp, and then releasing them into a field of undervaccinated girls (and boys under six). But even as these ideas emerged, I felt them being interrupted by the imagined freebirther in my head, sunnily informing me that my thoughts were the paranoid products of a medicalized lifestyle. Or maybe that was unfair. I reminded myself that I did not know any of these people.

As I packed a suitcase, I made a mental list of the things that I suspected might mark me as an outsider to the group. The absence of my children. The automatic breast pump that loudly announced the mother-baby bond I had severed to be there. My C-section scar, which I imagined being glimpsed in a communal shower or an uninhibited dance circle. Then I made a list of the things that I thought might mark me as one of them: I was white, and I had a travel bottle of Dr. Bronner's lavender soap. I picked through my closet and pulled out a straw hat and my most tradwifey maternity dress from my pregnancies. When I plucked a book off the shelf to take with me—a biography of Sigmund Freud—Marc warned me to keep it close.

"They're all going to be Jungians," he said.

After I deplaned in North Carolina, the attendant at the car rental counter took my name and then typed silently and at length. "There are no more cars," he said finally. He instead offered me something in the "SUV/four-by-four range." I agreed, pleased that my transportation would fit the ruggedly individualistic nature of my expedition. When I wound my way to the parking spot, I found one model left: a fire-engine-red Ram truck called the Warlock. I climbed into the cab as if scaling a rock's face. I peered down at the asphalt far beneath me. Then I engaged a sequence of switches and levers until the Warlock rumbled off. As I followed my phone's instructions to the land, I added one more item to my list of tells: *Drives a stupid truck.* A *warlock,* I learned, was a term for a male practitioner of witchcraft, and the main thing I knew about the Matriarch Rising Festival was that no men were allowed inside its outer gates. I had wanted to slip undetected into the community, but instead I would be riding a big red dick onto the land.

As I wound the Warlock through the hills of North Carolina, the terrain revealed itself to me in half circles of forest sliced with black slate cliffs. I pulled over outside a roadside gemstone dealer, pumped breast milk in the Warlock's expansive cab, poured the warm yellow liquid into the ground, and then trudged up to the shop, where I spent twelve minutes fingering smooth rocks until I found two green discs that I felt represented Alma and Brayden the best. As I rubbed the gems in one hand, I checked up on the WhatsApp thread in the other, trying to gauge the tenor of the group.

Tension was simmering regarding the accessibility of the festival to women with small children. One matriarch expressed frustration that kids' tickets had sold out so quickly, forcing her to find a babysitter for her four kids for the first time ever. A festival organizer quickly posted back. She was hurt at the idea that she had not adequately anticipated everyone's needs. The needs had in fact been meticulously anticipated. Then she said: *As the mom of a toddler, I recognize that this is a season of life that I might miss things for as long as I have an extended attachment relationship with my child—I don't go on one-on-one dates with my partner, I don't go to the movie theatre or concerts, and I certainly don't expect events who have to consider things like liability, the curation of events, and the enjoyment of the group as a whole, to make an exception for me, only one woman out of 300, simply because of the stage of life that I am in.* This was the rare place where mothers were summoned to a community created just for them, but it was not a fucking McDonald's PlayPlace, and those with young kids were, as ever, going to need to suck it up and stay home. When I thumbed over to the festival's Instagram page, I saw a video of Saldaya and the organizer zooming around the land in a golf cart, each with one breast out and a toddler latched on.

I climbed back into the Warlock and pushed its buttons. It guided me through a rural neighborhood and past signposts in wavy hippie lettering that said "SLOW" and "DOWN." Finally, I bumped into a line of vehicles idling outside the gates. I presented my ID and passed my finger across an iPad to sign a virtual waiver, agreeing to release the festival from liability and let it use my image, and received a millennial-pink brochure in return. An open-faced woman waved for me to park up a grassy raised bank, and the Warlock grunted angrily through the mud to reach it. Then I dangled my legs out of the cab and dropped unsteadily onto the soggy ground. Women filtered past me, joining an unpaved path toward the land. "This isn't my real car," I said to no one in particular.

I looked at the brochure in my hands. "When Women Gather, Magic Happens," it said. A map of the grounds was folded inside. I was to head up a gumdrop trail to an encampment called Nyx Valley. An organizer offered me a wagon with a lazy back wheel. I threw in my bags and struggled up the muddy incline past a series of shrines: groupings of fertility idols, harvest vegetables, votive candles, sheepskin fabrics, deliberate sprays of beans. It looked like a mudslide had hit a Hatch retail store. Then I came upon a woman sitting on a blanket, breastfeeding a baby who looked about

Brayden's age. I told her that her baby reminded me of my own, and she stared up at me with blank disdain. "Why didn't you bring him, then?" she said. My body pulsed with stress at the confrontation I had engineered for myself. *I don't know what I'm doing here*, I texted Marc as I continued up the hill. I was deep in the mountains, walking toward a tent set up just for me, just the kind of natural escape I fantasized about from within our New York apartment. But I had chosen a site at the internet's campground, the only one in the world that represented the opposite of logging off.

In Nyx Valley, I found a basic blue pup tent with a thin pad and fleece blanket inside. I lay down in my little bubble for a moment, then forced myself to join the crowd. I gravitated toward a very pregnant woman a few steps up the hill, struggling to draw a rain covering over her own tent. She had blond hair and brilliant teeth, and as she crossed her arms over her toadstool-printed coveralls, two other women poked their heads out of their own camps to help her construct her shelter. They both, I later learned, ran their own holistic women's groups in surrounding states. I suggested we rotate the rain tarp ninety degrees, and as we each took a corner, it seemed to float above us. We sank it into the ground with stakes as if completing a ritual.

When we were finished, the pregnant woman reached inside the tent and handed each of us a tender mango, freshly plucked from the organic farm where she lived and worked and, recently, prepared for her first freebirth. She had been eating well, getting exercise, basking in the sun. She was listening to the Free Birth Society's podcast and working her way through its online course. Nobody on the farm supported her plan to birth without assistance, so she lied to them about it. Now she was here, where she could speak freely. "I'm sorry I don't have a knife," she said of the mango. "I just bite right into them."

As she spoke, a wiry woman unzipped herself from the tent just below us. She wore gray camo pants and a black jacket with a hot-pink dragon stitched up the back. Curls of gray hair poked out the bottom of a baseball cap embroidered with a green luna moth. "It's so nice to be here surrounded by women," she said, and we reflexively agreed. "Real women," she clarified. A virulent and meandering rant followed, punctuated by feminist vocab lessons ("Do you all know about gaslighting?"), communal offerings ("I have weed if anyone smokes weed"), and her methods of intimidating trans people at pride marches ("I always keep three blades on me at once"). The egg-yolk sun dipped behind the hill as I stood frozen in place, watching her rage back and forth on our shared strip of grass.

The pregnant woman fetched her a mango, and I noticed that the woman's jacket was sewn with more patches: "LESBIAN NOT QUEER," "SAVE WOMEN'S SPORTS," "WOMAN IS NOT A FEELING." How quickly the festival's earth mama vibe had slipped into seething authoritarianism. It was dusky when the woman flipped a knife out and poked it at the air. "There might even be some women here who support trans," she said, and one of the women next to me replied softly that if any of them were here, they probably would not say so. And she was right; I did not say so. I just nodded at the knife and said, "That should come in handy for the mango," and everybody laughed.

When I zipped into the cloche of my tent, I rewound the encounter in my mind. It had started so pleasantly. But when the conversation turned, I said something neutral and ingratiating. In my defense, I had not expected anyone to be armed. I thought I had come to the land to test my own convictions about pregnancy and birth and parenthood. But as I made my bed and lay in it, I feared that my choice had been indefensible. Not my choice to get the epidural, the surgery, the robot bassinet, the breast pump, the baby monitor—whatever, that was all fine. The choice to keep pursuing the virtual abstractions of my second life. I could not drift wide-eyed down this rabbit hole forever. Now, confronted face-to-face by a fascist crone, I ducked back into my bubble and scrolled.

On my phone I looked up Nyx, the Greek goddess that the encampment was named after. She was the goddess of the night, and she had a whole brood of problematic children. There was Thanatos, the embodiment of death. Nemesis, the goddess of retribution. Momus, the god of ridicule and scorn. And the Keres: the many female spirits of violent and cruel deaths. Their bodies were all made of darkness. The sweet smell of weed filtered into my tent. Bugs with numerous legs alit upon the roof and cast shadows on the walls of my enclosure. I bit into the mango and its juice streamed down my chest. Tag yourself: I was Momus.

I awoke the next morning to an angry left boob. I had been away from Brayden for only twenty-four hours, and already my breast was knotted and sore, pressure building behind a clogged duct. I hooked myself to my pump and it pulled feebly at my nipples for thirty minutes. My left boob coughed up yellow spittle as my right one poured plentiful milk into its cup. I gathered some clothes in a plastic bag and headed to the shower area, past a wooden sign that said "SHE SHED" and into a stall hung with a spray of lavender. I massaged the knot under the hot water, slicking it with Dr. Bronner's, but nothing yielded. As I dressed and regarded myself in the mirror, l realized that the women around me were patting serums on their faces and easily hauling big woven baskets for their towels, like we were living inside a lifestyle brand activation. I looked at myself in the mirror and saw a rumpled summer witch.

Everyone was gravitating toward a raised stage, and Saldaya drove up past us in a golf cart, a walkie-talkie at her hip. The hood of the cart was decorated with a circle of what looked like brown pubic hair and glued with peach-colored baby trinkets. She ran through a couple of announcements. "If any of you brought placentas, per my request," she said, "please let me know so that I can put them safely into my freezer." I scanned the crowd, noting its mixture of dip-dyed skirts and matching athleisure separates. Babies hung on backs and hips. I saw a dream catcher tattoo, a salamander tattoo, a Medusa tattoo, a Celtic cross. I saw a tote bag for *The New Yorker* and one for the women's coworking space The Wing. I saw mothers lose patience with their children. ("Who are you saying no to? Stop saying no.") The kids were dressed in a familiar style of neutral knits, with beaded chains leading to gummy pacifiers. The skin on their mothers' faces appeared to fall normally, wrinkling and sagging in the appropriate places. I felt like I had walked into an ad for a postapocalyptic Pilates studio.

"The other thing is men," Saldaya said, and here her voice tipped into a kind of stand-up routine about men and their various practical uses. A nervous giggle skittered through the crowd. Her husband, she explained, might be seen from time to time on the land. "He is the brawn behind a lot of this," she explained. "He will need to be on site to fix an issue we're having in the kitchen. He's going to come, I think now, to minimize his presence. He will keep his eyes low." She continued: "Last thing about males. We have a Port-a-Potty-cleaner male. It's a women-owned business but the women don't clean the toilets." Sustained cheers.

As the opening circle closed, I was, for the first time that week, instructed to freestyle dance. I watched the women around me toss their arms into the air and squat and spring up repeatedly. I walked slowly backward down the hill, stole back to my tent, and reattached myself to the pump. At lunch, I joined a group of women who were recounting their birth stories. I told them that I had had two C-sections in the hospital but that I had, through a series of events, become interested in women who did the exact opposite of that. A woman in palazzo pants nodded knowingly and said, "Story medicine." She told the group that she wanted to birth at home because she didn't want to be tempted by a needle that could inject her with fentanyl at any time. "I had an epidural," I said, as if reporting back from the surface of the moon, "and it felt amazing."

I spent the day engaging in the designated activities of the rising matriarch. I danced the wheel of womanhood. I joined the solstice song circle and sang unfamiliar songs about various goddesses in a thin high voice. Then I went shopping. I picked through the makeshift marketplace and saw carved wooden dildos, little craggy handmade brooms, a baby onesie that said "100 PERCENT ORGANIC," and an incense holder that said "ANOTHER DAY, ANOTHER RABBITHOLE." I bought two carved wolf figurines for my two boys (under six). I bought *Portal*, Yolande Norris-Clark's unreadable self-published book recounting her painless ninth birth. Then I made my way to a café truck, where I bought a $9 espresso with a collagen shot from a woman who seemed—I'm not sure how else to put this—normal.

Later I was washing pumping parts in the communal sink when she appeared at my side. "Are you pumping?" she asked, and I admitted that I was. "I wasn't sure if I should bring my pump here," she said. She threw a thumb down the hill behind us. "I manually expressed behind that tree." Her name was Nev. She was a few years younger than me, but she had two children, girls, exactly the age of my own. She hadn't wanted to bring hers along, either. "I couldn't imagine them, like, sleeping here," she said.

We ate dinner together, and I asked what had brought her there. She told me that she had had a bad experience with the medical system during her first pregnancy. She had not wanted much prenatal intervention, but she did want to test the fetus for genetic defects. So she had her blood drawn for a NIPT, thinking that she was cleverly engaging in the least invasive test possible. The test came back high-risk for Turner syndrome—a false positive. Nev spent the coming days searching the internet for clues about the syndrome and the test. She underwent an amniocentesis she never wanted. When it produced a normal result, she knew she was done subjecting her pregnancy to examination. She stopped seeing her obstetrician and gave birth, unassisted, at home.

Our medical experiences were so similar. Our stories had intersected in the same place at the same time, and then they diverged. A few months after the festival, I called Nev over FaceTime, and she told me that, truthfully, she had always wanted an unassisted birth. As a kid she had watched a show on TLC, *A Baby Story*, and she had been disturbed by some of the installments, when the camera caught glimpses of hospital neglect. She felt like she would have to create a battle plan just to have a baby. Then she discovered freebirth and immediately knew it was for her. She lied to her friends and her parents and gave birth alone in her home with her husband and her sister at her side. When her placenta wouldn't come out, she called 911, and then she lied to the EMTs too, saying the baby had arrived unexpectedly fast. When she was finally wheeled down the halls of a hospital, her baby in her arms, she fantasized about burning the place down.

The birth was only the beginning of her disillusionment with the institution of parenthood. She said of the time after her first was born, "I had a vision of the kind of community that I wanted to be a part of, and it just wasn't there. I love my friends so much, but I just don't have the same culture that was around, maybe, when my grandmother was raising children, where you know your neighbors so much more intimately and you just drop in on each other and bring food and kind of do life together." She found that her friends were politely uncomfortable when she offered to babysit their kids for free, or to pool childcare on a more serious basis in the backyard where she was already caring for her own kids. She realized that she would have to cultivate such a community intentionally, and it was in that spirit that she came to the festival. "Women do not even realize what is available to us in community because we haven't seen it," she said. Our stories diverged, and then they inched back together again.

On the third day of the festival, I awoke to an angrier left boob. It was red and pulsing, and again the blockage failed to dissipate under the hot water of the shower. I swallowed three Advil and walked sheepishly to the village breast masseuse and asked if she could unclog my duct. I peeled off my shirt and lay topless before her. She placed a warm rubber water bottle on my chest and competently kneaded my breast. When the knot resisted her touch, she asked if I'd considered borrowing another woman's baby and having the child suck the clog out. I thanked her for the interesting idea, clothed myself, and wandered into a morning session that had just started under a large white tent. The session was called "The Bio-Logical Woman with Dr. Melissa Sell."

Who let a doctor in here? I wondered. I rubbed my tit absently as I neared the stage. Sell had a freckled face and red hair braided into pigtails and a flowy dress with a retro flower print. She looked like she could be my little sister, or my Wario. I tried and failed to make sense of what she was saying. She spoke of "the five biological laws," of our "powerful self-healing capabilities," of "conflict shocks" that created what we only perceived to be disease.

I called up my phone and googled *German New Medicine*. I discovered that it was an antisemitic conspiracy theory started by a doctor named Ryke Geerd Hamer. In the 1970s, his adult son Dirk had been shot and killed by an Italian prince, and Hamer soon developed testicular cancer, which he decided needed to be treated not with what he later called the "Talmudic scam" of institutional medicine but with his own attention to the "conflict shock" that had created the tumor. In GNM, the growth of a tumor was a good thing, a sign that the body was producing tissue to heal the conflict. Only once the psychic conflict was totally resolved could the symptom be cleared. Under the GNM rubric, anything could be a conflict shock: ball cancer, allergies, the common cold. Absolutely, Covid.

Speaking as the mother of a Jewish child with a cancer predisposition syndrome: this was not correct. I looked around the crowd. The pregnant woman with the mangoes was sitting on a folding chair, nodding, writing notes in tiny script until they filled the whole page of a notebook. Another woman raised her hand to ask a question, and Sell lifted her eyes to the sky in mock frustration, as if her answer could only skim the surface of the vast stores of knowledge and expertise upon which GNM was based. "We were indoctrinated from age zero. Pre-zero," she said. "Your mother was indoctrinated before you were even conceived, and *her* mother was indoctrinated before *she* was even conceived." Later, when I contacted Sell to ask whether she endorsed or rejected Hamer's anti-semitic beliefs, she did not respond.

I stalked back to my tent to pump again, where Sell's voice dissolved into a rhythmic sucking noise. Wasn't it perfect that the internet community styled most like a hippie commune was the most bizarrely individualistic of them all? The village doctor came around to tell people that if they had a heart attack, they didn't need to go to the hospital. They needed to reflect. I looked within and resolved not to spend the longest day of the year in the valley of darkness. I picked up my phone and leaned on a Delta representative to put me on an early flight. I packed my things and dragged them down the hill, and then I asked an organizer whether it would be possible to get out of there. She spoke into a walkie-talkie, and after some time, the golf cart appeared. Saldaya stepped off it and walked right up to me.

"You're the leaver," she said.

"I'm the leaver," I agreed.

She looked at me, nodded, pointed me back down the road to the parking area. As I followed the gumdrops out, it began to rain. I mounted the Warlock. I would need it to ford the muddy embankment while slipping it around all the other cars wedged around me. I turned the key and the Warlock grumbled. It lurched and whinnied as I tapped on its pedals. I twisted the steering wheel in random patterns as I rocked the truck forward and backward, willing the beast to escape the land. Finally an ethereal figure emerged from the edge of a wood. As it came closer, I realized that it was a man, making the universal symbol for "turn your car the way that I indicate you should." I did as he instructed, and as I finally released the Warlock from the mud, I stopped and rolled down my window.

"We are good for some things," the man said.

At the airport I pushed a heap of muddy clothes and tarps into a trash can like I was O. J. Simpson. I redownloaded an app on my phone to duck inside a lactation station called a Mamava, and I locked the door urgently behind me. As if I had been followed. I plugged in my pump and regarded myself in the mirror, which was painted with a smiley face and the message, "Lookin' good, mama!" The mirror was right: I was smiling. The Mamava app surfaced an old picture of Alma I had once uploaded as pumping inspiration. Twenty minutes later I realized that the bottle attached to my left boob was full and spurting warm milk onto the floor. As soon as I left the land, my body let go.

A few weeks later, Saldaya sent out a link to a set of hundreds of photographs shot at the festival. The images would fuel the society's social media branding for the next year. I paged through the collection nervously, waiting to be confronted by a picture of myself looking miserable in a crowd or nude on a massage table, but none appeared. From the perspective of the internet, it was as if I had never been there at all.

A few weeks after I returned from the festival, Marc and I took Alma and Brayden to the children's hospital, where Alma met with his care team like he had many times before. This time was different. The surgeon took one look at his tongue and recommended that he have a tongue-reduction surgery within the next few months. The tongue had kept growing large and quick, and it was interfering with Alma's speech, his teeth, and his jaw. Marc and I had been anticipating this possibility for three years, but still it was difficult to accept. I could understand everything Alma said perfectly, but I had to remind myself that he belonged to the world, not to me.

We made an appointment a few months out and spent the weeks preparing him to get his head around a procedure that Marc and I did not fully understand ourselves. We knew that the surgeon would make a U-shaped cut around the whole of Alma's tongue, and if necessary, he would cut inside it too, making a keyhole incision in the middle of the tongue. And we knew that it would cause him pain. The hospital advised that we inform Alma of the surgery only one to two days before, but this seemed cruel and intolerable. I did not want him to marinate in anxiety, but I also felt he had a right to know what was coming. We bought him a range of children's books about hospitals and surgery, though all the characters in them had something "wrong" with them that needed fixing: a turtle with a cracked shell, a girl with a punctured eardrum, a cousin bear with a broken arm. We had spent three years speaking proudly of Alma's special big tongue. Now we had to tell him that it was getting too big.

The day of the surgery, we arrived at the hospital and helped Alma change into a pair of medical pajamas, which were blue and red with little rocket men printed all over them, blasting around cartoon moons. I recognized the print from Theresa Thomas's Instagram account, @largerthanbws, from her pictures of her own son in the hospital before his tongue-reduction surgery. Though she maintained a seemingly exhaustive archive of her son's life and medical experiences, she had posted a photo of her son smiling in the pajamas pre-op and captioned it this: *Sharing this photo because I really can't bear to share what he's looked like today. Todays hard. There's no other way to put it.* She added: *I just hope when he's older he forgives me and understands why I've had to do what I've had to do.*

I have my own photo series of Alma on the day of his surgery. He's in the courtyard of a university, playing his guitar and singing at the top of his lungs. Then he's on the hospital bed, in those paja-mas, smiling optimistically with the guitar held to his chest. He had already been visited by the anesthesiologist, who had administered to Alma what he called "giggle juice." Alma felt faint, and then he wanted to lie down, and then they wheeled him out of sight. In the waiting room, the hospital sent us a series of text messages, as if we were waiting for our son to be delivered back to us via courier. They said:

Your child is in the operating room/procedure room.

Your child's procedure has started.

Your child's procedure is ending. The team will be in touch with you.

Your child has left the operating room. You will be notified when it is time to visit.

We will escort you into the recovery room as soon as possible.

All the surgery books said that Mommy and Daddy would be there when he woke up, but as I rounded the corner to his room I heard him screaming. He did not stop for a very long time. I won't describe the contours of his distress except to say that it was alarming and, from a medical perspective, largely ignored. Nurses kept walking into the recovery room, triggering more distress, then explaining that his distress was perfectly normal, that it was "just the anesthesia leaving the body." Every time they left I parroted the line in a singsong whisper to Marc: "It's JUST the ANESTHESIA leaving the BODY!" It was not the anesthesia leaving the body. It was that we had signed at the bottom of a form and let a doctor cut his tongue out of his mouth.

When we arrived home from the hospital, Alma's distress no longer seemed like a medical emergency. It changed shape but it persisted, day and night, for many months. Another passive-aggressive cookie plate arrived outside the door, this time from a different neighbor. Big Little Feelings posts passed my feed, assuring me that *toddlers are exhausting*, but that I was a *warrior parent* who could *prevent a tantrum* by following their commands. Its course's list of advice for highly specific situations did not include tongue surgery. Despite the brand's commitment to recognizing millennial parents' trauma, it did not appear to acknowledge traumatic events among children at all. Finally Marc and I did what Spock advised in his book: we called a child psychologist. She gave us the advice that no parenting social media account would: we should let him watch lots of television. An iPad, then pitched as the height of lazy and selfish parenting, was the greatest gift we could give him. A push-button ejection from his real life.

Alma's favorite television show was one that he first saw on the TVs at the children's hospital: *Mickey Mouse Clubhouse,* an insipid CGI program in which a flatly emotionless Mickey Mouse rules over a technocratic fantasyland. From the seat of a fully automated clubhouse built in Mickey's own image—and with the aid of a sentient, floating iPad called Toodles—Mickey and his friends make selections among the tablet's "Mouseketools" to solve the episode's central problem. Alma's favorite episode was called "Goofy Baby."

In "Goofy Baby," Ludwig Von Drake, absentminded professor and uncle to Donald Duck, invents a time machine. Von Drake leads Goofy through its enormous tube—it looks not unlike the MRI machine I encountered in pregnancy—in the hopes of turning Goofy into a medieval knight. Instead, Goofy reverts into a baby, forcing Mickey and friends to provide childcare while Von Drake adjusts his machine to turn him back into a grown-up.

Imagine your friend walks through a mysterious tube and comes out in infant form. A disturbing development, to say the least. And one that raises serious questions about the nature of time inside the clubhouse. *Mickey Mouse Clubhouse* runs for hundreds of episodes without any character appearing to age in any way, and yet a machine can de-age Goofy using a theory of time-space that seems not even to exist in the series? When Mickey Mouse is faced with these existential horrors, he responds by dispassionately summoning his iPad and ordering some tape for Goofy Baby's diapers. I wondered what it meant that my child's preferred form of self-medication was to dissolve into a dystopian future commanded by a narcissistic mouse.

As Alma watched the episode yet again, I sat down beside him and paid closer attention. Near its end, Daisy and Minnie try to feed Goofy Baby, but when they return him to his pram, he cries so loudly that he wakes Pete, a lumbering cat who is sleeping a few grassy hills away. Pete is Mickey's lightly villainous foil, and he storms over to the clubhouse to tell them to keep the noise down. But when he sees Goofy Baby, he softens. He waves his fingers in front of the stroller and says, "Aww, look at the little guy." Then he takes Goofy Baby in his arms and shows Mickey and his friends how to burp him, just like his mom used to do. He is, in fact, the hero of the episode.

I recognized the line, knew Pete's exact delivery. Every day Alma reached for Brayden, patted him softly on the head, and said: "Aww, look at the little guy."

As Alma escaped into Disney+, I too spent the weeks and months after the surgery disassociating into a screen. I had weeded out almost everyone on Instagram whom I didn't know, but I kept thinking of Dr. Melissa Sell. I wanted to know what her imaginary medical system would do when confronted with the reality of my son. I circled her account for a few days, and then I posted this: *My son was born with macroglossia (large tongue) due to genetic condition, does GNM have clues to why and how to treat?*

No response.

A few weeks later, I asked again: *My son was born with macroglossia (large tongue) due to genetic condition, does GNM have clues to why and how to treat?*

This time her answer appeared threaded beneath my own. She said: *The tongue is mostly muscle and the conflict that affects muscle is a self devaluation. There is tissue necrosis during the active conflict followed by tissue reconstruction in the healing phase. The biological purpose is to make the area more robust and better capable. The tongue is needed for speaking, sucking, and swallowing. During pregnancy did you experience a self devaluation related to one of these things? Did you need to "bite your tongue"? The goal would be to identify the conflict and talk about it. You can talk to children in their sleep about conflicts experienced during the pregnancy to help them release the conflict. Given that the tissue is larger the conflict was at least partially resolved. Talking about it and finding a full resolution will help resolve any potential tracks.*

This was nonsense, and yet it clarified the nonsense that had throttled my mind since I got pregnant. I had spent so much time worrying that my brain had somehow imprinted onto Alma's body. That my internal conflicts had manifested themselves in my child. That night, I showed the Instagram exchange to Marc.

"Wait, her name is literally *Sell*?" Marc said.

"Yes," I said.

"And she's a doctor?"

"She's a chiropractor," I said.

Marc read her paragraph again. She was wrong about everything, except for one thing. "You shouldn't bite your tongue," Marc said.

I wanted so much to have been there for Alma, the parent I needed to be, before he arrived. But I could not be her until he was here. Every day I seemed to unbecome her and become her again. I told Marc that I knew that I could not use an antisemitic conspiracy theory to *release my conflict* with Alma as he slept, but that I was going to do it anyway. I just needed to find the right message, the passphrase to whisper into his ear to resolve everything.

I put down my phone and opened the door to the bedroom that Alma shared with his little brother. I couldn't make them out among the dark shapes of the nursery, but I could hear them. Their breaths rose and fell above the mechanical fizz of the sound machine. Their breathing was synced almost perfectly together. I stood at the threshold, listening.

Acknowledgments

Thank you to everyone who cared for my kids while I was living and writing this book, in particular: Diana, Jaylin, Desiree, Chastity, Katherina, Julie, Lola, Hikma, Amanda, Jessica, Jayleen, Alma, Naomi, Michelle, Jose, and Gil. Also, babysitters Elana, Ruby, Patti, Leticia, and Tricia. And, and: Mom, Dad, Megan, Debby, Don, Lara, and Jeff. Thank you Jin Auh for believing that I could write a book, and Thomas Gebremedhin for helping me discover what it was. You have made me a better writer and a better parent. Thanks also to Anna Kelly, Emma Smith, Elena Hershey, Sara Hayet, Oliver Munday, and especially Johanna Zwirner. And to everyone at Doubleday, Wylie, and Little, Brown. Thank you to Maxwell Gillmer for your research, your fact-checking, and your wisdom. And to the friends who offered counsel on aspects of the book, among them Davey Alba, Kate Axelrod, Kerensa Cadenas, Lauretta Charlton, Michelle Dean, Tim Fernholz, Lauren Goldenberg, Megan Greenwell, Kamie Luna, Maya Salam, and the group chat. Thank you to MacDowell for giving me a place to write, plus freezer space for my breast milk. And especially to the staff for their care and feeding. To my editors who endured this, particularly Lorne Manly, Sia Michel, Gilbert Cruz, Caryn Ganz, and Sasha Weiss. To my doctors and nurses, and the BWS parents who shared their children's lives with me, especially Amanda Lawn, Christine Donnelly, and Aja. To Marc, for everything.

Notes

Chapter 1: Cycle

The Wall Street Journal article that characterized Flo's data privacy practices was reported by Sam Schechner and Mark Secada: "You Give Apps Sensitive Personal Information. Then They Tell Facebook" (February 22, 2019). Information on Flo's financial history and the business activities of its founders came from Crunchbase and from financial disclosure forms filed in the UK. Dmitry Gurski's comments on his vision for Flo are from Charlotte Tucker's interview in the online magazine *EU-Startups* (September 22, 2021).

For background on Marie Stopes, I am indebted to June Rose's book *Marie Stopes and the Sexual Revolution* (London and Boston: Faber and Faber, 1993) and artifacts in the Wellcome Collection's *Marie Charlotte Carmichael Stopes (1880–1958)* archive (London). My understanding of the life and politics of Mary Putnam Jacobi is indebted to Carla Jean Bittel's *Mary Putnam Jacobi and the Politics of Medicine in Nineteenth-Century America* (Chapel Hill: University of North Carolina Press, 2009). The quotes from Stopes's son and daughter-in-law are from Emma Brooker's *Independent* article "Sex, Libel and Eugenics . . ." (November 17, 1995). The origins of the Quantified Self movement are laid out in "What Is the Quantified Self," posted on the Quantified Self website, QuantifiedSelf.com (October 5, 2007). Rose Eveleth's "How Self-Tracking Apps Exclude Women," published in *The Atlantic* (December 15, 2014), articulates the critique of the movement.

Chapter 2: Bump

On the subject of the whiteness of pregnancy, I found these books especially useful: Kimberly C. Harper's *The Ethos of Black Motherhood in America: Only White Women Get Pregnant* (Lanham: Lexington Books, 2020); Nefertiti Austin's *Motherhood So White: A Memoir of Race, Gender, and Parenting in America* (Naperville: Sourcebooks, 2019); Camille T. Dungy's *Guidebook to Relative Strangers: Journeys into Race, Motherhood, and History* (New York: W. W. Norton, 2017); and Patricia Hill Collins's *Black Feminist Thought: Knowledge, Consciousness, and the Politics of Empowerment* (Boston: Unwin Hyman, 1990).

Ariane Goldman's essay "I Started a Maternity Brand Thinking That Pregnant People Needed Cute Dresses. They Need Way More Than That" was published in *Business Insider* (November 8, 2021). Hatch's newsletter sales figure comes from Greg Sterling's article "Why D2C Brands are the Future of Retail," published in *MarTech* (October 25, 2019). The *Page Boy* maternity catalog archive is a part of *Rescuing Texas History, 2018*, a project of the Portal to Texas History. The quote from the Boston physician was published in Boston Women's Health Collective's *Women and Their Bodies: A Course*, the precursor to *Our Bodies, Ourselves* (Boston: Boston Women's Health Collective, 1970). Molly Fischer's analysis of the prairie dress, "The Pleasure of Sitting Out a Trend," was published in *The Cut* (February 5, 2019). A representative for Lily's Garden told me that the game did not directly target users with ads tailored to their stage of life. "Instead, we strive to capture various relatable and interesting moments through storytelling," she said. "We create different ads and upload them to various networks. These networks use their algorithms to distribute the ads."

Charles Duhigg's *New York Times Magazine* story on predictive analysis is "How Companies Learn Your Secrets" (February 16, 2012), and the *Forbes* blog post highlighting the Target anecdote was Kashmir Hill's "How Target Figured Out a Teen Girl Was Pregnant Before Her Father Did" (February 16, 2012). To learn about my own online ad data, I used tools including BidFilter, the Headerbid Expert tool by AppNexus, and Blacklight by the Markup. My understanding of the ad-tech landscape is indebted to conversations with Jen Golbeck, David Hoffman, Ronald Robertson, Eric Seufert, Christo Wilson, and especially Shoshana Wodinsky. *Seahorse*, the documentary about Freddy McConnell, was directed by Jeanie Finlay (Grain Media, 2019). I'm also grateful to McConnell for insights he shared in a Zoom interview.

Chapter 3: Life

Jenna Karvunidis's essay reconsidering the gender reveal, "I Started the 'Gender Reveal Party' Trend. And I Regret It," was published in *The Guardian* (June 29, 2020). Ian Donald's full narration of a prenatal ultrasound can be found in Malcolm Nicolson and John E. E. Fleming's *Imaging and Imagining the Fetus: The Development of Obstetric Ultrasound* (Baltimore: Johns Hopkins University Press, 2013). I also found Janelle S. Taylor's *The Public Life of the Fetal Sonogram: Technology, Consumption, and the Politics of Reproduction* (New Brunswick: Rutgers University Press, 2008) and Barbara Duden's *Disembodying Women: Perspectives on Pregnancy and the Unborn* (Cambridge: Harvard University Press, 1993) invaluable in understanding the technology's rise.

Joanne Boucher's "The Politics of Abortion and the Commodification of the Fetus" was published in *Studies in Political Economy* vol. 73 (2004). Jennifer Denbow's article "Good Mothering Before Birth: Measuring Attachment and Ultrasound as an Affective Technology," published in *Engaging Science, Technology, and Society* vol. 5 (March 2019), is an insightful analysis; in it, she highlights Stuart Campbell's comments on "sub-optimal bonders." For a deeper understanding of the development of prenatal testing technologies, I am indebted to Rayna Rapp's *Testing Women, Testing the Fetus* (London: Routledge, 1999), and to my conversations with Rapp herself. Michele Goodwin's *Policing the Womb: Invisible Women and the Criminalization of Motherhood* (Cambridge: Cambridge University Press, 2020) was an invaluable resource. For more on the history of racist policing of reproduction, read Dorothy Roberts's *Killing the Black Body: Race, Reproduction, and the Meaning of Liberty* (New York: Vintage, 1997).

Chapter 4: Risk

"Memoir on the Morbific Elongation of the Tongue out of the Mouth" was published in *The Medical and Physical Journal* vol. 6, no. 32 (October 1801). For translations of the omens, I relied on Nicla De Zorzi's "The Omen Series *Šumma izbu:* Internal Structure and Hermeneutic Strategies," published in

Kaskal (January 2011). Catharina Schrader's diaries are published in *Mother and Child Were Saved: The Memoirs (1693–1740) of the Frisian Midwife Catharina Schrader* (Leiden: Rodopi, 1987). Ambroise Paré's book is *On Monsters and Marvels* (Chicago: University of Chicago Press, 1983). Other riffs on the maternal imagination are recorded in Michael T. Walton and Robert M. Fineman's "The Prevention of Infirm or Monstrous Births," in *Quidditas: Online Peer-Reviewed Journal of the Rocky Mountain Medieval and Renaissance Association* vol. 22 (January 2001). The workbook I consulted during pregnancy was Pamela S. Wiegartz and Kevin L. Gyoerkoe's *The Pregnancy and Postpartum Anxiety Workbook: Practical Skills to Help You Overcome Anxiety, Worry, Panic Attacks, Obsessions, and Compulsions* (Oakland: New Harbinger Publications, 2009). While Flo Secret Chat searches for *abnormality* and others came up empty in 2020, by 2024 many of them had been populated with article pages or comments.

Chapter 5: Nature

Brandy Zadrozny's article about Judith's freebirth is "I Brainwashed Myself with the Internet," published by NBC News (February 21, 2020). For the history of the demonization of midwives in America, read Barbara Ehrenreich and Deirdre English's *Witches, Midwives, and Nurses: A History of Women Healers* (New York: Feminist Press, 1973). I gained insight into Grantly Dick-Read's work through the Wellcome Collection's *Grantly Dick-Read (1890–1959)* collection (London). Statistics on American hospital births are from "From Home to Hospital: The Evolution of Childbirth in the United States, 1928–1940," published in *Explorations in Economic History* vol. 45, no. 1 (January 2008). Patricia Cloyd Carter's *Come Gently, Sweet Lucina* was self-published in 1957 and is available at the Library of Congress.

For more on the history of freebirth, I am indebted to Rixa Freeze's dissertation "Born Free: Unassisted Childbirth in North America" (2008), and to her chapter with Laura Tanner, "Freebirth in the United States," published in *Birthing Outside the System: The Canary in the Coal Mine* (London: Routledge, 2020, eds. Hannah Dahlen, Bashi Kumar-Hazard, and Virginia Schmied). I also relied on the freebirth chapter in Randi Hutter Epstein's *Get Me Out: A History of Childbirth from the Garden of Eden to the Sperm Bank* (New York: W. W. Norton, 2010). The quotes about twilight sleep were published in Charlotte Teller's

"The Neglected Psychology of the 'Twilight Sleep,' " in *Good Housekeeping* vol. 61, no. 1 (July 1915). Marie Stopes's own twilight sleep experience ended in tragedy: her first baby was stillborn.

Chapter 6: Birth

Amanda Little-Richardson's article on her experience filming *Lenox Hill* is "I Televised My Pregnancy—and Birth—as a Black Ob-Gyn," published in *Glamour* (October 1, 2020). For more on the impacts of inequity in birth, I am indebted to Khiara M. Bridges's *Reproducing Race: An Ethnography of Pregnancy as a Site of Racialization* (Berkeley: University of California Press, 2011); Aracelis Girmay's collection *So We Can Know: Writers of Color on Pregnancy, Loss, Abortion, and Birth* (Chicago: Haymarket Books, 2023); Jennifer C. Nash's *Birthing Black Mothers* (Durham: Duke University Press, 2021); and Dani McClain's *We Live for the We: The Political Power of Black Motherhood* (New York: Bold Type Books, 2019). Helena Andrews-Dyer's article "This Isn't Another Horror Story About Black Motherhood" was published in *The Washington Post* (September 4, 2019).

Lenox Hill's C-section rate was published as part of the Leapfrog Hospital Survey. Statistics on inequities in cesarean sections are from Michelle Debbink et al., "Racial and Ethnic Inequities in Cesarean Birth and Maternal Morbidity in a Low-Risk, Nulliparous Cohort," published in *Obstetrics and Gynecology* vol.139, no. 1 (January 2022). Jacqueline H. Wolf's *Cesarean Section: An American History of Risk, Technology, and Consequence* (Baltimore: Johns Hopkins University Press, 2018) was an invaluable resource. For more background on the commercialization of American healthcare, see Paul Starr's *The Social Transformation of American Medicine: The Rise of a Sovereign Profession and the Making of a Vast Industry* (New York: Basic Books, 1982). Mayim Bialik's quote about dead babies is from Taffy Brodesser-Akner's "Who Controls Childbirth?," published in *Self* (July 16, 2010).

Chapter 7: Work

My understanding of the care economy is indebted to Premilla Nadasen's *Care: The Highest Stage of Capitalism* (Chicago: Haymarket Books, 2023); Angela Garbes's *Essential Labor: Mothering as Social Change* (New York: Harper Wave, 2022); Angela Y. Davis's *Women, Race & Class* (New York: Random House,

1981); and bell hooks's "Revolutionary Parenting," published in *Feminist Theory: From Margin to Center* (Boston: South End Press, 1984). Nancy Fraser's analysis of breast pumps appears in "Contradictions of Capital and Care," published in *New Left Review*, no. 100 (July/August 2016). Antoinette Konikow's "What Socialism Will Mean to the Women Who Toil at Home" was published in *Socialist Appeal* vol. 4, no. 13 (March 1940). I also found Sharon Hays's *The Cultural Contradictions of Motherhood* (New Haven: Yale University Press, 1998) and Krista Lynn Minnotte's "Decentering Intensive Mothering: More Fully Accounting for Race and Class in Motherhood Norms," published in *Sociology Compass* vol. 17, no. 8 (August 2023), helpful. Zoe Hu's "The Agoraphobic Fantasy of Tradlife" was published in *Dissent* (2023), and Niloufar Haidari's "If This Is the Age of the Tradwife, Then I'm Ready to Die Alone" was published in *Dazed* (2022).

Chapter 8: Gear

For more on the technologies of parenting, I recommend Michelle Millar Fisher and Amber Winick's *Designing Motherhood: Things That Make and Break Our Births* (Cambridge: MIT Press, 2021) and Sophie Hamacher and Jessica Hankey's *Supervision: On Motherhood and Surveillance* (Cambridge: MIT Press, 2023). Leah A. Plunkett's book is *Sharenthood: Why We Should Think Before We Talk About Our Kids Online* (Cambridge: MIT Press, 2019), and Donna J. Haraway's is *A Cyborg Manifesto: Science, Technology, and Socialist-Feminism in the Late Twentieth Century* (Minneapolis: University of Minnesota Press, 2016). Harvey Karp's quotes are from an interview with Helen Rosner, "Harvey Karp Knows How to Make Babies Happy," published in *The New Yorker* (April 9, 2023).

Chapter 9: Growth

Victoria Lucas's essay discussing *Dumbo* is "Reclaiming Nemo," published by the BBC (August 19, 2004). Jessica Joanne Gibson's dissertation "'Conceal, Don't Feel, Don't Let Them Know': A Critical Analysis of the Representation of Disability in Disney Animated Films," for the University of York (February 2023), discusses *Dumbo*'s tropes. For more on the intersection of disability and parenthood, I relied on Sunaura Taylor's *Beasts of Burden: Animal and Disability Liberation* (New York: The New Press, 2017); Eliza Hull's fabulous collection *We've Got This: Essays by Disabled Parents* (London: Scribe, 2023); and Faye Ginsburg and Rayna Rapp's *Disability Worlds* (Durham: Duke University Press, 2024), the culmination of their decades of work on the subject. Angela Frederick's insight into the burden of intensive mothering is outlined in her article with Kylara Leyva and Grace Lavin, "The Double Edge of Legitimacy: How Women with Disabilities Interpret Good Mothering," published in *Social Currents* vol. 6, no. 2 (April 2019). The bell hooks essay "In Our Glory: Photography and Black Life" is from *Art on My Mind: Visual Politics* (New York: The New Press, 1995). Fortesa Latifi's thought-provoking article "'Medical Moms' Share Their Kids' Illnesses with Millions. At What Cost?" was published in *The Washington Post* (May 11, 2023). For more about the Orchid genetic testing startup, read Julia Black and Margaux MacColl's "Dawn of the Silicon Valley Superbaby," in *The Information* (July 19, 2024).

Chapter 10: Judgment

I highly recommend Alison Gopnik's *The Gardener and the Carpenter: What the New Science of Child Development Tells Us About the Relationship Between Parents and Children* (New York: Farrar, Straus and Giroux, 2016) and Malcolm Harris's *Kids These Days: Human Capital and The Making of Millennials* (New York: Little, Brown and Company, 2017). For more background on the cultures of parenting, I relied on Ellie Lee, Jennie Bristow, Charlotte Faircloth, and Jan Macvarish's *Parenting Culture Studies* (London: Palgrave Macmillan, 2014); David F. Lancy's *Raising Children: Surprising Insights from Other Cultures* (Cambridge: Cambridge University Press, 2017); and Harry Hendrick's *Narcissistic Parenting in an Insecure World: A History of Parenting Culture 1920s to Present* (Bristol: Policy Press, 2016).

ABOUT THE AUTHOR

Amanda Hess is a critic at large for *The New York Times*. She writes about internet and pop culture for the Arts section and contributes regularly to *The New York Times Magazine*. Hess has worked as an internet columnist for *Slate* magazine, an editor at *GOOD* magazine, and an arts and nightlife columnist at the *Washington City Paper*, and has served as the second vice president for the NewsGuild of New York, a union representing media workers. She has also written for such publications as *ESPN The Magazine*, *Wired*, and *Pacific Standard*, where her feature on the online harassment of women won a National Magazine Award for Public Interest.